Memories of Development

About the Author

Roland Jaquarello's credits include periods as Assistant Director, Royal Court Theatre; Director, Abbey Theatre Dublin; Associate Director, Welsh Drama Co.; Artistic Director, Green Fields and Far Away Theatre Company; Artistic Director, Live Theatre Newcastle; Artistic Director, Lyric Theatre Belfast; Artistic Director, Redgrave Theatre Farnham; and Senior Producer, Radio Drama, BBC Northern Ireland, working for BBC Radio 4, 3 and 2.

MEMORIES OF DEVELOPMENT

My Time in Irish Theatre and Broadcasting

Roland Jaquarello

The Liffey Press

Published by

The Liffey Press Ltd

Raheny Shopping Centre, Second Floor

Raheny, Dublin 5, Ireland

www.theliffeypress.com

© 2016 Roland Jaquarello

A catalogue record of this book is
available from the British Library.

ISBN 978-1-908308-79-5

Printed in Dublin by SprintPrint.

Contents

HATCHET IN LONDON

ON THE ROAD WITH GREEN FIELDS

LYRIC THEATRE BELFAST

Contents

FREELANCE JOURNEYS: RADIO

MY IRISH JOURNEY

ACKNOWLEDGEMENTS

Acknowledgements

I would like to thank the many friends and colleagues who, by re-calling their own experiences or submitting various programmes and photos, not only substantiated fact but helped stir memories of our work together.

I am particularly grateful to Michael Loughnan, the redoubt-able Samuel Pepys of Green Fields and Far Away, whose prodigious recollection of the minutiae of the company's tours is unrivalled. Talented designers Peter Ling, James Helps, Alison Böckh and Van-essa Hawkins also helped me enormously by providing both visual material and descriptions of their work on my productions. Roger Simonsz gave me the too often neglected perspective of the lighting designer. Actors Des Nealon, Alan Stanford and Kevin McHugh were most considerate in trying to recover material relating to my early Dublin days. Another thespian, Derry Power, kindly gave me a copy of a photo from my production of *Loot*, and Tessa, Kate and Deborah Vale politely withstood my persistence and managed to find a picture of *It's a Two Foot Six Inches Above the Ground World* in a family attic. Jeanne Laffan generously embraced a voice from the past and allowed me to quote from her late husband's play. Mairead Delaney, the Abbey Theatre's archivist, sent me a whole range of visual material. John Dooher from the Strabane Histori-cal Society confirmed some local history and writer Christopher-Fitz-Simon did likewise regarding queries about the Abbey's past. From New York, brothers Denis and Joe O'Neill sent me a variety of *The Scatterin'* photos, as did former Green Fields regular John O'Toole. Patch Connolly, another old touring colleague, also contributed photos of Green Fields and Far Away productions. Lyric Theatre stalwarts B.J. Hogg and Noel McGee clarified information about work during my tenure there. While in Belfast, Mike and Caoimhe Blair gave me warm hospitality and Gavin Carville, from that impressive bastion of research, the Linen Hall Library, let me look at their splendid collection of Lyric photos. Ophelia Byrne from BBC Northern Ireland also steered me towards some profitable areas of research. Tim Woodward earnestly pursued photos of *After the Fall*. Simon Goldrick and Andrew Forsythe in the Lyric marketing department provided me with many photographs from their archive. The effervescent Nora Connolly sent me much useful material regarding *The Death of Humpty Dumpty* at Live Theatre Newcastle, and playwright Graham Reid reminded me about personnel at Belfast's Musgrave Hospital. Druid Theatre Company and NUI Galway managed to help me find a photo of *Cheapside*. I also appreciated the assistance of agents Steve Nealon of Steve Nealon Associates and Lisa Cook from the Lisa Richards Agency in gathering material and information from their clients.

I'd especially like to thank Myrtle Johnston, John Lynch and Mike Blair for drawing attention to my errors in earlier drafts, David Givens for his belief in the book and, last but not least, to Mira Faber for putting up with a volatile first-time writer!

Photographs

The author would like to thank the following for giving their kind permission to reproduce production photographs:

- The Abbey Theatre Dublin
- The Lyric Theatre Belfast
- The New University of Ulster for the photo of Green Fields and Far Away's production of *Moby Dick*
- Denis and Joe O'Neill for Green Fields and Far Away's *The Scatterin'* photos and accompanying publicity shots
- Amelia Stein for the photo of the Druid Theatre Company's production of *Cheapside*

- Vanessa Hawkins for the photos of the Lyric Theatre Belfast's production of *The Butterfly of Killybegs*
- BBC Northern Ireland for the radio cast pictures
- *The Irish News* for the radio studio photo of the writer.

In addition:

- The Green Fields and Far Away photographs of *The Ikon Maker* were taken by Adrian Spalling.
- The illustrator for the Radio Times *Flaherty's Window* design is Iain Phillips.

Quotations

The author is grateful for being granted permission to quote from the following;

- *It's a Two Foot Six Inches Above the Ground World* by Kevin Laffan, Faber and Faber, 1970
- *The Entertainer* by John Osborne, Faber and Faber Main Edition, 1974, by kind permission of the Arvon Foundation
- *Hatchet* by Heno Magee, The Gallery Press, 1978
- *Comedians* by Trevor Griffiths, Faber and Faber, Main Edition, 1979
- *Our Lady of Sligo* by Sebastian Barry, Methuen Publishing Ltd., 1998
- *Molly Sweeney* by Brian Friel, published in Ireland by The Gallery Press 1994 and in Great Britain by Faber and Faber, 1994
- *After the Fall* by Arthur Miller, Penguin Books (revised edition 1980) and Arthur Miller letter, both by kind permission of the Arthur Miller Trust
- *Over the Bridge* by Sam Thompson, forward by John Keyes, Lagan Press, 1997
- *The Property of Colette Nervi* by William Trevor (radio dramatisation) 1999
- The Grainne McFadden article is reproduced by kind permission of the *Belfast Telegraph*.

To Mira

Theatrical Beginnings

1 – An Innocent Abroad

My introduction to Ireland was a glorious accident. I was to have gone to Durham University. I made a long journey to the north east in hopeful anticipation, only to be interviewed by a beagle-eyed academic, who seemed more interested in my sporting prowess. I had played in both the first XV and first XI for my school, Christ's Hospital, and despite my efforts to talk about literature, he seemed more interested in getting his three-quarter line sorted out than my views on the modern novel. Apparently, Hatfield College had a sports reputation so I was offered a place.

This all became irrelevant when I didn't get the necessary grades. Consequently, I had to start all over again. I was then informed about Magee University College by my English teacher, David Jesson-Dibley, an imaginative man who had directed me in a school production of *A Midsummer Night's Dream*, in which I had played none other than Hippolyta, Queen of the Amazons. He told me that in essence Magee was a back door to Trinity College Dublin. In those days, you did two and a half years of a Trinity College degree course in Derry and the final year and a half in Dublin. A previous Christ's Hospital pupil had been there and had enjoyed it. Unbelievably, in the early sixties, there were sometimes adverts in London's *Evening Standard* looking for pupils.

Fortunately, my erratic A Level grades were accepted and I made my way across the Irish sea. Up to that point my knowledge of Ireland was sketchy. Although one of our closest family friends was Irish, at school Irish history was only touched upon as a footnote to the wider British story, and I therefore knew little

1

about Ireland's turbulent past. My only insight came when we read *Juno and the Paycock* aloud in class and its heady brew of anarchic comedy and redemptive tragedy miraculously survived our awful public schoolboy oirish accents. Consequently, as I made my way off the ferry at Belfast, bleary-eyed after a rowdy night amidst hard-drinking revellers, I was entering a whole new world. As I sat on the train to Derry passing Castlerock I started fatally romanticising my surroundings, thinking of that small village and its environs as isolated and mysterious as the barren Mediterranean setting in Antonioni's film *L'Aventurra*, where a woman on holiday with two friends mysteriously disappears. However, by the time I reached Derry station it was pouring with rain, and dreams of the Italian avant garde had swiftly disappeared as I was brought harshly back to reality.

I was ushered in to lodgings at Dill House where I was planted into a third floor attic room with a sloping ceiling and two other students. Magee was a bizarre mixture of Presbyterians studying to be Ministers, other Northern Irish students, Brits like myself who couldn't get into an English university and a spattering from the Commonwealth. The prospective Ministers preached about 'sin at Magee', the Ulster folk drank hard at Joe Cassidys on the Strand Road or the Castle Bar in Shipquay Street, willingly supported by us renegade Brits of course, while Kenny from Ghana regaled euphorically about the merits of Nkrumah's autocratic reforms, despite the fact that his beloved leader was seemingly bankrupting the country.

There were a lot of dances which I found terrifying. This was the era of Dickie Rock and the Miami Showband and the beginning of The Beatles as exemplified by groups with names like Gene and the Gents. There was a defined mating ritual and after each set of dances, an announcement from the stage would state with chilling authority, 'your next dance please'. Then both sexes would go to separate sides of the hall before the next set of dances were called. It took me some time to get the hang of this but come to think of it, it wasn't that much different from the Hammersmith Palais.

2

There were periodic college dances but the regular weekly one was the Rugby Club Dance off the Diamond. On Saturday the place was heaving after the pubs. There was a fair amount of drink taken but very little trouble. Mind you, the steep incline of some Derry streets could be difficult to navigate in such circumstances. One of the absurdities of that time in the mid-sixties was that because the pubs closed so early in Derry, we had to rush over the border into Donegal to continue imbibing. Whoever had a car was very popular, but if one wasn't available we crammed into a taxi, speeding away to get there before closing. The opening hours were, shall we say, more 'flexible' in the Republic. Such adventures had all the thrill of a chase. However, if you got stuck in the wilds of Donegal it could be difficult. I once went to see a girl friend in St Johnston, which is in the middle of nowhere. I got a lift from a young businessman going on a date. When I got to the house, the lady in question was out. I'd got the wrong day. Her father looked at me with aggressive suspicion and was determined to get rid of me. With nowhere to go I was 'banjaxed'. I meekly attempted to hitch a lift from the sporadic traffic. After several futile attempts, I decided to sleep. I lay down by the side of the road until awakened several hours later by the businessman. He stopped –thank god – but then started to illuminate me in exuberant detail about his wonderfully successful evening, how he'd hit it off with his lady, which was not exactly what I wanted to hear. As he dropped me off he looked at me with earnest confusion, 'are you all right mate?' 'Fine', I lied as I staggered forlornly home.

Later during my time in Derry I stayed in Northland Road, opposite the college, at the home of the McCaffertys. This consisted of Helen McCafferty and her mother, a woman in her seventies. Both were genial and helpful as were so many of the Derry people. The town had a high unemployment rate but there was something special about their sense of community. At that time it was expected that Magee would graduate to becoming the University of Ulster, however that didn't materialise and the predominantly Protestant Coleraine was chosen instead. It was a decision that alienated more moderate middle class nationalist opinion and accelerated conflict. While I was at Magee, I gradually got a sense of the sectarianism that led to 'the Troubles'. I became aware that political gerrymandering led to boundaries being rigged, that Catholics were at the bottom of housing lists and being discriminated against in jobs. This was an eye-opener for me as I wasn't politically well-informed. In fact, in those days I read *The Daily Telegraph*, mainly for the sport. A group of us used to go to the XL Café on the Strand Road, an idiosyncratic haunt for workers, students and the disabled. When my fellow student Jerry Castle opened the pages of *The Guardian* with pride and made a disdainful comment about my choice of journal, it made me think and I wasn't seen at the XL with *The Telegraph* again. Although I became aware of the injustices in the North, it wasn't yet a smouldering inferno. I remember going to parties in the Bogside and sitting around the fire as Bob Dylan songs were sung. Nonetheless, looking back there were prophetic signs even in little things. For instance, I was arrested by an authoritarian RUC man for 'jaywalking' – jumping the lights before they turned green. I got off with a caution at the local police station but was alarmed that so much trouble could be taken about something so trivial. In London, every other citizen would have been arrested.

Sunday was a day that seemed like the end of the world. There was no activity whatsoever, everything was closed There were jokes that if he could, Paisley would have tied the legs of ducks in local parks together. It was regarded as the Lord's Day and many students went to Dublin where the weekend wasn't victim to such Protestant restrictions. At college we had to make our own fun.

I had joined the college football team and enjoyed visits to the likes of Limavady and Ballykelly but was more interested in something artistic. I suggested to the fledgling dramatic society that I directed *Ghosts* by Ibsen. Looking back, this was a ridiculous choice, far too difficult for such an inexperienced group. However, it was encouraged by the English Department, probably for academic reasons, and the fact that the play had a small cast meant

4

that it could be satisfactorily funded. I had offered to direct mainly because no one else wanted to do so. I became really interested in the play and particularly the way Ibsen dramatised the past through present action. We were to start with a tour and then perform the play later at Magee. My first experience of directing was a disaster. Before our opening at Castlederg Intermediate School, the student playing the servant Engstrand had a bad accident and could only appear with an inappropriately huge cast on his leg, slowing proceedings down to a halt. When we played our second and final date at Strabane Town Hall, some audience members were snogging in the stalls. When it came to the last act, where the central character, Mrs Alving is in torment, while her son pleads to be released from the pain brought about by syphilis, there was a cacophony of laughter. I had succeeded in making one of Ibsen's great tragedies a comedy. When I went backstage I had to console our leading lady who was in tears. Strabane Town Hall was later bombed by the IRA. I can't remember us ever doing the play at Magee. I think we died on the road.

Although it had been a baptism of fire, I wasn't put off. Previously I'd been interested in acting but, apart from not being good enough, directing satisfied my diverse interests more fully. I discovered that direction can be what you want to put into it. After failing with Ibsen, I needed to do a play closer to my own age group and one that could be simply staged. Luckily, I managed to direct *The Knack* by Ann Jellicoe, the sixties comedy about sex and power. All the parts were young, the set was simple and it was a lively ensemble piece with a wonderful musical rhythm. As we rehearsed, I got more confident in my ability to orchestrate a production. The play's few performances were a great success. There was the wonderful sound of audiences laughing and enjoying themselves. This gave me the impetus to start another venture involving a bigger cast. In this case, it was *The Taming of the Shrew*. Not many students were that keen on making a commitment to act, so rounding them up was like herding cats. However, the main parts were in good hands, not least those of my friend John Pine as

Petruchio. I'd been at school with John and he was a highly intelligent actor with a good sense of comedy, who later worked in both Dublin and the West End. The production was in modern dress, set in the sixties; Petruchio was an outlandish rebel, Kate a stuck-up debutante bound by a conventional family. The final wedding scene was set in a registry office with Petruchio in casual clothes. Maybe in hindsight the sexual politics of the play were insufficiently explored, but it was great fun and engendered a real sense of ensemble. Our production played mainly to students. Getting the wider community interested was difficult. I remember going around the town, knocking up houses to tell people about it. One woman opened her door and told me she wasn't going to come but that she'd buy a ticket anyway!

2 – Trinity Adventures

I HAD GOT THE BUG NOW AND WAS determined to try to direct another play when I arrived at Trinity. Fortunately, I was lucky enough to get *When Did You Last See My Mother?* by Christopher Hampton accepted by the redoubtable Trinity Players. Hampton's drama about a young gay relationship in London became a *succès de scandale*. It was probably the first time there was a homosexual kiss in Irish theatre. Written when the writer was only seventeen, the play had humour and an accurate, honest insight into adolescence and sexual discovery. When it was revived, the Gardaí came to see it but no charges were made. A pity really because it would have considerably accelerated box office. Despite its understandable immaturities, *When Did You Last see My Mother?* had a touching humanity which communicated strongly with the Trinity students. It's success led to me directing a production of *Romeo and Juliet* which went on to represent Trinity in the annual Irish Universities Drama Competition. Although I got complimented by the official adjudicator for 'a talent for big production', we didn't win and my production was too long and derivative. Sometimes, when you've seen many shows it can have a negative effect. Nothing wrong with influences – after all, wasn't it Olivier who said we were all scavengers? But when the imprint of others lies too heavily on your imagination, it stops you thinking through the play for yourself. My production was half-baked between the passionate Italianate (shades of Zefferelli) and something more obscurely doom-laden.

Trinity in 1967-68 was a wonderful place to be. In those days, it was distinctive, international and very social. Essentially a conservative university, it was surprisingly immune to the various sit-ins and rebellions that were transpiring in Britain at the likes of Hornsey Art College and Essex University. I think that was because it was eccentric and flexible. It seemed to have an unwritten rule – have fun but don't get caught! I always got the impression that a benign eye was conveniently looking in the wrong direction when something untoward was going on – as long as you dropped the porter the odd fiver, of course. Consequently, 'revolution' was unnecessary. This, added to excellent lecturers, an attractive town with a vibrant culture, made it an exciting place to study. So when, after finishing my final term, it was suggested that a group of us from Trinity and UCD, aided by some miscellaneous others like my sister Mandy, got together to present a season of four plays, I was more than happy.

The season ran throughout the summer and proved very successful. Most memorable were the performances of Sorcha Cusack as the mute Dodo in Ann Jellicoe's *The Sport of My Mad Mother* and the sexually mesmeric Ruth in Harold Pinter's *The Homecoming*. These two parts showed the contrasting sides of her emerging talent; an ability to convey deep thought without words as well as menace and powerful eroticism. As one who played Lenny opposite her in *The Homecoming*, I can vouch for literally being blown away by her performance. I also acted as Ricky, the dubious brother of the warm-hearted prostitute in Charles Dyer's *The Rattle of a Simple Man*. Ricky didn't appear until over half way through the play, which I found difficult, not least because of the temptations to leave my flat in Leeson Street too late and then get into a panic before my entrance. Being more preoccupied with developing my directing skills, I found it difficult to revert to being an actor. However, these experiences certainly helped give me a grounding in the actor's world.

I had some knowledge of acting because my father was a thespian. He had worked as Raymond Young (foreign-sounding names like Jaquarello being inadviseable in those days) in several West End productions in the forties and fifties, including the musical *Ace of Clubs*, written and directed by Noël Coward, and *The Brothers Karamazov*, adapted by and starring Alec Guinness, as well as several feature films including *Adam and Evelyne*, in which he co-starred with Stewart Granger and Jean Simmons. In fact, I have childhood memories of my father telling me that 'Jimmy' Granger confessed to him that he was only in show business for the women. Unfortunately, the vicissitudes of the profession had contributed to the divorce from my mother, a talented pianist, who had performed at the Wigmore Hall and later taught at the Royal Academy of Music. However, even though I came from an artistic and performing background, nothing could prepare me for the process of going on the boards myself. Such an experience should be compulsory for all directors.

3 – You're a Big Boy Now

As we came to the end of our season, I was contacted by a Dublin company called Theatre '66. This was run by three actors: Julie Hamilton, Ritchie Stewart and Vincent Smith. They produced plays in Dun Laoghaire, the nearby coastal resort, at the Gas Co Theatre, the theatre being at the back of gas showrooms. In fact, you passed the cookers and fridges on the way to the auditorium. Usually they produced more tried and tested plays, but during the Theatre Festival at the Eblana Theatre in central Dublin they were presenting a new Irish play, *Watershed*, by G.P. Gallivan, an experienced Dublin writer who had written historical plays about Parnell and Michael Collins. His latest drama was about the menopause and how a middle age crisis effected one woman, her husband and his close friend. Suddenly, I was being propelled into professional theatre. In those days there were no courses for direction, you learnt from experience. In *Watershed*, I was fortunate to have a cast of consummate professionals – Des Nealon, Robert Somerset and Joan Stynes – who all responded to my ideas and guided me into the professional world. I remember being very nervous before the first rehearsal, sitting in my flat, planning moves in the set's model. Inevitably, most of them went out of the window.

While it's good to have a basic sense of the play's physical journey, predetermined moves aren't the way to direct creatively. Having been used to directing students of mixed ability who needed more steering, I created a false structure before directing professionals. Once I got into a dialogue with the actors, I found the physical shape by responding to what they were doing, the moves coming more organically out of the text. However, in those days, there were some who still believed in the imposition of moves. One celebrated Dublin director, when reviving a play, blew the dust off the old prompt copy and got the actors to move exactly as the original cast did many years previously. I suppose we could call this the Samuel French School of Direction, as their acting editions used to have all the moves of the original production.

Watershed was a moderate success, enough to get me up and running. The houses were good and the reviews, although mixed, were respectable, with the *Irish Independent* amusingly referring to me as 'the Italianate director from TCD'. While I was wondering what to do next, Des Nealon got in touch and told me that he wanted me to work for a company he had helped to set up called Amalgamated Artists. The board consisted of an actor, Des, a director, Frank J. Bailey, a studio manager in RTÉ, Alan Gibson, and Tony Murphy, a genial accountant. They wanted me to direct a comedy about contraception, *It's a Two Foot Six Inches Above the Ground World*, by Kevin Laffan.

Kevin, who was later the creator of *Emmerdale Farm*, was born in Liverpool. One of fourteen children, his father was a disabled Irish photographer and at one point his family were thrown out of their home by bailiffs. Kevin claimed to have escaped the workhouse by jumping off a lorry. Later, he slept on the kitchen floor of an elderly actress, who advised him that 'if you want to be serious, be funny'. He never forgot her advice. He'd written a hilarious comedy about a Catholic family agonising over whether to use contraception. Today the play is dated but at the time, it was very relevant. As the sexual revolution of the seventies gathered pace, there was great pressure on a couple to adhere to Catholic doctrine or break free. It wasn't easy to get contraception in Ireland during this period. This was the era of women protesting by smuggling condoms over the border via Belfast, so the theme had direct relevance to the audience. Mick (Des Nealon), the husband in the play is caught between his more liberal wife, Esther (Angela Vale) and his friend, Father Yeo (Kevin McHugh), a doctrinal priest, who wants him to obey the church's teaching. Things are complicated by a visiting lorry driver, Baker (Frank Kelly), a born hedonist who sees sex just as an outlet for pleasure, two children intent on asking embarrassing questions at the most inopportune moments and a babysitter (Bairbre Dowling) who invites her Swedish boyfriend (Shane Briant) to the house.

I approached the play with the seriousness that I thought the subject demanded, so that the characters were believable and their point of view clear. I didn't want the humour signalled in a self-conscious way but to develop out of the situation. Then a distinct world would emerge. The cast responded to my approach with well-judged performances, which helped the play to oscillate easily from laughter to pathos. And what laughter there was. I will never forget three moments. First when Father Yeo, tired and upset, mistakenly swallows a contraceptive pill thinking it's an asprin. It seemed the laughter would never stop. It was so loud that it seemed to take an age before it started to subside and the next line could be spoken. There was also a moment in the opening breakfast scene when one of the children asks Mick, 'have you got hairs on your wee wee, daddy!' Again, the theatre erupted with the laughter of recognition. The third instance was what we might call the Irish 'Tynan' moment when Baker, in an escalating argument with Mick says, 'you like a good feed, we like a good fuck.' Just as critic Kenneth Tynan was the first to say the four letter word on British TV, I think Frank Kelly (later to find TV fame in *Father Ted*) was the first to utter the profanity on the Irish stage. During the run, when several priests and nuns left after hearing such language, they were ironically applauded as they departed. In the play, Mick struggles with his conscience as his wife implores him to accept contraception. At one performance, when he tells her that such an idea 'makes me sick', a woman in the audience piped up, 'you make me bleedin' sick!'

The first night was one of those rare moments when everything seemed to come together. We had a good play, a talented cast who enjoyed working together, good notices ('attendance should be compulsory for all' – *The Irish Times*) and big audiences. In fact, the play quickly packed out its initial run at the Eblana and ran with different casts for eighteen months. The Eblana wasn't the Abbey or the Olympia, it was a small, 230-seater, an ex-cinema under Busáras, located past the toilets in the basement of the central bus station in Dublin. Its stage was small and cramped and making exits could be hazardous as you could immediately smack into a brick wall. Despite these limitations, there was an energy and commitment to make the production work. This was commercial theatre and if enough people didn't come, the play would close. In those days, we rehearsed for two weeks, not something I'd encourage anyone to do for long, but of necessity you honed many practical skills, which you might have avoided in more comfortable circumstances. Also, the fear of closing early could knit people together in a unique bond to do their best to make the play successful.

Working on *Two Foot Six* was a lesson for me in comedy. It gave me a grounding that I needed. Kevin Laffan was a very professional craftsman. He was hardened in the British rep system as a director and writer. I think he had learnt a lot from it. Certainly his construction was immaculate. He set up a recognisable family and then allowed conflict to seep in gently between the family

11

It's a Two Foot Six Inches Above the Ground World by Kevin Laffan, designed
by Peter Avery. Eblana Theatre Dublin, 1970. Angela Vale as Esther Goonahan
and Frank Kelly as Baker.

and a friend. Just as this intensifies he introduces an anarchic outsider who threatens the status quo. This accelerates both the crisis
and humour to farcical proportions only for it to dissipate on the
outsider's departure. The main protaganists, weary and exhausted,
were then left to face themselves and their future. The play had
that essential theatrical virtue – rhythm. I often think of a script as
a musical score with similar changes of pace, emphasis and contrast. Kevin's play was perfectly composed. The excessive laughter
came because the play never forced its humour. The audience got
to know the characters before we laughed at them. When familiarity was established the conflict accelerated, sometimes using a
split set to hilarious comic effect. Attitudes and incident collided
in a final farcical denouement, which earned the pathos of the last
scene. The play was very funny because the actors strongly held
to the truth of their characters, trusted the writing and resisted
overembroidering their performances.

While working on a successful comedy, I made one of the biggest mistakes of my career. In my contract for *Two Foot Six*, like all directors in a commercial production, I got a small percentage of the gross takings. This was a very welcome stipend for a young director starting out. However, after a few weeks of the run, Tony Murphy came to me and spelt out the company's financial woes and asked me to forfeit it. Apparently, the money made by *Two Foot Six* was being absorbed by their losses on previous productions and the company needed to cut back to get on an even keel. Because I understood what Amalgamated Artists were trying to achieve, and I liked them all personally, I agreed and *Two Foot Six* went on its long run. Was I naïve? Possibly. But there are times when, after you've reasoned the arguments, you have to trust your instinct. In any case, on the strength of the production, I went on to direct a successful English national tour of the play, starring Linda Thorsen, *The Avengers* star, as Esther, and Abbey stalwart Pat Laffan as the beleaguered Mick. Furthermore, AA asked me back, giving me the opportunities I needed to get experience.

The next play I directed for AA was *Loot* by Joe Orton, a black comedy about robbery, murder and corruption. What's more we got Donal McCann, the most talented Irish actor of his generation, to play the lead, Inspector Truscott. *Loot* had been a big success in London after the initial overplayed touring production with Kenneth Williams had failed disastrously. Now, with Donal in place, the time was right for the Irish premiere. Donal had already made a big splash in the Abbey Theatre's production of Boucicault's melodrama *The Shaughraun*, which had gone to the World Theatre Season in London, and in *Tarry Flynn* by Patrick Kavanagh, after which girls were waiting for him at the Abbey stage door. Donal had an inbuilt suspicion of directors, maybe fearing that they'd stultify his brilliant instincts, but in my case we seemed to get on. Maybe it was because we both liked cricket and reading papers. For a short time, Donal had worked at *The Irish Press* and he enjoyed working his way through all the current politics, sport (particularly the horses) and scandal. In any case, Donal loved the part and attacked it with relish. He was a major actor leading from the front. I think he also enjoyed the challenge of realising the character quickly. His father had been a successful playwright for the Abbey at the old Queen's Theatre in Pearse Street, when public funds were limited and commercial success essential. Donal understood the nature of the gig. In those days, not so many Irish actors did an English accent that convincingly, but Donal caught the character's estuary voice perfectly. This, coupled with a natural sense of comic timing, made him a brilliant Truscott. Nonetheless, we did have one altercation.

During one of our run-throughs, Donal started indulging, try-ing to make the other actors laugh by 'mugging'. I was annoyed about this as it was the main principle of the production that we were going to play it straight within the style of the piece and not indulge in wink-wink, nudge-nudge acting. I reminded Donal of this in no uncertain terms. He didn't take it well and dramatically left the theatre with a departing outburst. After a few minutes talk-ing to the Stage Manager, I suddenly saw that Donal had been so enraged that he had left his coat and possessions in the theatre. I continued the meeting, only later to be interrupted by an embar-rassed Donal returning furtively to take his belongings. Cautiously, I pointed them out to him. As he departed, he moved towards me. Apprehensive of further conflict, I thought 'what now?' I needn't have worried as Donal proceeded to whisper mischievously in my ear, 'fancy a pint in PJs?' PJs was Molloys, a friendly pub not far from the Eblana. Run by P.J. O'Connor, it had become a haunt for many theatre folk, not only Donal but other leading lights from the Abbey. It was warm, friendly and inviting. I really felt part of the community there. Donal explained that he was trying to get a response from the cast and was frustrated, so he resorted to camp-ing it up. He reassured me it wouldn't happen in performance and we proceeded towards the opening.

Everything progressed well until the first preview, when Mau-reen Toal, as scheming nurse Fay, looked in a wardrobe, saw a dead body, slammed the door and the top of the wardrobe got dislodged and hung perilously above her head. The audience found it hilarious and laughed uproariously, although the situation was both precarious and dangerous. Maureen thankfully survived and we went on to have a very successful run. The Irish audience took to Orton's anarchic satire on religion and corruption, a mixture perfectly attuned to the times. Unfortunately, because of Donal's prior commitments, the production had a limited run. There were talks of possibly getting a replacement but I don't think anybody could come up with an actor nearly as good, so it was thought best to close. When Donal died, nobody in the Irish press mentioned this performance. Maybe because the production only had a short run, or it didn't fit into the scheme of things, not being in an Irish play. That was a pity as it was one of Donal's best – a brilliantly inventive, comic interpretation by an Irish actor in a modern English classic. For those fortunate to see it, it was truly memorable. On the last night, at his final exit, Donal, as the corrupt cop departing with the loot, decided to improvise and on turning to the widowed Irishman, the very Catholic McLeavy (Derry Power), he said his own line, 'Give my love to the Pope.' It got one of the biggest

Loot by Joe Orton. Eblana Theatre, 1970. Derry Power as Mr McLeavy and Donal McCann as Inspector Truscott.

laughs of the night. I have to confess that I think even Orton would have enjoyed that.

With two successful comedy productions, I managed to get the start and confidence that is essential for a director beginning his career. I was still learning but rather absurdly I found myself being categorised as a successful commercial director. I never thought of myself as such, rather a lucky beginner who had recently been given two fine plays to direct. At that point I was more interested in learning by directing good plays and working with good actors. At the time, Ireland didn't have a full-time drama school, only a few part time ones at the Abbey and the impressively serious Focus Theatre. Some Irish actors had been trained in England but most learned by performing. This made them hardened practitioners, but in a culture of short rehearsal time and few directors, it sometimes made them take short cuts. There was certainly an abundance of talent but often it wouldn't develop sufficiently, becoming bludgeoned by the pressure to get a performance together too quickly. Today, there are many more directors resident in Ireland. Then everybody just wanted to act and everything was centred around Dublin. Irish regional theatre relied on touring productions or thriving amateur groups.

Although Dublin theatre was small it was vibrant and not lacking characters. Frank J. Bailey was one of them. The play director on the Amalgamated Artists board, he was warm, ambitious and neurotic. He was also gay which was difficult in the seventies, being against all religious and social norms. Frank was from Cork where his family ran a successful hotel business. A bespectacled, haunted figure with a propensity for hyperbole, he had an infectious enthusiasm which sometimes ran away with itself. For instance, when he went over to England, he saw Cliff Richard in a play at Bromley and sent a long and expensive telegram back to the board in Dublin stating that Cliff was willing to perform at the Eblana. This was pure fantasy and Frank was hauled back by the board's much shorter telegram saying: 'Come back, Frank. Now!' Frank was always in the middle of off stage drama. Just before directing *Two Foot Six*, he met me in a pub opposite the Cambridge Theatre in London. After buying me a drink, he looked at me earnestly and said, 'You've got to back down. Or should I say, I'm asking you, Frank to Roland, to back down. I've got a deal for a musical but the backers need to see my work. This show's going to be the next *Hair*.'

When he described it, it sounded ghastly. Apparently, it took place in Trafalgar Square where a naked chorus were chained to Nelson's column singing about society's injustices! More like a sixties parody than the next landmark musical. I politely prevaricated and got in touch with Des Nealon who told me not to take any notice of Frank's antics. On another occasion, Frank got morbid over the set for *Loot*. He was in the front row of the stalls staring at it on the afternoon of the first performance. I asked him if there was something that he was worried about. 'No, it just reminds me of Orton's death,' he said with exaggerated camp inflection. I took this as a compliment as designer Peter Avery had created a deceptively eerie atmosphere, ordinary on one level, with its suburban trappings, but with hints of the macabre with its ostentatious crucifix and tomb-like wardrobe.

The most celebrated character in Dublin theatre was Micheál Macliammóir, who ran the Gate Theatre with his partner, Hilton Edwards. Micheál and Hilton were now elderly gentlemen but this didn't stop Micheál applying more rouge and miscasting himself in younger parts. Actor, writer and scholar, he was undoubtedly able. He had played Oswald opposite Peggy Ashcroft in Ibsen's *Ghosts* and was Iago in Orson Welles's film of *Othello*. He and Hilton had founded the Gate and provided an imaginative alternative to the Abbey in the thirties and forties, concentrating more on international work interspersed with strong new Irish plays. However, in the sixties, they were past their best. Their productions seemed mannered and old-fashioned, full of imitation West End production values. They indulged in continually playing the style at the expense of the truth of a scene. However, this didn't stop conservative critics like Desmond Rushe of the *Irish Independent* consistently eulogising their outmoded productions. Other theatres had at least one foot in the modern world, but the Gate seemed to delight in refusing to accept the liberal social and artistic changes that the sixties brought. To many of these Irish critics, this new freedom was like a bad rash they'd couldn't erase. Instead, they just kept scratching. For instance, the *Evening Herald's* film critic had a star system which in those days was unique. Nearly every good modern film of the era was fortunate to get one star from this reactionary gentleman. In fact, there was an absurdity at the centre of Irish cultural life that such an obviously gay couple like Micheál and Hilton were feted by a political and religious establishment who totally refused to acknowledge the rights of homosexuals. I think they were tolerated because they were both eccentric and successful. They had undoubtedly contributed significantly to Irish theatre and were seen as 'theatricals' or 'luvvies' as actors are now deridingly called, apart from main stream society. Stories were legendary about Hilton and Micheál and many actors of the day enjoyed imitating their grand Victorian theatrical tones. When they were criticised, their housekeeper staunchly defended them by insisting that they were very good gentleman because in all her time working there she'd never seen a woman in the house!

I once went to tea at their Georgian home in Harcourt Terrace. I was seen as a young director they should meet. I never got a word in edgeways, as they proceeded to entertain me with their double act. 'Oh Hilton, for god's sake shut up and give the boy some tea!' I remember we discussed the celebrated playwright Harold Pinter, who had worked as an actor with Anew McMaster's company in Ireland. 'Oh those dreadful plays,' exclaimed Micheál. 'Not enough speeches. Just awful mundanities.' He then parodied Pinter's dialogue brilliantly. 'Lovely man. Good actor but oh those ghastly plays!' The irony was that Macliammóir could have been very good in such plays as *No Man's Land* but didn't stretch himself anymore. His occasional performances were solo affairs performing his own myth rather than the character. He was most likely to be seen coming to the Gate's rescue resurrecting his one man show *The Im-*

portance of Being Oscar. If a Gate production flopped and came off early, when it finished on a Saturday, Micheál would be back with *Oscar*, by public demand of course, the following Monday. I went to see the show on one of these occasions. When Micheál got to his Dorian Gray section and talked of 'a painting of a most beautiful boy', and of Lord Henry being 'suddenly interrupted', a Dublin working class voice piped up, 'Oh for jaysus sake, why don't you give us "Melancholy Baby"?' Micheál responded by looking askance, facing his heckler with an icy camp stare and retorting, 'as I was so rudely then'. Inevitably, he got a round of applause and dismissively turned away from his assailant before continuing his excessive performance. When I made certain noises in the press that Joe Orton was the new Oscar Wilde I had difficulty convincing the two Gate 'boys'. There were, in fact, similarities – both were gay and wickedly satirised society. If Orton had lived he might well have built a body of work to challenge Wilde. I think he would have had a particular field day during the Thatcher era.

I was fortunate to get so many opportunities so early in my career. Directors need a home to develop their work and Amalgamated Artists gave me that. Dublin in those days had a slower pace, conviviality and humour that was irresistible, and it wasn't long before I was very much part of its theatrical culture. For instance, I was warmly welcomed when I made the odd sojourn to Groomes, the hotel opposite the Gate which housed late night drinking for politicians, police and inveterate theatre folk. Mrs Groome was the wife of the General Secretary of Fianna Fáil, Ireland's ruling party, and when, after the pubs closed, you made your way up O'Connell Street and knocked on the door of the celebrated hotel, she would cautiously appear and in ripe country accent declare, 'Roland. The Guards. Come back in fifteen minutes'. I never quite understood this ritual as many of the Gardaí were in the pub! However, while I never had trouble gaining entry, others were less fortunate. For instance, when veteran actor Arthur O'Sullivan decided to take a taxi from County Kerry to Groomes, as a break from the interminable filming of *Ryan's Daughter*, he got out of the cab, paid his £100 fare, only to be greeted by the indomitable Mrs Groome telling him in no uncertain terms, 'Archie. You're barred!' Groomes was the communal green room of Irish theatre. It was Ireland's long days journey into night. Ostensibly a hotel, I never remember anybody staying there, apart from when they were too drunk to go home. As you entered, you were confronted by a homely saloon bar, often peopled by the good and the great. I remember seeing John Hume and Paddy Devlin there, looking worse for wear after discussions about the escalating tension in the North. The back room was more of a public bar, sparse and minimal. It was here that you'd see actors arguing about a production, writers vehemently debating the merits of Dublin whores, musicians playing a melancholy Irish air or a leading literary figure surprising us with a moving rendition of an operatic aria. It was a unique meeting place, a focus for drink, frustration and dreams, but also a centre for artistic fraternity. When the Groomes sold up and it closed, theatre lost a focal point. It was back to taking brown parcels of drink to the suburbs. The other notorious late night attraction of the day was the Manhattan, an infamous all night café in Harcourt Road, near Kelly's Corner, not far from Rathmines. There in the middle of the night, you were likely to see a distinguished actor stagger in looking for his egg, sausage and beans amidst young ones canoodling after a night of dancing at the likes of Sloopy's and Zhivago night clubs.

Such distinctive experiences made me glad that I stayed in Dublin after I completed my degree. I'd made a lot of new friends, fell in love with both the city and Irish drama, while learning my craft with people who believed in me. Thankfully, it wasn't long before Amalgamated Artists asked me to direct another Orton play, *What the Butler Saw*. They hoped it would do as well as *Loot* and run longer. In truth, while it had a perfectly respectable run, it didn't, probably because it hadn't the macabre ingredients of death and religion which made *Loot* so successful with an Irish audience. In fact, it's more of an English comedy, albeit an ambitious one. It satirises not only the police but the family, psychiatry, medicine and a hypocritical establishment, while parodying great English and Irish comic writers in the process. Orton had been in prison for stealing library books. It was while he was doing time that he seemed to acquire a huge knowledge of comic writers like Wilde and Congreve. Consequently, it's not surprising that in his plays the young are always being exploited by the authority of their elders and can only survive by being criminals themselves, in this case, bellboy Nicholas Becket (Chris O'Neill) and secretary Geraldine Barclay (Dearbhla Molloy). They are depicted as relative innocents in a corrupt world, who have to resort to disguise and guile to survive. At the end of the play, there is an apocalyptic scene in which a dim policeman (Des Nealon) descends from the heavens and the remains of Winston Churchill are celebrated. If this was the last scene Orton ever wrote, we can surmise that he might have started his next play with an angry but hilarious Swiftian satire.

Sadly, Orton was murdered by his partner Kenneth Halliwell, an unsuccessful writer, who in turn killed himself. Initially, Halliwell's career was advancing quicker than Orton's so maybe he couldn't live with his lover's success. I was told that when a director went to discuss a play at the flat they shared in Noel Road Islington, he found a dark room with the blinds drawn, a room full of cream cakes and a collage of defaced library books on the wall. However, Orton wasn't only an idiosyncratic maverick but a uniquely gifted comic dramatist who had great vision and is sorely missed.

What the Butler Saw presented me with greater stylistic and technical challenges than *Loot*, especially on such a minute stage. The play moves from being a sophisticated comedy of manners to an outright farce with a surrealistic epilogue. Despite the physical limitations, it was a wonderful experience to direct a play written by such an original comic talent. Orton wanted to comment on society not through more traditional straight drama or via an issue play but by the power of laughter. He exposed the folly and vice of the establishment through his own blackly absurd vision. I wish we had more overtly comic playwrights today to reinvigorate

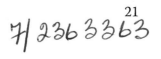

commercial theatre. I suppose, to an extent, alternative comedy has taken on that mantle, but it's no substitute for the longer, more challenging form of the comic play.

Although I didn't know it at the time, this was to be the last production I directed for Amalgamated Artists. After *What the Butler Saw* closed, AA brought back *Two Foot Six*, until their finances ran into trouble and they called it a day. Even when they had a success, I think they were probably playing catch-up, subsidising their losses, handicapped by playing to a limited seating capacity. In the history of Irish Theatre, AA are blithely ignored. Along with the Pike Theatre, Gemini and the Globe Theatre earlier, they produced modern plays that were gateways to a more liberal Ireland, and provided public discussion about important and previously taboo subjects. It was, for instance, AA that produced *Boys in the Band*, the first openly gay play performed in Ireland, and new Irish work like *Savages* by James Douglas. As there was no landmark Irish play, they don't easily fit in to a more obvious narrative. That's a pity as they opened the doors to new talent and challenging subject matter with intelligent popular theatre. Sadly, the strains of commercial production finally wore them down.

4 – Festival Frolics

DURING THIS PERIOD, I DIRECTED my second production for the Dublin Theatre Festival, *Ah Well, It Won't Be Long Now!* by Mary Manning. At first I was hesitant as the play wasn't very well written and the subject matter was deeply conventional. However, after further consideration, I realised that I needed to have the experience of working in bigger spaces. What's more, the leading part was going to be played by Milo O'Shea, an Irish star, which would present another new challenge. Consequently, I decided to accept the offer, especially as the fee was good and I hadn't much money. In any case, the play was only running for two weeks. The Festival in the early seventies was run by Brendan Smith, a squat, owlish figure who always put his glasses up on his forehead like a deep sea diver coming up for air, as another crisis was averted. Brendan was also producing the play, a country house Anglo-Irish comedy, which he saw as a vehicle for Milo, who was now living in the United States, and this production was seen as his homecoming. The play was about two Americans looking for valuable cultural documents which they eventually discover under the commode of an ageing professor played by Milo. It was an amiable, rambling country house piece with very little tension. However, due to Milo's presence, the Olympia Theatre was full every night so the play became an event, an occasion that went beyond the drama itself. I discovered that this can happen in Ireland in a unique way. There can be an amazing bond between the people in the play and those watching it, probably the result of being a small society where everybody knows everybody else. Also I found out that a play at the Olympia never seemed to start on time, and when it did there were always latecomers making their way conversationally to their seats as if they were in a bar. No wonder the theatre had music hall roots. Although for a serious-minded young director like myself, it was annoying to see one's work ignored in this way, I soon realised that the Olympia had a wonderfully eccentric spirit. This was the perfect place for popular drama that engaged a wider audience. There was none of the bourgeoise aloofness of the Gate with its Dublin 4 audience and pseudo-West End values. There was something earthy, accessible and eccentric about this warm Victorian theatre, which would welcome anybody and had a barwoman who'd worked there for forty years and had never seen one production!

Ah Well, It Won't Be Long Now! was written by Mary Manning, an Irishwoman who had lived in Boston for many years. She was warm, opinionated and well-connected. The only problem was that she was also an acerbic critic for *Hibernia*, the now defunct Dublin magazine which had extensive coverage of politics, literature and the performing arts. Mary had trashed a lot of people in this publication. I think she saw herself as a combination of the acerbic Dorothy Parker and the powerful *New York Times* theatre critic Clive Barnes. She certainly had a very American way of being crudely forthright. Inevitably, she made enemies and people were looking for revenge. After the first night of her decidedly average play, they got it. Venom poured forth like blood from a bad wound. Dublin became decidedly Sicilian as those with vendettas relished payback time. The irony was that it had no effect on the box office. Cleverly managed by Brendan, the play was a big hit.

The actors deservedly survived the local critical debris. They were a motley international crew. There were two Americans, Philip O'Brien and O.Z. 'Zebbie' Whitehead, who now lived in Dublin. Philip had real estate to manage and Zebbie started a highly successful new Irish play award and was heavily involved in the Bahai religion. Prior to coming to Ireland, Zebbie had also been in many Broadway shows and John Ford's film of *The Grapes of Wrath*. Then there was Susan Hallinan, the able and beautiful English wife of Producer and Agent Richard Hallinan. Liam Sweeney, a brilliant doleful Irish clown, played a gloomy butler who would mournfully intone various announcements from a gallery in Peter Avery's attractive Georgian library set. Emmet Bergin was the dashing, handsome juvenile lead and Zoë Wanamaker, the highly talented young English actress, his girlfriend. Brendan trusted my judgement, and probably thought it was also good to bolster the play with another name, given Zoë's father Sam was a well known American actor/director who had fled to England to escape Mc-Carthyism. In fact, Zoë was brilliant in the role, creating an eccentric scatty Anglo-Irish character that was both funny and oddly touching.

Milo was an endearing and comic leading man. During breaks, he would play the piano and sing old music hall songs in the big Olympia bar, where we were rehearsing. When it came to the work, he took me aside after a week or so of rehearsal. 'The text work you're doing is good. But now we need to find the sense of humour of the characters. This play is a soufflé and we need to cook it right!' It was good advice. While my initial work had laid the groundwork, we didn't want to overload a piece that wasn't Chekhov. As a result of Milo's advice, I looked to get the actors to lighten their vocal delivery, have more of a sense of fun and a twinkle in their eye, without resorting to indulgence. This didn't resolve all the play's problems, but the production did have an Anglo-Irish charm and the audience laughed a lot. Several of the British press, uncontaminated by Mary's *Hibernia* abuse, enjoyed the piece, John Barber of *The Daily Telegraph* describing it as 'an intriguing country house play'.

We were followed at the Olympia by Hugh Leonard's play *The Patrick Pearse Motel*, a scurrilous satire depicting the Irish bourgeoise cashing in, quite literally, on history. One of the actors in the play was Godfrey Quigley, a warm, swarthy, stocky figure with an actor-manager demeanour, who seemed to always start speaking with the declamation 'Dear Heart'. Having seen *Ah Well*, he came over to me in the expansive Olympia bar and gave me some advice. 'Dear heart, Susan is looking very pretty but has the demeanour of an actor apologising for the play's dialogue. You know, dear heart, I have one rule about bad writing. Be definite. If a writer writes bad dialogue I shove it down the audiences throat so he or she will never write such crap again!' Godfrey was later in *Staircase* by Charles Dyer at the Eblana with that most versatile of Irish actors, David Kelly. They were playing two gay barbers. While there, Godfrey got a call from a Broadway producer asking him to take over in Brian Friel's *The Mundy Scheme*. Godfrey had already appeared in the play in Dublin so he was ideal to replace an actor who had become ill. When the producer phoned, Godfrey audaciously bargained for more money but the producer refused. Godfrey forgot about it and continued with *Staircase*, only for the producer to ring him again. When he accepted the increased fee, Godfrey decided to go for broke and insist on billing. By this time, the producer had had enough and slammed down the phone. Godfrey again continued with *Staircase*, thinking he'd blown it. Twenty-four hours later, the producer rang the theatre once more and ruefully accepted Godfrey's demands. However, Godfrey knew that Brian Friel's play didn't have the commercial legs of *Philadelphia Here I Come* so he told the company. 'See you in a few weeks – with the poster!' Godfrey's prophecy was right. *The Mundy Scheme* closed after four performances and he was soon back in Dublin – with the aforementioned souvenir.

During the Festival, I stayed at Mrs O'Shea's lodgings in South King Street opposite the Gaiety Theatre. Mrs O'Shea was a warm, country lady who had a real understanding of theatre people as was evident of her toleration of the various comings and goings in her guest house. She and her imposingly tall husband, who worked for the Gardaí, created a very friendly family atmosphere. When I was ill suffering from a virulent flu, during the technical rehearsal of *Ah Well*, I felt comforted by both the surroundings and the various medicines Zoë had kindly given me. During rehearsals Zoë and I had become good friends and we went to see a Maureen Potter show at the Gaiety where in one of the supporting novelty acts we saw a seal go on strike. The trainer had ordered the seal to go on to one of its assorted perches but it refused and belligerently walked off the stage as the curtain was hurriedly brought down. Zoë and I burst into laughter like giggling school children revelling in such a defiant animal creating such chaos.

A feature of the Festival was the daily press conferences chaired by Brendan Smith. The highlight was usually the jousting Brendan had with *Irish Times* critic Seamus Kelly, a Shavian figure, resplendent with appropriately white beard, who multiskilled as Quidnunc, the author of the *Irish Times's* diary. He could be a good observer of Irish plays but through personal ware and tare the impact of his work gradually declined. However, that didn't stop him from hogging the limelight and endlessly questioning Brendan about every detail of the Festival's organisation. Sometimes it was fascinating, on other occasions tedious. It was more consistently entertaining to see the bemused looks of the attending international press as the two locals crossed swords about matters the foreign visitors couldn't comprehend. Brendan was often criticised unfairly for being mean. In fact in my production, he summoned me to inform 'Miss Wanamaker that in a modern play you have to supply your own costumes!' And he did always suggest his wife, Beryl Fagan, for parts. 'You know Ronald (he repeatedly mispronounced my name) you could consider Beryl. She was splendid in the Butlins season at Mosney this summer.' On this occasion he won as Beryl did in fact play a foreign Countess in *Ah Well*. However, for all his eccentricities, Brendan kept the Festival together on meagre resource for many years. Thanks to him, it's survived to this day and has been the launching pad for many new writers and actors.

5 – Avant Garde Exploits

AFTER *AH WELL*, I WANTED TO EXPAND my horizons. Consequently, I directed three unusual Irish premieres. *Police* by the celebrated Polish writer in exile, Slawomir Mrozek, a surreal comedy about a totalitarian state, with Frank Kelly, Tom Hickey, Des Nealon and Alan Devlin, which transferred from the Project to the Eblana. *Fando and Lis* by the Spaniard Fernando Arrabal, which dramatised the volatile, violent and moving relationship between

Police by Slawomir Mrozek, designed by Peter Avery, Eblana Theatre, 1971.
Frank Kelly as Chief of Police and Tom Hickey as Prisoner.

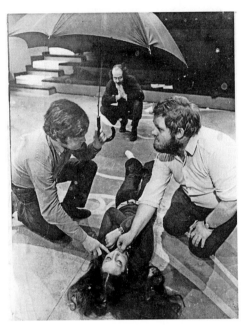

RJ directs a rehearsal of *Fando and Lis*, by Fernando Arrabal. Peacock Theatre, 1971. With Alan Devlin, Terry Donnelly and Gerard Walsh.

a young couple (Terry Donnelly and Bryan Murray, both excellent at extending themselves) as they travelled on a sand-filled set to a mythical destination, at the Peacock. And finally, *The Pedagogue*, by English writer James Saunders, a monologue about a teacher trying to control a class in the wake of an imminent nuclear attack, a tour de force by John Pine at the Project as the audience sat in school desks. The Project was primarily a visual arts centre and I remember before one late night performance of *Police*, a sculptor came in and completely destroyed his work in a drunken rage. It was an image that's always haunted me, reflecting the way we can all be our own worst enemies. However, despite such a debacle, the productions went well and reflected a growing international repertoire in Dublin in the early seventies. Working on such varied plays not only gave me confidence, but helped me understand the importance of the distinctiveness of each writer's individual voice and the need to create a different world for it.

ABBEY THEATRE DUBLIN

6 – Manoeuvring through the Minefield

IT WAS AFTER *THE PEDAGOGUE* production, that I was approached by Lelia Doolan, the newly appointed Abbey Theatre Artistic Director, to become a Director there. My first reaction was one of delight. It was an honour to work at one of the first National Theatres in Europe, the home of Yeats, O'Casey and Synge. Little did I know that I was entering a political minefield. The Abbey Theatre Company had only returned to Lower Abbey Street in 1966. After a fire destroyed the original building in the early fifties, it had moved to a temporary site at the Queen's Theatre. There it was managed by the redoubtable Ernest Blythe, an Ulster Protestant, Republican convert and former Finance Minister, who absurdly saw the Abbey as an instrument of national defence. I was told that when RTÉ was in its infancy, British director Peter Collinson, later of *The Italian Job* fame, used to practice his zoom lens shots as the controversial Blythe was asked how many people he had killed in the earlier 'Troubles'. Blythe ran the Abbey with a rod of iron. The Abbey had low public funding and could only survive by achieving a high level of box office. This led Blythe to indulge popular taste to too great an extent. The Royal Court in London became well known for their revolutionary 'kitchen sink' plays, but the Abbey had been producing similarly set plays much earlier, in the forties. This prompted Brendan Behan to remark that the Abbey was the best-fed theatre company in Europe because of their diet of kitchen comedies. Unfortunately, the company were also badly paid, overworked and artistically under-nourished, being forced to act in too many pot boilers. This led to frustration and bitterness culminating in the strike of 1964 which was the beginning of the end for Blythe.

When the company moved to the new theatre they had a good deal. There were contracts for life, better working conditions and a Players Council protecting their rights. While the actors certainly deserved more of a voice, this policy became an albatross around every Artistic Director's neck. Then there was the quality of the new building. When I asked a senior Abbey actor his reaction to the new edifice, he replied 'Horror!' Certainly the main house was unwelcoming with bad acoustics and a stage which was remote and inaccessible. You got the sense of a theatre which was only half-developed. Nonetheless there was an optimistic response from the public, the theatre became better subsidised, and with the help of good writers like Brian Friel and Tom Murphy, the plays improved considerably.

Leila Doolan was the first female Artistic Director of the Abbey. She had come from RTÉ where she had been a successful Producer/Director. She had a good understanding of writing and administration. She was a competent director and had a real eye for talent. The company was stuck in its ways and needed a kick into modernity. Most importantly, she had a vision for what was necessary. Given the paucity of formal training in Ireland at the time, it was a brave initiative to bring in voice and movement coaches, and to try and loosen up the Peacock as a genuinely experimental space rather than a mini-Abbey. Unfortunately, most of the experienced actors rejected her ideas and did their best to voice their discontent.

7 – Hatchet Success

MY FIRST PRODUCTION AT the Abbey was *Hatchet* by Heno Magee. Heno is a working class writer from Oliver Bond House, one of the estates down by the River Liffey. His play is about violence in a working class Dublin community and a mother who puts pressure on her son to not only protect her but to uphold the family gang tradition handed down by her husband. However, Hatchet is now married to an aspirational wife who is looking for him to defy his mother and get out of gangland. Hatchet tries to extricate himself from violence but becomes tragically ensnared by it. By the time the script got to me I was fortunate that it had been worked on by others. Phyllis Ryan of Gemini had held a reading directed by Vincent Dowling, one of my fellow directors at the Abbey, and he had given the play to Lelia. Vincent had other projects so it luckily came to me. I was delighted. Although the play was set in Dublin and I was a middle class English boy, I certainly had an affinity with the play from growing up in post-war Battersea in the days of teddy boy gang culture. After all, those were the days of moral panic as the teds fought turf wars and danced in cinema aisles to 'Rock Around the Clock'.

Hatchet was to be performed in the Peacock, the smaller Abbey space which could be converted into the round with accompanying loge, if necessary. In fact, we did the play on the proscenium stage, which was more suitable for such a mainly naturalistic drama. The set by Brian Collins was a simple raised rostra with a cyclorama daubed with red paint framed by metal bars, emphasising the play's heightened, primal quality. The furniture on the rostra changed the location which moved between Hatchet's home and the local bar. The cast was a combination of those in the resident company and freelancers. This had a creative tension which helped the production's success. Some of the resident company didn't seem to be keen on the play, and there was an air of sneering, middle class resentment that emanated from a few. In contrast, most felt like myself that we were introducing an exciting new voice to Irish theatre. However strains came to the fore once one strayed from the conventional path and wanted to explore areas of the play through improvisation. Also, some of the

Hatchet by Heno Magee. Peacock Theatre, 1972. Arthur O'Sullivan as Joey, May Cluskey as Mrs Bailey and John Kavanagh as Hatchet.

more conservative members of the cast wanted to be dressed in a sanitised way which made them more appealing to the audience. In fact, quite often in productions you'll see costumes being worn immediately off the peg, insufficiently broken down, with no sense of either being inhabited or relevant to the character's income or environment. I didn't want a clean, polite production but a rough, earthy, passionate one – naturalistic on the surface but gradually becoming more heightened, for at its core *Hatchet* has an element of Greek tragedy with a mother destructively willing her son to violence to defend family honour against the wishes of his wife. Therefore it needed to be a fully fledged, unapologetic, working class drama which could fly.

The cast was certainly well contrasted, not least in the acquisition of Danny Cummins as the barman. Danny was a brilliant comic who was regularly in the Gaiety pantomime supporting Maureen Potter. I remember seeing him do a solo sketch about the last waiter in the old Metropole restaurant before it was to be demolished. It was a play in itself, both funny and moving about the end of an era of old Dublin. I wanted him involved because he would bring a different slant to the play. This was something I learnt from being at the Royal Court, where they cleverly mixed up the casting so you could bring diverse perspectives to a production. Comics like Max Wall had played straight roles successfully there and Danny brought similar enrichment. The barman was a small but crucial part in the second act, when tension in the pub leads to Hatchet's friends beating up gang leader Johnnyboy's brother, Barney, in a nearby lane. Not once did Danny resort to tricks or his music hall persona. He immersed himself in the character by listening and, with focused bar activity and accompanying looks, he observed the escalating tension in his pub with increasing concern. Another freelancer who gave a brilliant performance was Donal Neligan as Johnnyboy. When Barney (Bryan Murray) is beaten senseless outside the pub, Johnnyboy, looks for immediate revenge, suspecting incorrectly that Hatchet was the main perpetrator, unaware that he was in fact trying to pull his mates away from the fight. Donal was a fireball of contained, psychopathic anger in a riveting performance of danger and passion. His scene in the final act with Mrs Bailey when he storms her house looking for Hatchet was always seething with electricity. Sadly Donal, often nervous and hesitant offstage, died tragically young, which meant we never saw the full flowering of his talent. At least he left us with a truly memorable performance. One of Johnnyboy's silent sidekicks was played by Colm Meaney, who was then at the Abbey School and would go on to be not only a very successful film actor but a good Hatchet himself. It was Lelia, with an eye for talent which has never been fully recognised, who alerted me to Colm's considerable potential. *Hatchet* produced a gallery of good performances. At the core of the play were its leading actors: May Cluskey as a powerful, seering, rat-like Mrs Bailey, John Kavanagh, lean, taut, macho but vulnerable as Hatchet, and Terry Donnelly, sensitive but unsentimental as Bridie, his wife, who did the play particularly proud.

Hatchet's first night was that rarity, a really exciting performance. The overall rhythm wasn't totally there, but that would come with time and confidence. What we did have was a great visceral sense of the power of the play and its irresistible Dublin humour. Alun Owen, the celebrated Welsh-Liverpudlian playwright, told me that while he could have written the first act, he certainly couldn't have written the second and third. The second act bar scene was particularly arresting. It was full of orchestrated activity which never lost focus, and the opening song, 'My My Deliah', sung by the assembled throng with the odd cries of 'get 'em off ya' thrown in by Hatchet's mates, created a wonderful contrast to the impending violence. The final scene, when Mrs Bailey pressurises her son to go back to gang violence and fight Johnnyboy, while Bridie, Hatchet's wife, hurls abuse at her, is one of the most powerful scenes in modern Irish theatre. New plays are the most risky undertakings but they are also the most exciting. When a work gains acceptance as *Hatchet* did, there's no better feeling than being part of the team that brought it into the repertoire. As the response was very positive both from audience and critics alike, it soon became apparent that we had a success on our hands.

It was during *Hatchet* that I started to come up against the Abbey's politics. As most of the audience at the Peacock were middle class, I was interested in taking the play into the working class community. I suggested Ballyfermot, a troubled south Dublin estate. Leila thought it was a good idea but that it had to be run by the company. There were some dissenting voices and we had some interminable meetings where I witnessed unwarranted negativity. I thought it was only Ulster that always said 'no'. In the end after negotiative exhaustion, we came to an agreement and performed the play in a hall near the estate. I'd always been interested in this kind of work ever since I became familiar with Jean Vilar's TNP in France, the RSC's Theatre-Go-Round and Joan Littlewood's early work for Theatre Workshop. Theatre is many things but it certainly shouldn't just be about getting 'hits' in big theatres in a capital city. Outreach work is vital if a wider audience is to be engaged and developed. Theatre isn't just about the bourgeois.

When we got to Ballyfermot the locals looked at us with initial suspicion as if to say, 'you think you know how we live, do ya?' However, once the performance got going they began to appreciate the play. I remember in the second act when two of Hatchet's mates are in the lane waiting to attack Barney Mulally and they chant the refrain, 'I'll give you a song and it's not very long, all coppers are bastards', there was immediately thunderous applause which stopped the show. However, whatever their feelings about the Gardaí, the audience seemed to enjoy our visit. During my time at the Abbey, mainly for financial reasons, we never did another project like this. I regret not pushing harder for similar ventures. Subsidised theatres have a wider responsibility to engage with the more disadvantaged members of society.

During this period, I had been living with one of the actresses in the company, Veronica Duffy. In fact, we had been going out before I got the Abbey job. Veronica was attractive and ambitious with a good sense of humour. At the time, she had played supporting parts at the Abbey where she had been regarded as an actress of considerable promise. Although I had now lived in Ireland for a fair length of time and had seen and read many Irish plays, I had only directed one indigenous Irish play. Maybe I'm the only director to have become a Director at the Abbey on the basis of having directed plays by an Englishmen, a Pole and a Spaniard. Although theoretically I was reasonably informed about Irish drama, it was Veronica who would correct me on a certain emphasis in plays, or help me when I had to write up cast lists with actors who had Irish language names. Veronica was equally busy, playing parts in *The White House* by Tom Murphy, *The Iceman Cometh* by Eugene O'Neill and *The Silver Tassie* by Sean O'Casey. I think living with her helped me gain acceptance with certain members of the company. However, to a few, a resident English director was anathema. Going to Trinity was insufficient.

At that time, the resident company were often resentful and bitter. Even though they'd left the drudgery of the Queen's, this didn't stop many of them from moaning about relatively trivial issues. It was as if the culture of the Queen's days was still there with its 'us against the rest of the world' mentality. Now that many of the company had lifetime contracts, they were both inflexible and powerful. In those days, it was difficult to judge the tenure of Abbey Artistic Directors because their hands were so tied. They had to use the resident company whether they liked it or not. In some plays, this was fine because there were talented and skilled company actors, but when it came to more diverse material, they were often inadequate or miscast. As was the case with *Hatchet*, there were opportunities to employ freelance actors but with a big company wage bill, the opportunities were limited. What's more, the Players Council could wield disproportionate power. Their members knew that Artistic Directors came and went but they were there forever. One particular frustration was that if an actor was playing at night, you could only work with him or her until 1.00 pm. You sometimes felt that it didn't matter whether it was Peter Brook or God himself directing, at 12.50 pm there would be a certain older Abbey actor looking out of the rehearsal room window, indiscreetly practising their drive to the tee, thinking they'd be on the golf course in an hour or so. While actors should be protected, it wasn't as if they were in every play; on occasions, some were playing a very small part. There was no flexibility to take into account particular circumstances. This was debilitating for the younger actors who were hungry to develop their talents. If they wanted to put in extra work they were discouraged and an awful atmosphere ensued. What was particularly depressing was the lack of curiosity in too many of the older members of the company. They didn't have much interest about how the theatre and the world were developing. Many were so bruised by their Queen's experience that they became over-obsessed with it never happening again. As Vincent Dowling, a director/actor of the same generation but a person who was willing to move forward, said to me, 'It's still Blythe's theatre.' If some of the company had spent as much time developing their craft as they did internal politics, the Abbey would have been the best company in the world.

When Lelia pulled off the brilliant coup of getting Michael Cacoyannis of *Zorba the Greek* movie fame to direct Yeats's version of *Oedipus,* the Cypriot director couldn't believe that many of the actors broke at 1.00 pm. He offered an ultimatum: either they were to be available to 4.00 pm or he wouldn't accept the job. The Players Council sensibly acceded to Cacoyannis's wishes and an excellent production was the result. Not that everything went smoothly. After a rehearsal, Leila had arranged to show one of Michael's films to the company. We all duly assembled in the Peacock, the lights went out and the film began. Suddenly after five minutes, Michael's voice could be heard in the dark saying, 'this print is terrible where did you get it?' 'RTÉ,' Lelia replied. 'You mean to say that the whole of Ireland are seeing this travesty of my work.' Michael then sulked in the dark as we continued to watch the film. A few minutes later the picture spun out of control and all you could see were a series of numbers flickering manically on the screen. Suddenly Michael catapulted from his seat. 'No. I can't stand it! This is unbearable.' Leila asked for the lights to come up, then made a brief speech suggesting that we stop the showing and that maybe we'll see a better print another day. We all retreated meekly out of the theatre while Lelia consoled the bruised Cacoyannis who continued to wail: 'I can't believe that they are all looking at this awful version. There weren't any decent subtitles. How can they understand it?' In fact, it transpired that Cacoyannis looked to rigidly control all elements of his productions. This also led him into conflict with his designer, Alan Barlow. Barlow was a good if somewhat conservative English designer who had worked a lot for former Abbey Director Hugh Hunt. I always got a sense that he saw himself as rather superior to young, struggling artisans like myself. However, in Cacoyannis he met his match and at the costume call, the Greek took some scissors and started cutting away at his costumes. Barlow looked aghast as if the Mona Lisa had been defiled. Unwisely, he challenged Cacoyannis:

'Michael, are you saying that my designs for the play are wrong?'

'Yes,' said the director casually, continuing to snip away.

8 – Wheelchair Blues

AFTER DIRECTING *HATCHET*, I WAS asked by Lelia to direct *An Evening In*, a play by an English writer, Paul Shephard. It's a sub-Beckettian drama set in a blossoming garden (Ionesco being another influence) – picturesquely designed by Mary Farl Powers – and inhabited by an old couple in wheelchairs, who recall the vicissitudes of their life. It's a serviceable piece but very derivative. However, it was a good acting opportunity for two older actors, May Cluskey, who had been so good in *Hatchet*, and Arthur O'Sullivan, an eccentric, bespectacled character actor who had played Joey, Mrs Bailey's friend, in the same play, and the menacing, lunatic Dr Rance in *What the Butler Saw*. During the rehearsal period, I had to record an aural flashback of them having sex in their younger days. This was a hilarious undertaking and I had to stop Archie from sounding as if he was sawing trees! Although Archie and May gave strong performances, I didn't really understand why we were doing the play. Then it dawned on me that the economy of there being only three actors (there's a very small supporting part) might have had something to do with it. Having recently been given *Hatchet*, I wasn't in a very good position to complain, such being the hazards of a contractual residency.

Paul, the writer, lived in Brighton and when I visited him I discovered he was gay and lived with his companion in a flat not far from the seafront. Brighton has a wonderful combination of the regal and the sleazy. Its Regency architecture gives it style and its dubious characters underworld drama. It's also a well known area for gay people and theatricals (Olivier used to live there) and this couple fitted the scene perfectly. When Paul and his friend came for the first night at the Peacock, they appeared in very camp tight black leather trousers and accompanying accoutrements. Like a version of Village People, their incongruous presence certainly livened up the proceedings of a rather desolate first night bar.

As a director of a new play, you are more exposed to criticism than if you direct a classic which has been tried and tested over many years. A good established play can be directed badly and survive while a new play, particularly by an unknown writer, can have a good production but vanish quickly without trace. Of course, there are bad new plays, but too often critics use vitriolic language to dismiss new work that never transpires with established plays or writers. I sometimes think it would be illuminating to put on a new play by Friel or Stoppard and change the name to Joe Riordan or Philip Winstanley. Would the critics respond in the same way if they didn't know that the writer had a track record? I doubt it.

For writers to develop they must have the right to fail. If theatres have faith in their talent, they must hold their nerve and stay committed to developing their work. Unfortunately, today with pressure for accountability, short-term expediency means that hits are more important than developing a real company ethos or a vibrant play culture.

9 – The Enemy Within

IN THE SEVENTIES, LELIA DOOLAN saw that the Abbey had to modernise in this direction. For some years it had been stuck in a conservative rut with a narrow repertoire, average productions and internecine politics. She wanted to bring in a new energy to expand the repertoire, build up the skill base, develop the existing company and reach out to a wider audience. With this in mind, she employed new outside talents like voice coach Patrick Mason (later to be Artistic Director of the Abbey), two talented designers – the aforementioned Alan Barlow, ex-Old Vic, and the idiosyncratic Voytek from Poland – John Lynch, a good RTÉ director with an acute understanding of acting, the exciting and imaginative Jim Sheridan, later to be a successful film director, and myself. She also got the innovative Tipperary-born designer Sean Kenny involved, and although he suddenly died at forty-three before he was to direct *The King of Friday's Men*, thankfully his designs had been completed. His many sets in London included those for *Oliver*, *The Hostage*, *Uncle Vanya* (with Laurence Olivier) and *Hamlet* (with Peter O'Toole). He was a trained architect and would been an imaginative choice to design the Abbey, but amazingly no one asked him.

Lelia also contracted new young acting talent to revitalise the company and challenge the status quo. This was evolution rather than revolution. However, that didn't stop change being resisted at every turn. There was a reluctance to attend voice and movement classes, to adapt to different rehearsal methods and to see the Peacock as a genuinely experimental space. Things came to a head with an event I organised in the smaller theatre. It consisted of my production of *Picnic on the Battlefield* by Fernando Arrabal in the first half and improvised pieces in the second directed by myself and Jim Sheridan. *Picnic* is an anti-war play, a surreal comedy with a typical Arrabal blend of innocence and cruelty. A soldier, Zapo, is in the front line. His father and mother, oblivious to the dangers of warfare, visit him so that they can have a picnic. When an enemy soldier arrives Zapo takes him prisoner but invites him to

Picnic on the Battlefield by Fernando Arrabal, designed by
Stephen Devaney. Peacock Theatre, 1972. May Cluskey as
Madame Tepan, Bernadette McKenna as Zapo, Nuala Hayes
as Zepo and Colm Meaney as Monsieur Tepan.

share their picnic. As they happily proceed, a burst of machine gun
fire kills all of them. The play was produced in a stylised way. The
soldiers were played by women (Bernadette McKenna and Nuala
Hayes) and ultra violet light accompanied the shooting. We used
the loge for stretcher-bearer characters with white faces to emerge
almost dream-like out of a puppet show. I like to think that the play
became a grotesque version of a Chaplin comedy. An example of
theatre naïve perhaps, but with what was going on in the North at
the time there were relevant echoes.

However, it wasn't the Arrabal that instigated the fuss but the
improvised drama in the second half of the evening. The first part
of this section was an argument between myself and Colm Meaney
about football, but continued with more personal matters and then
extreme national ones. We started the improvisation in the bar
like 'happenings' of the day, and one night an upper class Anglo-
Irish woman complained to Bob Seale, the resident usher, that he
ought to evict us. Now Bob, a lovely genial man, was conservative

by nature but he milked this moment. 'They're okay,' he said to her with a wide grin, 'they're grand.' The bemused Anglo-Irish woman, unaware that we were acting, then left the theatre in disgust. My argument with Colm would finally spill into the theatre and end in an English–Irish rupture. This was followed by another improvisation about violence in colonised countries. I remember Jim and I directing a piece about Vietnam and some members of the audience partaking in an improvisation set around 'the Troubles'. One of the more senior members of the board, Gabriel Fallon, who'd been a good friend of O'Casey's and always reminded us of the fact, liked it. 'Good to see something different,' he declared. Mind you, he was less enthusiatic when, after missing a board meeting, *The Ken Campbell Roadshow's* Sylvester McCoy (later a Dr Who) put a ferret down his trousers and then dropped them to reveal all in the Peacock. 'It wouldn't have gone on, if I'd been there,' said Gabriel. Was that the first nudity in Irish theatre, in the hallowed portals of the National Theatre of Ireland? Quite possibly.

Fallon may have encouraged our experiment but some of the members of the company certainly didn't. A gang of them came down to see the improvised part of our performance like Stalinist invigilators. They looked puritanical and grim-faced as if we'd breached some religious order or political belief. After the show, there was a discussion and on this occasion there was an electric tension in the air. The cast looked on bemusedly as these die hard Abbey actors started criticising us, their colleagues, in front of the public. Now having a disagreement in the green room, in rehearsal or the pub is one thing, but showing such an outward display of public hostility towards an attempt to do something different was unforgiveable. The audience seemed to disagree with their comments. On the night of the diehards' visitation, Paddy Holden, a famous ex-Gaelic footballer, was there with members of his family. After listening to the gang whingeing on about improvising in front of the paying public, Paddy suddenly stood up and said, 'What are yous doing? Yous are meant to be their side. Me and the family decided to come out tonight. We thought we'd take a chance coming here like. But as far as we're concerned, we got our money's worth.' Although I would make no claim for the evening being fully successful, it built on Tomás MacAnna's earlier progressive work in the Peacock and was an attempt to be adventurous, to engage an audience in a more interactive way and to explore some different forms. Visiting RSC Director Clifford Williams thought it was more interesting than many productions he'd seen. More importantly, it was a marker for trying to make the Peacock a more flexible, challenging space, as the founders intended, not a replica of the Abbey. Unfortunately, the project revealed the genuine splits in the company and the very hard job that Lelia had to move the theatre forward.

10 – Further Feuds

THE PEACOCK GANG WEREN'T the only group trying to undermine the regime; there were many cabals meeting in corridors and whisperings that made blood thirsty Jacobean drama mild fare. What was particularly upsetting was that people employed and given an opportunity by Lelia weren't giving her a chance but talking behind her back currying favour with actors to aid their career. They were positioning themselves for any successful coup. This was a betrayal of trust. I have a rule regarding such matters: if you haven't the guts to say it to someone's face, don't say it at all. This poisonous atmosphere began to infect productions. Matters came to a head when Lelia started directing her first Abbey production, *St Joan*. Bernard Shaw's play isn't easy to direct as it's long, wordy and very rhetorical. To make it work, you've got to have a strong central performance. Much to her delight, Veronica had been given the lead part. Certainly she had the passion to be a resolute, independent St Joan and her casting was a bold attempt to remove the play from Irish whimsy. Unfortunately, the rehearsals were full of problems. Most of the older actors didn't seem to buy into Lelia's rehearsal methods, and some seemed to have trouble being directed by a woman. I happened to catch a rehearsal in the theatre when Lelia was asking the cast to improvise scenes.

The older actors in particular were struggling and there was an air of resentment permeating the atmosphere. The production became political. You could sense that the actors were unhappy and wanted Leila out. Maybe Leila wasn't the most experienced theatre director and was more naturally suited to other areas of the job, but that didn't excuse the attitude of some of the cast. They seemed to have an investment in the production's failure. On the first night, I was sitting next to the columnist Bruce Arnold, who whispered to me after the first scene that one of the actors didn't seem to be enjoying his part. Well, that's one way of describing it, I suppose. In the middle of this fracas was Veronica, a young actress in her first leading part, caught in the crossfire of theatrical politics. Inevitably, she wasn't given the support she deserved. Leila did her best but was having to fight on too many fronts. I'll never forget Veronica in tears in her dressing room after the first night. It was a natural consequence of the pressure that was unfairly put upon her. I felt guilty myself. I did give her support but as I was about to direct my first main stage Abbey production, I was also preoccupied. It was a difficult time for both of us.

11 – My Irish Scandal

ST JOAN WASN'T A DISASTER, but it wasn't a success either and it failed to give Lelia the launching pad as a director that I had hoped. On the contrary, it gave her detractors the ammunition they wanted. Amidst this ferment, I was due to direct Richard Brinsley Sheridan's *The School for Scandal*. Initially, Leila invited me to direct *Philadelphia Here I Come*. However, I reread the play and although I thought it was inventive and well written I didn't think it was right for me at the time. I didn't have any experience of emigration. There was also a nagging English voice in me saying, 'so he has a problem with his ignorant Dad, then get out and go to London, New York wherever'. After all, working class English writers had written of characters with similar difficulties with their uneducated families, who had just unsentimentally uprooted to start a new life elsewhere. Yet I was keen to work with Brian Friel as I liked and respected him. I remember one conversation we had in Del Rio's Cafe opposite the Abbey. It was about a celebrated Abbey actor who insisted on milking a round of applause every time he made an exit. 'Every time he exits and the audience applaud, I want to puke,' said Friel. He was right. Such external acting belonged to an amateur tradition of effect over truth that needed to be expunged. If only southern Irish productions had a similar northern terseness and avoided a tendency to sentimental lyricism. Memory plays like *Philadelphia* and *Dancing at Lughnasa,* as well as Tennessee Williams's *The Glass Menagerie,* easily reassure audiences so they need a particularly tough approach.

Unfortunately, I still couldn't get my head around *Philadelphia* despite its incredible success in America. I was beginning to sound like a friend of my mother's in the Epsom of her youth who, after seeing Chekhov's *The Three Sisters,* said: 'You know, Pam, those girls were very silly moaning about Moscow all the time. They could have got a copy of the train timetable and left!' Maybe, I was also missing the Chekhovian point, but I needed to be honest about what I could give to a production. My ruminations were interrupted by meeting Donal McCann in the Plough Bar. He told me that he'd been asked to play one of the leads in *Philadelphia.* 'You'd have a great *Philadelphia,*' he advised me. Even though, he was probably right, I was becoming increasingly enamoured with *The School for Scandal.* I'd seen Gielgud's production in London and thought it was a brilliant, very funny play. I wanted to take the opportunity to direct a classic period comedy. As it transpired, Donal never actually appeared in the Abbey's revival of *Philadelphia Here I Come.*

I prepared avidly for *Scandal.* I looked at a whole range of paintings, cartoons and graphic design – Rowlandson, Cruikshank, Hogarth and so on. I read widely about the period, the code of manners, as well as the deportment of a lady and a gentleman. Most importantly, I read the text incessantly, making notes about the language and how it reflected character. I was helped by designer Bronwen Casson, who had a good graphic sense and pro-

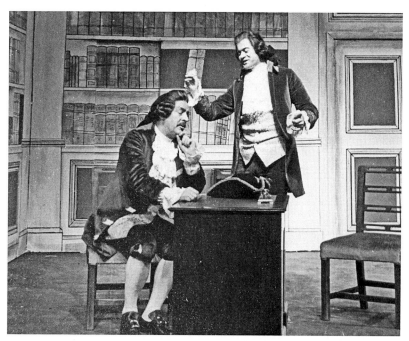

The School for Scandal by Richard Brinsley Sheridan, designed by
Bronwen Casson. Abbey Theatre, 1973. Geoffrey Golden as
Sir Peter Teazle and Desmond Cave as Joseph Surface.

duced a set that moved easily between front cloth exterior scenes
and diverse interiors. I decided to set the production in Dublin.
I wanted to capture the Irishness of the play, the love of talk, the
imaginative humour, the bitchy backbiting, the sense of an intense
community. There was no point doing it like an English company.
We needed to find our own way. While I still think this was a good
idea, I realise now that I wasn't bold enough. It was there in my
production but too tepidly. I should have more fully embraced the
particular qualities that the Abbey actors gave to the play. I think
I was a bit haunted by the technical brilliance of that Gielgud production and his actors' total command of the language, particularly the ability to talk quickly and clearly and to move with supreme
elegance. Consequently, I found it hard to accept a rougher way of
doing the play. Sometimes, it's best to forget the good productions
of others!

When we started rehearsals some of the senior actors continued their display of negativity which had corroded *St Joan*. In fact,

The School for Scandal by Richard Brinsley Sheridan, designed by Bronwen Casson. Abbey Theatre, 1973. Ronnie Walsh as Sir Oliver Surface, Bill Foley as Moses and Bob Carlisle as Charles Surface.

there was a split between the Lady Sneerwell gossiping set and those in the Charles Surface scenes. Lady Sneerwell was played by Angela Newman, an experienced Abbey leading actress, with whom I'd never worked before. She had a good presence and could be very powerful, but she didn't have a natural lightness of touch for high comedy. Unfortunately, she resented my direction from the start and created a tense atmosphere. Despite this, good performances did emerge. Raymond Hardie, inexplicably one of the few Ulster members of the company, was insidiously effective as the manservant Snake. May Cluskey was an energetically loquacious Mrs Candour and John Kavanagh an amusingly scathing Sir Benjamin Backbite. Edward Byrne as Crabtree was an adequate but rather too effeminate Crabtree and seemed to be even more gossipy than his character. I wanted Philip O'Flynn, a natural comedy actor, to play it, but he had a Houdini way of being unavailable when he was cast in parts beyond his comfort zone. Most successful of all was Des Cave who played the difficult part of Joseph Surface, 'a man of sentiment', with style, humour and considerable physical precision. It was the most complete performance in the production. Unfortunately, he was a leading figure on the Players Council, which was at the heart of the offstage political drama. Consequently, it wasn't easy following *St Joan* as there was a lot of bad feeling around, and in some quarters it was being transferred directly into my production.

However, the atmosphere in the Charles Surface scenes was totally different. The actors were more comfortable in this earthy Hogarthian part of the play and they didn't have an axe to grind. Bob Carlisle was a charming, dissolute rake and was well supported by other likely lads, Niall O'Brien, Eamon Morrissey and Emmet Bergin. The added fun was that the character Sir Toby Bumper, who sang a song in the middle of the revelry, was played by the silver-haired, craggy veteran Harry Brogan. Now Harry was an Irishman with no time for the English. Consequently, I was wary of working with him, so I had consciously set him up with a 'star turn'. It was my way of dealing with Harry's barnstorming, outdated acting style. I think he appreciated that because near the opening night, when tension amongst the cast was high, he turned to me and said, 'don't worry, son, the song will be good'. Of course, this was only three minutes of the whole play or at most maybe five if Harry strung it out (inevitably he played it drunk), but I think he saw me as an underdog fighting against the odds. For all his eccentricities, I never found any malice in Harry, only impish devilry. He wasn't one for all the politicking, more of a loner who came in on the number seven bus from Dalkey and went straight back home after the show. And for all his indulgence, when he was well cast he could be most effective. My best memory of him was as Harry Hope in the Abbey production of *The Iceman Cometh*, unable to leave his bar, hovering at the threshold of the door, blinking fearfully into the harsh light of the outside world.

Another larger than life character in the production was Ronnie Walsh. Ronnie joined the company especially for *Scandal*. Genial, stylish, warm with a good voice and a command of language, he liked gambling and drinking. A successful broadcaster at RTÉ, he was very suitable for Sheridan and gave the production solidity as Sir Oliver, returning home from the East Indies, to judge the relative merits of the Surface brothers. However, he could struggle with remembering lines and sometimes an eccentric paraphrase would pepper his speeches. In a later production, in which Ronnie played a large leading part, he suggested to director Vincent Dowling that he might have a telly prompter in the set's fireplace to feed him his lines. I remember hearing Vincent's sharp response reverberate out of the darkness of the Peacock auditorium: 'No Ronnie, No!' In *Scandal*, Ronnie was often in scenes with the morose Bill Foley, who seemed to complain about everything. He was the Abbey's resident Cassandra. He always seemed scarred and bitter. He had been at the Queen's during the Blythe years and it made him suspicious of progress. This didn't help the quality of his work, which I often found one-dimensional and obvious. He never seemed to express enthusiasm for acting or anything else for that matter. Everything seemed to be a chore. I felt that he'd really prefer to be somewhere else if he could have similar security. Bill played the Jewish money lender Moses, a mercenary conduit between Sir Oliver and the Charles Surface. As it was a section of the play energised by the colourful Ronnie and a good group of young actors, many of whom weren't permanent company members, Bill didn't have such a ready audience for his litany of grievances.

At the heart of the domestic side of the play is Sir Peter Teazle, an old man of society who has married a young wife from the country. Geoffrey Golden was one of more sensitive of the older actors and his Sir Peter certainly had warmth and vulnerability. The trouble was that his endearing performance was too small for the size of the theatre, its cavernous acoustics and lack of intimacy. It needed projection but Geoff was locked in a naturalistic tradition and didn't embrace the heightened style of the language. I probably should have done more to get him to 'act up' and relish size without sacrificing the truth of his performance. Matters were complicated by the fact that the actor playing Rowley, his servant, was Micheál Ó hAonghusa, the lover of his wife. During one rehearsal with just the two of them, he announced that he'd just been

The School for Scandal, by Richard Brinsley Sheridan, designed by
Bronwen Cassson. Abbey Theatre, 1973. Micheál Ó hAonghusa as
Rowley and Geoffrey Golden as Sir Peter Teazle.

told that Micheál was apparently the father of one of his children.
There was very tense silence before I suggested we take a break. I
don't think they talked off stage during the whole run.

Lady Teazle was played by Terry Donnelly who had a great
sense of comedy and was an actress of considerable potential.
She had already shown the range of her ability in *Fando and Lis*
and *Hatchet*, but although she was a lively, humorous, rustic Lady
Teazle, she was undermined by a shrill vocal delivery that lacked
range. Big theatres easily expose actors technically, especially in
classical drama where the challenges of language and movement
are more demanding and precision and vocal variety are essential.
Despite these limitations, Geoff and Terry played well together
and successfully got across the humour of the relationship. I just
felt it could have been better, like my production. Unfortunately,

my dreams of a memorable *Scandal* weren't realised. The production had mixed notices and a perfectly respectable run. For my first production of a classic comedy, it was decent without ever fully realising my original vision.

In fact, *The School for Scandal* was the kind of play the Gate tended to appropriate with superficial dexterity. I found their productions external and lacking detail. However, some of the Abbey actors weren't that well equipped to deal with the technical demands of classical acting. Sheridan, like Shaw, combines an Irish imagination with English linguistic precision. Vocal and physical specialist support became available, but the older company members were very defensive and suspicious about such input. In rehearsal, some were more comfortable performing rather than exploring. Because they were afraid, they didn't enter a journey of discovery but wanted to bask in the reassurance of repetition. When a young director like myself started looking at the text and meaning in more detail, Angela Newman, in particular, became resentful. I think she wanted a more broad brush approach and was afraid of being particular. Sadly, she never really articulated to me what she really wanted, preferring to moan behind my back. I got the unpleasant feeling that she didn't like being directed by a young Englishman in a form of theatre with which she wasn't very familiar. She was the Grande Dame of the Abbey and she knew best. This was in startling contrast to Milo O'Shea in *Ah Well* generously taking me aside and giving me the benefit of his considerable experience. Eventually, my *bête noir* left the production mysteriously indisposed and was replaced by Veronica, who had been playing the minor part of a maid. Despite very little rehearsal, and being too young for the part, she rose to the challenge brilliantly, kick starting the production into a new life, bringing energy, clarity and humour to the role. We joked that she was not Lady but 'Baby' Sneerwell!

12 – Experimental Retreat

AFTER *SCANDAL* I WAS KEEN to retrench. Although audiences seemed to enjoy it, it wasn't a pleasant experience. When you are venturing on your first big professional production, you need a feeling of support. I certainly got this from Lelia and my fellow directors, but the rest of the company was so mired in political dissension that it became very difficult to work creatively. I was beginning to get depressed by such feudal strife. All I wanted to do was direct plays and do some good work, not spend a disproportionate amount of time dealing with theatrical politics. Moaning, bitching and jostling for position, while part of theatre culture, shouldn't be allowed to supersede artistic commitment. Unfortunately, the Abbey seemed to exhibit such activities with a distinct brand of vitriol that paralysed the whole of the building.

After such a baptism of fire on the Abbey stage, I wanted to start again on a small scale with something different. Luckily, my proposal to direct *Escurial*, an avant garde play by the Belgian dramatist Michel De Ghelderode, was accepted. Lelia was keen to keep the Peacock more active and so we got a lunchtime slot. De Ghelderode's play is hallucinatory and surreal. A Belgian dramatist who had dabbled in puppetry, he had written a bizarre piece about a King and a clown left alone in a palace. Around the existing set, Brian Collins imaginatively created an isolated throne surrounded by darkness and shadow. Off stage, while the Queen is dying, the King uses his clown to get through the last gasps of her life. However, the clown rebels and looks to overpower the King. The King fights back and sends for his strangler, who kills the clown. The dead clown is then dragged away as the Queen dies. This quirky play unfolded like a nightmare with off stage screams of death punctuating the chiaroscuro setting.

I had managed to expropriate four members of *Scandal* – Bob Carlisle, Niall O'Brien, Raymond Hardie and Colm Meaney – to work with me on this 'guerrilla' production. We were a tight, subversive group away from the whingers and moaners. Bobby gave a memorable performance as the King. He showed that rare ability of first-rate actors – to suddenly change mood. One minute he was charming, the next cruel and sadistic. He would be vulnerable fearing the loss of love, only to then turn vengeful with hatred for his dying spouse. At the time, Bobby was going through the break-up of his marriage. We all knew it but obviously the audience didn't. Bobby did what a good actor does –uses himself. He didn't emote or indulge but exposed considerable depth of feeling while the King lost love in the midst of death. It was one of the best performances I've ever seen in Irish theatre. He was brilliantly assisted as the Clown by Niall O'Brien, an actor of honesty, who radiated truth. Rarely seen in a lead role, the production gave him an opportunity to show a greater range than many may have expected. Together, they were a wonderful double act, hand in glove, superbly supported by Ray and Colm. The play was received very well, played to good houses and revived for a further run in the evening. For me, it was a redemptive experience after the politics of *St Joan* and *Scandal*. It's not the first time that a director has enjoyed working in a small creative context rather than the more corporate one of a big production.

13 – Departure

It was clear that my time at the Abbey was coming to an end. Pressure was building on Lelia and there was little likelihood that one of her main appointees would have his contract renewed. One day in her office, Lelia told me that the board didn't want me to stay. She paused seeing I was upset and said bluntly, 'You'll be better off somewhere else'. Of course, she was right. I was relieved to be getting away from such a conservative, self-destructive, monocultural organisation. Yet, at the same time, I'd become part of a family there, even if it was a fratricidal one. I'd done some good work and genuinely wanted to make a further contribution in developing the company. While there was such good young talent available there was always hope. Unfortunately, such optimism became unrealistic. The Players Council seemed to have a stranglehold on the board, who showed a lack of courage in supporting Artistic Directors. The contracts for life given to a permanent company were an unmitigated disaster. I believe strongly in the idea of a company sharing common artistic values and aspiring to an ensemble style, but I don't believe in making theatre an adjunct of the civil service. If only the company had been chosen from the widest range of Irish talent rather than the select few, it could have progressed more radically. The sensible policy would have been to have had actors on short-term contracts, focused on a series of plays or projects as Druid currently do. This would have given flexibility in casting, stronger commitment and clearer artistic goals. Instead, the theatre was hijacked by an old guard that lacked ambition and rejected change. While the modern Abbey has thankfully got rid of these excesses and recently stabilised the finances during difficult economic times, it has moved too much in the opposite direction. The theatre these days has no company and the Peacock is too often dark when it should throw open its doors to artistic innovation. The Abbey has become just another place where people do plays rather than share an artistic vision. Hopefully, the 1916 centenary programme will give the theatre a new sense of purpose.

14 – Final Farewells

INEVITABLY, IN SUCH CIRCUMSTANCES when you're seeing out a contract, you have to put ambivalent personal feelings aside, and be professional. Of course, I was grateful for the opportunity the Abbey gave me, despite the nature of my departure. However, I was looking forward to finding work in a more progressive and creative climate. Given these circumstances, my last productions at the Abbey were relatively enjoyable affairs.

The first of these, *King Herod Advises*, was written by Conor Cruise O'Brien, a formidable intellectual and writer who had been a cabinet minister. Although the play was cloaked in the trappings of the New Testament, it was essentially about the North and whether violence was justified. A short, lively Shavian piece, the cast included Angela Newman's tall, bald husband, Philip O'Flynn, my houdini man. Despite my fracas with his wife, I got on well with Philip, an endearing character who amusingly alluded to the critics coming to the Abbey as the pilgrimage to Knock! He was also a natural comic actor of considerable ability. He had given a

King Herod Advises by Conor Cruise O'Brien, designed by Brian Collins. Peacock Theatre, 1973. Peadar Lamb as the Minister for Underground Development, Veronica Duffy as Salome and Ronnie Walsh as Herod.

wonderful performance in Hugh Hunt's exhilirating production of Sean O'Casey's *The Silver Tassie*, which had successfully toured Poland and Russia. I have particularly fond memories of the scene where Philip struggled to deal with the modern invention of the telephone: jumping around like a frightened animal, so terrified of the transmission of the human voice, it was if he was confronted by aliens from another planet. Philip was loquacious and had an amazing habit of moving seamlessly from talking to somebody in the wings one second and then departing to the stage on cue the next. He'd been among the many Irish actors who had been employed on David Lean's epic, *Ryan's Daughter*, which led him to endless name dropping. Apparently, one day Donal McCann was in the Plough doing an excellent imitation of Philip – 'As David said to me...' – when the man himself suddenly entered the bar, interrupting Donal in full flight with a venomous, 'you bastard McCann!' One afternoon, while rehearsing the O'Brien play in the Peacock, Philip arrived very late. This was unusual as he was reliable, so he did the old pro trick of getting his excuse in first before he got reprimanded. 'Roland, there's terrible traffic in Moore Street' he yelled before I could speak, while looking around to the cast for support, who in turn sheepishly averted their eyes in a different direction. Philip was the best O'Casey actor I've seen. His comic ability made me dream of an Irish version of Ben Johnson's *Volpone* with Philip in the title role and Alan Devlin as Mosca, his servant, who finally fleeces him. Theoretically, it would have been hilarious. Sadly, in reality neither of them could really take that leap of responsibility into playing leads consistently, so it never happened.

My very last production for the Abbey was *The Night of the Rouser* by Sean Walsh, an ex-priest who had previously lived in London. It was an early 'Troubles' play and another attempt to embrace the political situation in the North. Impressionistically staged on the raked steps of the Peacock stage, characters came in and out of various pools of light to dramatise the story of a doomed love affair between those on either side of the divide. With hindsight it sounds clichéd and predictable, but at the time it had an immediate reality. The production worked well. Bob Carlisle, Belfast actor Maureen Dow and Eamon Morrissey gave strong performances and the play did give a sense of the personal suffering being endured by those in the conflict.

15 – Political Turbulence

IN FACT, DURING MY TIME in Ireland, there were many tumultuous political events, not least Bloody Sunday and the consequent burning of the British embassy in Merrion Square. I remember witnessing the latter first hand and feeling very uncomfortable. For somebody who had actually lived in Derry for two and a half years and seen such tensions unfold, it was a very sad spectacle. Nonetheless, I sympathised with the protestors at the time. There was a feeling that something had to be done to show solidarity with those who had suffered and disgust at the British government's handling of the situation. Despite the high emotion, the protest was very well planned. The embassy staff were warned well in advance and were easily evacuated. The burning went ahead, a point was made, followed by an apology from the Irish government. A new embassy was later built in Ballsbridge. Nonetheless, it was alarming to witness such an attack, especially as the Gardaí didn't seem to try very hard to stop anybody. A writer said to me at the time, 'we could be in the Weimar Republic soon'. Certainly, the splits in the Jack Lynch government and the ensuing Arms Trial made such assertions not so fantastic. As the B specials' reckless behaviour in the Battle of Bogside and that of British soldiers during Bloody Sunday helped recruitment to the IRA, so attitudes in the south hardened. I remember one night in the lighting box at the Abbey, one of the technical staff saying, 'see that audience down there, Roland, in normal circumstances none of those people would support the IRA but now just one incident could tip them over the other way.' We were very near that point at that time. However, despite this political turmoil and its anti-British sentiment, I don't remember any Irish person abusing me personally. People seemed to make a distinction once handed down to me by an Irish colleague. 'The Brits? As individuals, nice people. As a government, a shower of shits!' I was certainly grateful not to be tarred with the same brush as the British government.

16 – Moving On

ON LEAVING THE ABBEY I WAS determined that I was never going to be hijacked by theatrical politics again. I came into theatre to direct plays and engage audiences, hopefully about what's going on in their lives and society. Now I realised that it wasn't that simple. Theatre is also a political battle. If you didn't have the right conditions to do a play, you were going to have an uphill fight, whatever your talent. A director has to be determined to get the best resources available. If these aren't sufficiently realised, he or she will struggle against the odds. Many directors with successful careers are better politicians than artistic interpreters because they are good at getting themselves in a comfortable position to function. As far as the Abbey board were concerned, I was an external appointment, and English to boot, during a time of bad relations between the two countries. Most people at the Abbey took me for who I was and what I did. They were perfectly happy to work with me. However, I was always vulnerable to a few more doctrinaire company members. They were quite happy to see the back of me for no other reason than the apartheid one of race. During *Scandal* a few actors appeared disinterested. It was the only time in my career where some of the cast seemed not to be trying their best. I was never going to let that happen again.

Although I really enjoyed living in Ireland, I didn't know where I could develop my work. There were so few alternative outlets in those days, so I needed to get back to London. However it wasn't easy leaving. In many ways I felt at home both in Dublin and in Irish theatre. Then there was Veronica. The turmoil at the Abbey had certainly affected our relationship. After all, she had gone through a baptism of fire in *St Joan* as well as getting flak about me. We agreed that I'd go ahead to London and she'd join me. As Colm Meaney, Niall O'Brien and Veronica helped me with my trunk to the boat, we all said we'd meet again soon. In a sort of way we did, although Veronica never came over until several years later, when she did good work in English theatres.

HATCHET IN LONDON

17 – East End Exile

'WHERE ARE YOU GOING MATE, to see how the other half lives?' asked a taxi driver, as he drove me and my belongings to Whitechapel, where I was going to move to a squat with Abbey exiles Colm Meaney and Alan Devlin, among others. On my return from Dublin in 1973, I had been living in my mother's Georgian house off the Kings Road. We weren't rich but she had managed to get a short lease on the property in the early sixties. This made me rather popular during that seminal decade. However, it was too easy and having gone through a difficult period on my return to

London, I felt I needed to stand a bit more on my own feet. However, joining a communal squat wasn't exactly what I had in mind. When it was my turn to cook, I suddenly found myself on the other side of London, panicking and returning late to a volley of abuse from hungry squatters.

This was the era of political activism. In fact, Colm went on to work for John McGrath's 7:84, a radical company whose name was based on an article published in *The Economist* stating that 7 per cent of the UK population earned 84 per cent of the wealth. I think it was a seminal point in his development as an actor. Fortunately, I'd managed to work on a challenging season at the Welsh Drama Company in Cardiff directing Strindberg, Brecht and Arrabal, while reuniting with none other than my friend from Trinity, Sorcha Cusack. Alan appeared for various companies, establishing himself as a distinctive character actor. Colm and I lived on the top floor of the squat. His room had a picture of Bobby Moore pinned on the wall as he was a strong Hammers supporter. My room was bigger but full of my own chaos. I was a humble supporter of then lowly Fulham, so I had no suitable football icons. We'd all escaped Dublin theatre and split up with our Irish girlfriends. Our abode was in Parfett Street not far away from the Half Moon, an exciting fringe theatre near Aldgate East.

The Half Moon was an old converted Jewish synagogue and housed a series of radical plays. The left wing politics of the seventies informed the theatre and its commitment to the local working class community. There was a strong Irish input into their work. For instance, Shane Connaughton had written a successful agit-prop play about the wrongly convicted robber George Davis. London walls were scrawled not just with 'Clapton Is God' but 'George Davis Is Innocent OK?' I wasn't totally convinced about George, who later got rearrested on another robbery. My doubts led to an altercation with a boozy Devlin, who managed to bang my head against the non-plastered kitchen wall of the squat. As soon as blood started pouring from my head, a shocked Alan spewed forth an aria of repentence. 'O jaysus Roland. Sorry.' I immediately went to A&E at the local hospital where, when I got squirmish about stitches, a tough East End nurse dismissively crowed, 'Men, they're such bloody cowards.' On my return to Parfett Street, there was general sympathy for my wound but also a feeling that because of my interest in cricket, I was more annoyed at the George Davis protestors stopping a Test Match by digging up the Headingley pitch than any other concern. This wasn't entirely true.

During this exciting period, the Half Moon got a high profile. They were leading not following. I even saw the likes of such notables as the flamboyant Kenneth Tynan waxing loud and lyrical in the White Swan, the pub next to the theatre, run by Ida, a Jewish refugee, and her husband Victor. Colm and Alan appeared in plays there. For me, getting to direct was a slower process. I wanted to put *Hatchet* on in London and thought the Half Moon was the perfect place, because of its size of stage, audience and policy. However, I always got the sense that I was too middle class and not politically radical enough for some of the Half Moon management. Nonetheless, helped by Colm's prompting, we finally got a slot in the summer.

I passed the bucket around and got some money from Irish supporters. We called ourselves Equinox. I'm not sure how that name emerged but, more importantly, we managed to assemble a cast that would grace the boards of any theatre. From the beginning, there wasn't any of the shenanigans that surrounded the Abbey production. Nobody was going to make much money out of our profit share but the commitment from the cast was fantastic. I stripped away the expressionistic backdrop from the original production and looked to make it more concisely naturalistic, aided by Canadian designer Peter Hartwell. As an act of faith, Laurie Morton came from Dublin to play Mrs Bailey. Colm played Hatchet, Alan Johnnyboy and we were supported by an array of good Irish actors based in London, including Bernadette Shortt, Donal Cox, Chris Gannon and Ritchie Stewart. Casting is a matter of insight and luck and with *Hatchet* we had a very good cast indeed. They inhabited their parts very naturally. Consequently, my role was to guide them into an ensemble, make sure that the rhythm of the play was respected, that there was sufficient variety in the production and that the performances didn't peak too soon. In particular, to make certain that they didn't reveal everything about their character too early. An actor should always withhold something until the end, then you seduce the audience to want more.

One major addition from the production at the Abbey was fight director Malcolm Ransom, who orchestrated the most brilliant stage fight that I've ever seen. Because the Half Moon was an old synagogue, we were able to attach corrugated iron to a brick wall, which meant that when Barney Mullaly (Niall McCabe) was beaten up, he could be thrown against a solid, hard surface and in filtered darkness, while banging and kicking the iron, we created a very menacing atmosphere indeed. Stage fights are about timing and choreography, and how an audience's imagination is teased and diverted into thinking about what might be happening. Malcolm created a fight of such rhythmic intensity that by the time Barney was left utterly bedraggled in the lane with Hatchet's mates departing, cynically singing 'why why Delilah?' and 'get 'em off ya', the audience were stunned. So much so, that when the lights came up for the interval there was no applause. I think the audience were genuinely frightened by such a powerful fight, especially in the heart of the East End. Who said you just need to get applause to show appreciation?

Hatchet went on to get universally good reviews ('nightly kicking life and laughter into London theatre' – *Time Out*; 'an unflinchingly honest piece of work' – *The Times*; 'it ought to be given a showing in a larger house' – *Financial Times*), the actors were highly praised ('brilliantly acted' – *New Statesman*) and the theatre went on to be packed out for its three-week run. Morale was high and there was a strong sense of unity in the cast. It showed Irish actors have unique qualities, which can stand comparison with any around. Laurie was magnificent as Mrs Bailey, a glowering tribal queen of a mother, bent on possessing her son and defending the family honour at all costs. The final scene when Johnnyboy waits for Hatchet outside his house and Bridie (Bernadette Shortt), Mrs Bailey's daughter-in-law, decides to confront her for destroying both her son and her marriage, worked particularly well in this environment. Bridie is essentially a polite and generous woman, but Mrs Bailey has driven her to anger and hate. Language breaks down as she berates her tormentor crying, 'ye bitch, ye bitch ye, ye dirty rotten, cowing, whoring, pigging bitch'. However, it's too late, and Mrs Bailey challengingly seduces her son into violence, 'come on love. I'm with ye. Come on chicken love.' It was a scene that had the force of hideous intimacy. At the Half Moon, Johnnyboy confronted them both behind the audience, in the foyer of the theatre, whispering menacingly, 'come on fuckin' Hatchetman'. The feeling of him being in the street made the tension even more eerie and real.

Alan Devlin was a good Johnnyboy. He looked a bit like James Cagney in those thirties Warner Bros movies: dark blue suit and hair parted in the middle. Alan seemed to be nervous about the part, probably because he knew that Donal Neligan had set a high bar for Johnnyboy at the Abbey. He needn't have worried because he made the part his own, more psychopathic playboy than Donal's hard chaw. Alan was an actor of considerable talent who went on to win an Olivier Award for Best Supporting Actor, ironically for the same part for which, many years later, Colm would rightly win acclaim in an Old Vic production with Kevin Spacey – Phil Hogan in O'Neill's *The Moon of the Misbegotten*. Alan couldn't deal with success and instead of it propelling him into the character roles vacated by the death of Jack MacGowran and Patrick Magee, he drank too much and became unreliable. He returned to Ireland, and when off the wagon still gave the occasional good performance in films. Directors wanted him because he was creative and unpredictable, and if you caught that it was memorably watchable.

However, there were times when he let even his friends down badly, not least those who gave him leading parts or lent him money. He was worse than a modern banker as most of what he borrowed was never repaid. I remember when I gave him a loan, and he still hadn't returned the money, I jokingly mentioned inflation (it was the seventies after all), to which he eloquently retorted, 'Fuck inflation.' Diminutive Alan emanated a cuddly attraction to certain women. Was this the Dudley Moore syndrome? He certainly didn't lack admirers. The run of *Hatchet* saw a lot of partying and I remember one night, Colm and I were watching the Olympics at the squat on a clapped-out television when Alan came thundering in with two Scottish sisters. When Alan greeted us with the customary, 'howya lads?', I noticed how he seemed to be out to impress us. Colm and I were dismissive. Alan was never interested in sport so he gave up and retired with his ladies. Unfortunately, the bedroom was next door and we proceeded to watch the Olympics to the sounds of his cavortings. Alan was a lot of fun and full of insight. In true Irish fashion, he would pinprick pomposity, not least many years later at the celebrated London theatrical restaurant Joe Allen's when, after opening in a play, he saw two national critics, Nicholas de Jongh and Jack Tinker, smugly eating their late evening meal. 'What makes you think you're important?' challenged Alan. The critics then tried to wave him away. Alan responded by reiterating, this time more forcefully in his best Dublin vernacular, 'What makes you think you're so feckin' important?' De Jongh and Tinker then panicked, called for the manager and asked for Alan to be evicted. When the manager arrived he informed them that if he got rid of every theatrical person who has been in an argument, there wouldn't be any customers left!

In the seventies it wasn't easy for an Irish play to be successful in London. *Hatchet* was an exception. It travelled well because it had the universal theme of a working class man struggling to escape the violent legacy of his background. There was a similar story in every country so the play was very accessible. In fact, during the run I heard a cockney voice pipe up that the formidable Mrs Bailey was just like his Mum. After our series of good reviews in the national press, we were full every night. Craig Raine, the celebrated English poet, then drama critic for the *New Statesman*, asked me for the script. He gave the play an excellent, well written rave review but then didn't mention any actor, let alone the director. Bloody poets! Despite these eulogies, we couldn't extend the run as the theatre was already booked. My efforts to get a transfer were undermined by the cast size and an irrational fear by managements of the play's bankability.

ON THE ROAD WITH GREEN FIELDS

18 – The Birth of a Touring Company

AT THE END OF THE RUN, THERE was talk about why there wasn't an Irish company in England. At the time, every ethnic group seemed to be served but there wasn't any representation for a significant Irish community. It was as a result of these deliberations that I formed Green Fields and Far Away. Talk is one thing, action another, and it was left for somebody to initiate the proceedings. Most of the actors had their own careers to pursue and nobody seemed to want to deal with all the funding bodies and administration. Consequently, the onus fell on me. I didn't think that I was a natural administrator; still I was willing to learn and given my commitment to Irish theatre, the success of *Hatchet* and the coverage it got, I felt it was a good time to apply for funding. With the help of my family, I formed a company. It was clear that the best funding route was touring and this was something that always interested me. Touring puts you on the street. Some directors just go from one university in their education to another similar environment in a subsidised theatre building. They've never experienced the less rarified rigour of small-scale touring with its one night stands, constantly varying venues and changing audiences. I embraced such an opportunity as soon as I realised that touring gave one the challenge of visiting places where there was little theatre and the audience were mainly unfamiliar with the Irish repertoire. Given this context, my aim was to crossfertilise a classic with a new play and offer them both in repertoire to a venue. This seemed to satisfy the Arts Council of Great Britain, who were then seen to be getting more bang for their bucks. The Arts Council in those days were more committed to taking good work to new audiences than rigid accountability. They had a sense of a mission. The touring department was led by Ruth Marks, an imaginative and innovative administrator. It was an act of trust that she committed money to an embryo company.

Our first touring repertoire in 1977 was *Hatchet* and *The Shadow of a Gunman* by Sean O'Casey. I wanted to capitalise on *Hatchet's* London run and pair it with an Irish classic that is a known title. Assembling the company wasn't the easiest task. It's difficult getting actors to tour when the pay isn't big and they are away from home for eight weeks. Nonetheless, we managed to get together a strong nucleus including some very good young actors. One of those was Liam Neeson, with whom I'd worked previously at the Lyric Belfast. He was to play the leading part of Donal Davoren, the poet who gets caught up in the Irish War of Independence of the 1920s, and the smaller part of a policeman in *Hatchet*. That was also part of the deal: that a bigger part in one play was complimented by a smaller one in the other, and that you also helped with getting the set in and out of venues. Liam had shown enthusiasm to come over and work with a new Irish company and the first week's work at our rehearsal space in North London progressed satisfactorily. Then one day he asked to speak privately to me and told me that he couldn't continue. When I tried to establish the reasons for his defection, he informed me in somewhat vague terms that he had to return to Ireland, implying that it was a private matter. I was taken aback as Liam had initially been one of the project's enthusiasts. Obviously, I was finding my feet trying to run a new company and there were a few teething problems in those early days. However, I don't think it was any particular inefficiency that led to Liam's departure. I had no idea why he had to return home but an actor, however talented, who wasn't interested in committing to the tour was no good to me or the company.

After Liam left I heard in Belfast that he just didn't fancy doing all the contracted getting in and out of the set. I was disappointed that a good actor and, at the time, a leading one of considerable potential, was leaving at such an early stage of the first tour, particularly when an Irish company based in the UK hadn't toured for many years. From the experience of my close involvement with Liam in Belfast, I'd discovered that he was a very committed and hard working actor. Now I was finding out he was also a very driven one. In previous conversations, he'd mentioned his particular interest in film acting. This was the path he was rigorously pursuing and maybe our venture was too much of a detour.

Some business manuals say that every problem offers a new opportunity. In fact, Liam's departure led to the introduction of somebody who was to become a regular member of the company. As I looked for an actor to take over at short notice, it was suggested that I should try Michael Loughnan. While working freelance as an accountant, Michael had been getting valuable experience acting at the Sugawn Theatre, a well known north London venue for Irish plays. This was the call he was waiting for to take the plunge fully into the profession. Michael was with us within forty-eight hours and we lost little time in maintaining rehearsal momentum. In fact, it soon emerged that Michael was more suited to Donal Davoren. Where Liam was certainly a strong romantic presence, to the impressionable Minnie Powell, Michael brought more complexity to the role, being both a believeable poet and a more likely coward. It doesn't rain but it pours and before we went on the road there were three other actors who wanted to drop out – Ritchie Stewart, Vass Anderson and Tom McCabe. Again, I think when the reality of small-scale touring kicked in, they weren't willing to deal with the necessary rigours. This time I insisted that the departing thespians stayed until I got replacements. Certainly their imminent departure was a nuisance, but everybody was too busy to allow it to cause too much disruption. Over the years, I've learned that a certain type of actor is just unsuitable for touring. All this species does is moan the whole time rather than embrace the experience and the inevitable ups and downs it brings. Consequently, however talented they might be, you're better off without them, as you can never satisfy their demands and they can severely

Green Fields and Far Away Theatre Company, 1977.
Back row: RJ (Artistic Director), Don Foley, Ian MacPherson, Ann Scott,
Ritchie Stewart, Ann O'Connor, Liam Neeson, Maire O'Hanlon,
John O'Toole, Mick Walsh, Vass Anderson. Front row: Tom McCabe,
Tony Sampson and Brendan Ellis.

damage morale. Mind you, with four of the original company departing so quickly, there were times when anyone went out of the rehearsal room, I wondered if they were coming back!

Our first date on the road was at Basildon in Essex, later to become notorious during the Thatcher years, when it went Tory, creaming off the skilled working class vote. On winning the seat, the local MP mentioned the town ad nauseum in the House of Commons. So Essex Man got a lot of publicity. So later did Essex Woman and when Chigwell-born Sally Gunnell won an Olympic gold medal, the *Sun* splashed one of their most salacious headlines telling us about Essex girls coming first!

In fact, Basildon's Towngate Theatre is a big auditorium but thankfully *Hatchet* is a play that can embrace size and so it proved. The performance went well and gave us a good start. Having got over the hurdle of our debut, we settled in to our motel at Teynham, Near Sittingbourne, Kent, which was our base for the South East leg of the tour. Our abode had its inadequacies so some wags in the company, nicknamed it the Bates Motel after Norman in Hitchcock's *Psycho*. It was there in a cramped lounge that we finished rehearsing *The Shadow of a Gunman*, much to the apprehension of the residents. When it came to the scene where bombs are discovered in the tenement and there were shouts of 'bombs, bombs, bombs', an alarmed proprietress arrived in her dressing gown threatening to call the police. Eventually, she accepted our explanation but only with great reluctance and brooding suspicion. Despite this hiatus, *Shadow* duly opened at Nonnington College. I don't think I fully got to grips with the play. On a naturalistic basis it seems to stretch credibility within its given timeframe. There are also intruding neighbours more in the style of Jacobean caricature. I didn't find a distinct enough way of integrating these two areas into a sufficiently cohesive vision. Maybe the problem is that if a production is too naturalistic it's unbelieveable, and if it's too stylised it loses it's political edge regarding the tragic intrusion of 'the Troubles' on ordinary people. I should have been braver in finding an imaginative solution. Still, there were some good performances and the audience seemed to enjoy the production. O'Casey, the great writer that he is, won them over in the end.

During our time in Teynham, the IRA and UVF bombing campaign was going on apace, the blanket protest had started but at least peace leaders Betty Williams and Mairéad Corrigan helped provide a window of hope by winning the Nobel Peace Prize. However, it didn't seem to stop audiences attending in reasonable numbers and initially there was no extreme English objection to our presence. However, when the tour progressed to Scotland, we were to discover a different response. As we made our way north, the roads were frozen. There were diversions and it was agreed that the van carrying the set should go on ahead and the main body of the company in the transit van should follow. However, while we were waiting in a traffic jam at the Scottish border, we suddenly saw our Company Manager, Tony Sampson, driving the three ton van in the opposite direction, back to London. We all shouted and screamed to no avail, there being no mobiles in those days. However, eventually Tony figured it out and we all reached our destination. This was a lodge run by two Scotish gay gentlemen, who had so many ornaments in each room that you were in constant danger of tripping up every few yards. It was meant to be a break in our journey but Celtic tension emerged when one of the landlords told us that for having a bath we'd have to pay an extra fifty pence plus vat for the plug. This didn't go down well with the company, although when stereotypes become a reality you can only laugh.

It was around this time that the new cast members bedded in. One of them, Ronan Wilmot, was an old friend of mine from my Abbey days, where he was the Publicity Officer. I had amusing memories of him going in and out of the Artistic Director's office to the accompaniment of increasing curses and slammed doors as his copy was continually rejected. He also regularly greeted me as I ascended the stairs of the rehearsal room with a hearty, ironic English welcome of 'Good morning, Roly!' Then he'd proceed to discuss the latest sport and in particular the spiralling fortunes of of my beloved Fulham FC. Ronan had strong social skills, communicated well to the company and was interested in the world beyond Ireland, which was rare in that organisation. However, he really wanted to be an actor not a publicist. He had left it late as he was then in his thirties. He'd already played some parts on the fringe in Dublin but was eager to expand so when I gave him the call, he grabbed the opportunity. His debut as the Ulsterman Adolphus Grigson in *The Shadow of a Gunman* was one of the best performances of an alcoholic I've ever seen. However, I can't say that I contributed much to it because we had such a minimal time to rehearse. Even though Ronan just relied on his familiarity with the play and his instinct, what he produced was a miraculously rounded characterisation of a sad, bigoted Orangeman, which communicated particularly well with the Scots. Often when actors are faced with such a crisis, they rise to unprecedented heights. In a perverse way, it simplifies the process and forces the performer to make choices quickly and trust their instinct and imagination. This can often free up a performance, whereas a longer rehearsal process can sometimes get actors so locked in their heads that their performances lose spontaneity. I remember when a Russian was directing *The Cherry Orchard* at the Abbey, she had a Soviet length of rehearsal, that is, very long. One Abbey actor was quoted as saying that he was afraid of feeling stale on the first night. Although I'm not an advocate of instant acting, and for more complicated texts you certainly need a longer process, sometimes when actors are well cast and the piece is not long, an artistic short sharp shock can work wonders. Look at the good acting in those film noirs which were made in a few weeks.

After Ronan joined us in Fife, we went to the Third Eye Centre in Sauchiehall Street, Glasgow, an art gallery which in those days occasionally housed theatre. As John O'Toole and Ann Scott were acting the opening domestic scenes in *Hatchet*, establishing the leading character's struggle over loyalty to his widowed mother and his wife's middle class ambitions, we heard guttural Scottish interjections. Initially, John and Ann took no notice but as the scene progressed the noises got louder and more persistent until you could sense unease amongst the audience. When the heckler started saying, 'why do we want to listen to the Irish for fuck's sake? Aren't they just a lot of fuckin' trouble?' John had had enough and did an Albert Finney (in the early sixties, Finney berated an audience member during the run of *Billy Liar* and got front page headlines). He leapt off the sofa, came downstage, stared at the protagonist at the back of the gallery and told him in a thick *Hatchet*-style Dublinese, 'are ya going to shut up or am I going to have to bleedin' shut ya up?' The uneasy audience now responded with a burst of heartfelt applause. The Scottish gentleman was hauled away by some officials and from that moment a rather ordinary performance became electric. It ended with a warm ovation concluding a bizarre evening.

Such behaviour was repeated when we arrived in Edinburgh at the Netherbow, a small, compact theatre run by the Minister of a local Protestant Church. During one of our earlier performances we encountered another heckler shouting similar slogans, 'why are we bothering about the Irish etc.' I was backstage at the time and several of the cast were demanding that something be done. It was agreed that Michael Loughnan and Tony Sampson, who were playing policemen, should go into the auditorium and 'arrest' the perpetrator. The Irish Gardaí uniform wasn't that dissimilar to that worn by the Scottish force and our friend was so drunk that he wasn't able to discern the difference. Surprisingly, he came as meek as a lamb. A good thing, too, as I later heard that he'd been in prison for breaking a policeman's arm! Our time in Edinburgh ended with us transporting the takings in a black bag. While on the road, a couple of the company went for a meal. After they'd eaten, they made their way back to the van only to discover they had left the bag in a motorway café. And this was when IRA bombs were going off. We rushed back and, mercifully, the bag was still there. An inquest among those involved led to a series of self-flagellating arguments but at least the money hadn't been stolen.

During the tour, we performed at my old school Christ's Hospital. I nervously anticipated the company's response to an English public school, given their elitist reputation, and in particular to CH's traditional uniform of blue greycoat, leather belt, breeches with brass buttons, white bands (like a priest), yellow socks and black shoes. At least CH wasn't typical of such an institution, having been founded by King Edward VI to give education to the underprivileged. In fact, in my day if your parents earned too much money you couldn't go there. Today families are means-tested and a range of governors subsidise the cost of fees for lower income families. Consequently, the school still attracts a wide cross-section of society.

My own time at CH consolidated my love of drama. I played several parts in school productions, including a one dimensional Duke of Exeter in *Henry V* and the previously mentioned Hippolyta, Queen of the Amazons, in *A Midsummer Night's Dream*, which later toured Holland. In the latter, my 'breasts' were scrunched pieces of *The Daily Mirror*, suitably cupped. Unfortunately, they seemed to go down too well with the actor playing Theseus, who during rehearsal started to put his hand around my waist. This was greeted by a short sharp elbowing in the stomach. This didn't put him off as at the end of the run he chased me across the school quadrangle. A narcissistic performer with a very deep broken voice, he thought of himself as God's gift to classical acting. On the first night, farce ensued. After making our initial regal entrance to the accompaniment of live trumpets, Theseus took a ring from the cushion provided by the servant Philostrate and placed it on my finger. However, as I held it up to the light, I didn't hear the fruity opening declamations from our bass-voiced genius but something rather more vernacular. 'Oh fuck!' he wailed. He'd forgotten the first lines of the play. I listened to his demented ramblings for a short time, then leapt in with my first speech. Theseus looked upset and ashamed, his reputation in tatters, but he stumbled through the performance, despite his diminished status.

Many years later, while walking down a West End street, I suddenly saw a much older Theseus in a restaurant with a woman I took to be his wife. Rather childishly, I peered through the front window making faces at him. He looked bemused and bewildered, unable to recognise me. I was tempted to go in and remind him and his wife of his over-familiarity at rehearsals, but I just couldn't quite pick up enough courage.

All these bizarre memories came flooding back on my return to Christ's Hospital. However, eventually I refocused on the school's splendid new theatre which had opened in 1974. It has wonderful acoustics and is fully adaptable to either an open, thrust or proscenium setting. Several pupils worked on getting *Hatchet* ready for presentation at the theatre. I was relieved to observe that the company were intrigued by the school's traditions and impressed by both the attitude and the skill of the boys as they dextrously clambered over lighting rigs and set sound levels. I think it was a bit different to what they had expected. As our first tour also included Canterbury, Swindon and the Sherman Theatre in Cardiff, we certainly managed to establish an initial network of dates. The idea of taking two plays on the road in repertoire seemed to work and the audiences were good for a new company's first tour.

19 – Rural Rides

THE ARTS COUNCIL SEEMED TO agree as happily my plans for continuing our work were accepted. In the autumn of 1978, we started touring two new plays in repertoire. Synge's classic *The Playboy of the Western World* and Bryan MacMahon's *The Honey Spike*. Bryan was Headmaster of the Boys National School in Listowel but he also wrote novels and short stories as well as plays. He had a most unusual sensibility with an eye for the nooks and crannies of rural life: its simple, breathtaking beauty as well as its cruelty and injustice. This particular play is about a young tinker couple who travel from the Giants Causeway in the North to Puck's Fair in Kerry, so that the wife can have her baby born in the 'the lucky spot', the honey spike of the title. On the way they have to encounter the police, prejudice, the IRA and finally tribal warfare at a Kerry fair. In the end, the wife doesn't make it to the honey spike, loses her baby and dies.

It's a moving folk play, a picaresque journey, full of hope, humour and excitement which ends in sadness and death. If the play has a fault, there's a tendency towards sentimentality. In getting actors from Dublin and Belfast to play the leading parts, I hoped to cast against type and bring a hard edge to the tinker's struggle. My approach had rich dividends, as John O'Toole and Brid Brennan were both excellent, bringing sensitivity and passion to their parts, while not looking for easy sympathy by eschewing false lyricism. Our production of *Playboy* was directed by Terry Palmer, who had pioneered many Shakespearean productions at Hoxton Hall in the East End. A Welshman, he has a strong imagination and a creative intelligence that fitted in well with the company ethos. His production had a clarity, simplicity and a good sense of both the play's domestic roots and its visceral sweep. Limerick-born Kevin Wallace, now a successful West End Producer, played Christy Mahon with charm and energy, Kay Dunn, a London-based Irish actor, was an attractive Pegeen, and they were supported by a lively cast. The set was designed by John Hallé, who had worked successfully at Hampstead and Leeds Playhouse. He always seemed to be wearing black leather clothes and riding a motor bike with his girlfriend Angie sexily perched on the back. Imaginative and technically able, John created a strong visual framework for both plays. *The Honey Spike* in particular was very effective. It was played on a small wooden rake, in which sections could be removed or raised and additional props and furniture added if necessary. This gave a brilliant, abstract sense of landscape on which lighting could simply change the mood. It also gave the production variety and speed. John was to become a Green Fields regular.

After producing two city plays, I was keen to get variety into our repertoire and purposefully chose two rural works. They were well-contrasted and audiences seemed to respond to them well. *Playboy* is probably the most successful Irish play of all time. Maybe it has to do with our ambivalence towards heroism, that we need heroes but often feel let down by them, that indeed there's 'a great gap between a gallous story and a dirty deed'. Certainly it's a play of dynamic mood changes that reflects such contradictions, moving from quiet introspection to physical violence, from infectious hilarity to naked cruelty. Terry's production caught this well. For Irish audiences, *Playboy* can be done to death, but this isn't true for British ones and certainly not those living in the provinces. So presenting a known title like *Playboy* was a constructive building block.

Developing a company is about establishing an identity and winning trust from your audience. Once that is gained you have a greater opportunity to expand your repertoire. We were certainly making progress and attendance for both plays was good, considering one was unknown. The company played similar dates to the *Hatchet* tour, a mixture of one night stands and split weeks. Such a schedule always puts a strain on personnel, but has the added excitement of every performance being a first night. Also, you are not playing to the great and the good or the chattering classes but ordinary people who come without the baggage of an agenda. Many nights in the Abbey or the Royal Court are ruined by having

The Honey Spike by Bryan MacMahon, designed by John Hallé.
Green Fields and Far Away Tour, 1978-79. (left to right) Kevin Wallace as
Shone McQueen, Sara Rae-Maddern as Tinker (hidden), Karina Knight as
Winifred McQueen, Gerald McAllister as Dickybird, John O'Toole
as Martin Claffey, Finola Keogh as Poll-Poll Sherlock (kneeling), Kay Dunn as
Tinker, Michael Loughnan as Tinker and Maurice Blake as Mickle Sherlock.

the air of a public audition, or do I mean hanging? In many ways, on tour you often get a more genuine reaction.

There was a good atmosphere with this particular company. They seemed to enjoy working hard and being in each other's company, if the reputed number of affairs on the road were anything to go by. What did that grand, old English actor say when asked if Ophelia slept with Hamlet? 'On tour, indubitably!' Certainly a good balance of the sexes contributed to high morale. As for the other pleasures, well, substances certainly seemed to waft around various vicinities, but they always seemed to be kept out of my range so I was able to plead ignorance of such calumnies. Stamina was important, especially if you imbibed after the show. It needed to be when the likes of Michael Loughnan was asked to play so many parts. For instance, in *The Honey Spike* he started singing a ballad before a scene change, then grabbed a balaclava to become an IRA man in the following scene, got wounded, then miraculously was reincarnated as a British Army officer in the next scene, only to then change costume again so he could sing another ballad, while the next scene change took place. There's the versatility of a touring actor for you! In fact, Michael's singing worked well and gave the feeling that the play itself was actually unfolding like a ballad.

At the end of the tour, which included a successful run at the Everyman Theatre Cork, we performed *The Honey Spike* for three weeks at the Irish Club in Eaton Square London. Despite its fashionable location, the Irish Club was a bit like an Irish Fawlty Towers. It seemed to be a refuge for alcoholics during the 'holy hour' and attracted a combination of émigrés, artists, politicians and general eccentrics. One afternoon, I saw a stumbling, white-haired, elderly woman coming up the entrance steps. The face seemed familiar but I couldn't put a name to it. Then suddenly I realised she was Winston Churchill's daughter, Sarah, an actor who lived across the street. She had a big drink problem and was desperately looking for a tipple.

Green Fields and Far Away, 1978. Maurice Blake, Gerald McAllister, Patch Connolly, Karina Knight, Michael Loughnan, John O'Toole, Brid Brennan, Sara Rae-Maddern, Gayle Runciman, Finola Keogh, Redmond Roche, RJ (Artistic Director) and Mick Walsh (Administrator).

Apart from meetings and Irish social events like bacon and and cabbage evenings, the club rooms were loaned out for rehearsal to the likes of the Royal Court. Consequently, John Osborne, Nicol Williamson, Samuel Beckett and Billie Whitelaw were among those who were seen during our sojourns there. In fact, one of the company had the distinction of peeing in the same toilet as the great writer. At least, he didn't ask him for his autograph as a fan did to Paul Newman while he was in a similar posture. The performances went well and the Irish ambassador came to see the production. I think he might have enjoyed it but took a nap during one section. After negotiaing with the the likes of Mrs Thatcher, can you blame him? Also during *The Honey Spike* run, Gerry Fitt, the Belfast politician, was staying at the Irish Club while he was being seriously threatened by the IRA. During our performance various actors were coming out into the corridor dressed as IRA men. All this in the vicinity of a politician who was allowed a body guard and a loaded gun. Who says art and reality never intercede? In fact, a similar fusion emerged at Aldershot, a staunch army town, where because there was limited access in certain areas of the arts centre, actors were forced to go outside and run around with balaclavas and rifles! More serious was the situation in Ashford, Kent, where because of the murder of Lord Mountbatten by the IRA, the local arts centre was under considerable pressure to cancel our booking. The tabloid press was also criticising the Arts Council for funding such companies as ours. Therefore it was to the credit of the manager of the venue that a significant number of people warmly received our performance. They refused to waver under such threats, even though Mountbatten's birthplace wasn't far away. This was the only time we had any significant problem regarding 'the Troubles', although we did hear from the person who hired us the vans that he had inadvertently given a vehicle to an IRA man, who was later arrested. Over a pint at one of our shows, after expressing his concern about the incident, he then smiled and said, 'mind you, he was a good payer!'

One of the uncommon aspects of *The Honey Spike* company was that it included several older members, which wasn't usual in small touring companies. One of them was Maurice Blake, who with his white beard was instantly recognisable as a Gabby Hayes (Hopalong Cassidy's sidekick) lookalike. Maurice was a larger than life performer. A Dubliner who left Ireland when he was very young, he was a product of the fit-ups and had served in the British army. He was both likeable and loquacious. While travelling in the van he would tell us to keep quiet and then proceed to talk more than anyone else.

The Honey Spike by Bryan MacMahon, designed by John Hallé. Green Fields and Far Away Tour, 1978-79. Kay Dunn and Michael Loughnan as Tinkers, Finola Keogh as Poll-Poll Sherlock, Maurice Blake as Mickle Sherlock and John O'Toole as Martin Claffey.

Maurice was what I would call a personality actor. My attempts to get him to be bring more depth and variety to his characterisations often failed. I think his days in the fit-ups meant that he was used to working fast and getting technically organised, without too much recourse to detail. Sometimes, after directing him, the scene would come out exactly the same as if I'd said nothing. It wasn't that Maurice was difficult or didn't understand, it was just that he was like a long playing record resolutely stuck in a groove. I think this can happen when you are forced to pick up bad habits early in your career. Unless an actor just takes the value of performance experience from the fit-ups and moves on, understanding a more creative process becomes increasingly difficult. Nonetheless, Maurice was genial, loyal and hard working with a sense of comedy and a striking presence. If he had been in Hollywood, he would have been snapped up by John Ford and fitted seamlessly into his stock company with the likes of Harry Carey Jnr. and Ward Bond.

Another older actor on the tour was Gerald McAllister, who gave a most imaginative performance in *The Honey Spike* as Dickybird, a character who whistled like a bird and had prophetic powers regarding the tinkers' destiny. Gerry, a small compact Ulsterman with whisps of greying hair on a receding hairline, was the opposite of Maurice. Where Maurice was extrovert and talkative, Gerry was quiet and introverted. A solitary figure with a newspaper always at hand, Gerry talked very quietly. However, on stage he sprang to life. His performances as Dickybird and Old Mahon were sensitive but lacked clarity and definition. I could never fully understand exactly what he was saying. However, he had such a strong spirit and emotional understanding that somehow it didn't seem to matter. The audiences were with him. The final older member of this company was Finola Keogh. Finola came from a theatrical Irish family, her father ran a theatre company in Dublin and her mother was an actor. She was a child performer for RTÉ in its early Henry Street days and later she went to RADA. She was a warm and intelligent person, who became the mother of the company. Eccentric and forgetful, she wasn't a brilliant technician but she brought a wayward charm to her roles. Playing an elderly tinker to Maurice Blake's blustering husband, they made a delightfully offbeat couple.

The Honey Spike–Playboy tour was one of our most successful and enjoyable. Two well contrasted plays, a very likeable company, a positive response from audiences and good reviews ('caught, the spirit of Ireland', *Edinbugh Evening News*; 'vigorously performed', *The Scotsman*). In both plays, there was certainly a genuine community on stage that was entrancing to watch. The ensemble's infectious energy and commitment seduced the audience into watching them. It was a highpoint for the company. We were doing good work, getting decent audiences and our profile was increasing. However, one of the difficulties of running Green Fields was that we were advised to apply for touring project grants. Apparently, this was the best way of establishing the company, as we were very unlikely to get revenue funding. This made continuity very difficult as there was no guarantee that we'd always succeed in getting the money for each tour. Consequently, it became impossible to hire staff in the gaps between tours. This didn't help us build a solid administrative base. However, as it became more manifestly clear that the Arts Council were impressed with our work, and that the company had at least an immediate future, we needed a stronger administrative hand on the tiller.

After the first tour, Mick Walsh, who had played Barney Mulally in *Hatchet,* became our administrator. Personable with a boyish charm, he had a lot of good PR skills and was excellent with the funding bodies and venues. Mick had played his part well in *Hatchet* but he wasn't obsessed with being an actor. I think for him it was more of a learning curve about the business. Sometimes it was a steep one. I well remember being with Mick pacing the marble floor of the National Westminster Bank, Sloane Square, while Mr Haines, the Manager's Assistant, went away to consult with his colleagues as to whether the bank could pay out the wages. This was our version of *High Noon*, a race against the clock.

I was never certain if Haines, with his pencil moustache, black suit and stern look, enjoyed torturing us or whether he was just frightened about giving money to a lot of 'artistic layabouts'. The suspense was built up by the Arts Council paying us in instalments which invariably arrived late. The bank certainly made us sweat but thankfully they always gave us the money in the end. It was an endless Friday afternoon ritual and both parties acted out their parts. The penniless artists on one side and the humourless guardians of the public purse on the other. In fact, Mr Pollitt, the bank's manager, was a genial, rotund man, who looked like a character out of Dickens and always seemed to be referring to his 'superiors'.

Once at one of our periodic meetings, he confided that he'd recently got divorced, while insisting that he still had good relations with his wife. He then proceeded to say that he was looking forward to his retirement in Cornwall. Actually, I think he was quite lonely and didn't really enjoy his job. Shortly after our meeting, Mr Pollitt was knocked down by a car while attempting to cross the road immediately outside the bank. He was taken to hospital but after making an initial recovery, he sadly died a year later.

20 – Emigration Rock 'n' Roll

OUR SUCCESSFUL AUTUMN TOUR meant that we managed to get funds for another production in the spring of 1979. I chose to present a revival of *The Scatterin'* by James McKenna, which was originally produced at the Theatre Royal Stratford East. What particularly interested me was the way its form, a play with rock 'n' roll music, matched its content, emigration. Emigration has been the curse of Irish life, and now after the disastrous recession of 2008 and the mismanagement of the Celtic Tiger it's back with the country again. In fact, I remember my accountant, Frank Dunphy, a Dubliner from Donabate who became Damian Hirst's manager, telling me that when as a youngster in the fifties he was idling with lads on a Dublin street, the Gardaí would come up and ask them, 'why don't you take the boat?' *The Scatterin'* is about the process towards 'the boat', following four working class lads before they leave Ireland. The play cleverly intertwines the theme of fifties emigration with the explosive birth of rock 'n' roll. It's an attractive urban brew with hard-hitting social drama mixing with beehive hairdos, drainpipe trousers and sexy jive. The writer James McKenna was a dark-haired, handsome, peripatetic artist. Essentially a sculptor, he also painted and later migrated to writing verse dramas which were performed in Dublin fringe venues. A genuine experimenter, he was a restless creative spirit who never seemed to find a suitable home. It was to his credit that he tried new forms and didn't look to write another version of *The Scatterin'*. However, despite his later efforts it's for his play with rock music that he's best remembered.

Our production had a strong cast: John O'Toole was charismatic and powerful, and was joined by Ronan Paterson, a burly Scot who had lived in Dublin, Dubliner Denis O'Neill who'd worked in London, and Kevin Wallace who had played Christy Mahon with great brio. Janet Behan, Brendan's niece, a detached, sexily aloof presence, played the main female part, and Alan Dee was our Musical Director. Alan had recently had a great success in the Irish production of *Jesus Christ Superstar*. A quirky Dubliner, talented and able, he corralled three other musicians to form a band, eccentrically called The Watchtower. Musicians and plays don't always mix. Musicians belong to a different and more volatile culture. I realised this when I was rehearsing a show in London musically directed by by Jona (*Stop the Cavalry*) Lewie. During the dress rehearsal, Jona asked for more drums. The drummer replied, 'okay, if you want more crap music'. Jona calmly turned round while still playing keyboards and retorted to the rebellious reprobate, 'yes, that's right mate, more crap music'. Not really the language of the average theatre rehearsal. Consequently, I was concerned that the musicians might not be disciplined enough to deal with a theatre tour. Thankfully, my fears were unfounded, Alan kept his group together, they played well, kept excesses to a minimum and maintained a good standard.

However, the tour wasn't without mishaps. I'd hired a smoke machine for the scene where the lads light a small fire in the Wicklow hills. Unfortunately, the smoke went out of control and the cast were plummeted into something more celestial as swirling smoke clouds obliterated their presence and the scene ascended from Wicklow into the heavens.

Then there the case of the policeman in a neck brace. Redmond Roche was playing a Garda and one of the flats fell on him during a performance because somebody had forgotten to lock one of the pivots. It wasn't long before our cop had to have a brace around his neck. Later, he and the other 'policeman' had been drinking in the afternoon before a performance. This contributed to Redmond misjudging his fight scene punches and hitting Denis O'Neill so hard that Denis's jaw muscles became so stiff that he found it hard to talk. It was fortunate that it happened before a three-day break in performances.

Seemingly at the centre of company lunacy was George Tarbuck, a small, talented lighting designer who had an awful stammer and was mischief incorporated. Some nicknamed him George the Terrible. Although he took an eternity to finish a sentence, he sang well (without a stammer) and was a good pianist. At the time, he also played in a punk rock group called Crass. Despite lighting the show well, I got fed up with some of George's antics. At Birmingham, where we had already gone round in circles trying to get off Spaghetti Junction and find Aston University, George brought things to a head at the digs. He infuriated our landlady

The Scatterin' by James McKenna. Green Fields and Far Away tour, 1979. Ronan Paterson as Patzer McLoughlin, Denis O'Neill as Con Geraghty, John O'Toole as Jemmo Fitzgerald and Kevin Wallace as Tony Riordan.

by bringing a wardrobe out of his room and putting it against the door so his roommate couldn't get out. I was very angry and about to aggressively confront George when Maurice Blake, who was playing one of the few older parts in the show, wisely pulled me away. 'Forget it, Roly, it's not worth worth it.' That didn't stop me railing at the impish Lighting Designer. This wasn't very dignified, but when you're tired after a lot of travelling, tempers are easily frayed. If you also feel that somebody is both undermining the tour and your company, you're likely to start the Battle of Brum. After all, to George it was only another job but to me it was a personal commitment. Apparently later that day, after our altercation, Denis and Dick Farrelly (one of the musicians) opened the door of the three-ton truck, ready to depart, only to discover George pulling a bottle of whisky out of the compartment and greeting them with an elongated 'gggggggoooodmoooorning!'

Despite such setbacks, when in a good venue, *The Scatterin'* was artistically one of our better shows. The trouble was that we had too many one-night stands for a production with a lot of equipment and a very heavy set. John Hallé's design was artistically effective but consisted of several heavy wooden frameworks, which made the get ins and outs slow and arduous. When I witnessed the company panting up to a sixth floor at one venue like breathless mountaineers scaling Everest, the penny dropped. This was a wake up call about touring design

The Scatterin' by James McKenna, designed by John Hallé. Green Fields and Far Away tour, 1979. (Top) Ronan Paterson as Patzer McLoughlin and Kevin Wallace as Tony Riordan. (Bottom) Kevin Wallace as Tony Riordan and John O'Toole as Jemmo Fitzgerald.

The Scatterin' by James McKenna. Green Fields and Far Away tour, 1979.
Kevin Wallace as Tony Riordan, Ronan Paterson as Patzer McLoughlin,
Denis O'Neill as Con Geraghty and John O'Toole as Jemmo Fitzgerald.

and the need for light and flexible sets. Also, getting bookings for
an unknown play and writer without a classic in the repertoire was
difficult. Nonetheless, *The Scatterin'* was well performed, there
was a poetic, raw sensibility about the production and we'd managed to keep the company going.

21 – The Tour from Hell

OUR ARDUOUS SPRING ADVENTURE was followed by one of those
nightmare tours you want to forget. It's not that it was unsuccessful – in fact, commercially it worked well – it was just that it
caused no end of problems. It started optimistically with me commissioning a play about Jack Doyle, the Cork boxer, who fought
Jack Peterson for the British Heavyweight title at Wembley in front
of 100,000 people, married Movita (later Mrs Marlon Brando), became a Hollywood film actor, sang, performed a music hall act,
'Punch and Beauty' with his wife and ended up a dosser in Notting
Hill Gate, cadging drinks from all and sundry.

I'd asked one of the company, Ian MacPherson, to write the
play. Ian had acted in the first tour and was articulate, witty, bright

and very imaginative. He would later become a very successful alternative comic. In many ways, it was through his hilarious comments and observations while travelling in the van that I thought he was the man to bring the reprobate Doyle to life. Not only did Ian produce an amusing script, but also lyrics to several good songs by musician Sue Van Colle.

The central character was split into Old and Young Doyle. The deceased Old Doyle recounting his life to a reporter while in heaven and Young Doyle actually performing it. For both Young and Old Doyle we needed actors who were charismatic and good looking, believable as heavyweight boxers, could sing well and were willing to tour for little money. It was particularly difficult to cast the older part but I eventually chose James Donnelly, an experienced, attractive actor with an Irish background. The only trouble was that I discovered he was a recovering alcoholic. For the younger Doyle, we found Luke Hayden, a raw, inexperienced Dubliner with bags of enthusiasm and charm. Given the needs of the script, we had to employ many new faces in the cast, several of whom weren't particularly loyal to the company. However, Donnelly was well cast and initially showed himself to be creating a strong, believable character. We rehearsed in the Irish Club where he proudly announced that he was off the drink. However there were signs of alarm when Donnelly invited Michael Loughnan into the bar after rehearsal. He reiterated his vow of abstinence but then proceeded to raise a pint of beer, proclaiming vociferously, 'but I deserve this!'

The Jack Doyle play was twinned in repertoire with Behan's classic *The Hostage*. I'd always liked Behan's work for its rich humanity and humour. While I was at boarding school, I read *Borstal Boy* and thought that it was a very powerful, well written novel. I suppose I was in a kind of borstal myself so I was reading it in an appropriate place. *The Hostage* has a unique feeling of improvisation which only such an Irish play could give you. You feel that anything could happen at any time. That's why songs and jokes seem to spring up quite naturally from nowhere. The Gaelic version of the play, *An Giall*, is meant to be a much tighter, more subtle, poetic work. In contrast, the English version is highly influenced by Joan Littlewood and her sense of carnival theatricality. She was after all in favour of making theatres fun palaces, accessible to all. Despite the raucousness and the broad humour there still lies at the play's core, a touching, sensitive love story of a soldier kidnapped by the IRA and falling in love with Teresa, a young maid. When time runs out to exchange the hostage for an IRA man facing execution, all mayhem takes place and leads to the soldier's death. Littlewood may have made the play a coarser, more commercial piece of work, but she certainly helped Behan find fame. He seemed to relish this, proving to be a brilliant self-publicist. It was reported that when *The Hostage* transferred to the West End, he read all his good reviews aloud while travelling on the tube.

While I was a student, I worked in the BBC film vaults at Ealing Studios and witnessed Behan recording an interview with novelist Colin MacInness, author of *Absolute Beginners*. They seemed to like each other: both wrote about outsiders and working class communities. However, there were two problems. Behan was drunk and after completing various sections of the interview, he insisted on singing, which he did most beautifully. Eventually, he got through the interview but it was a bit of an eye-opener to this naive student to see a writer turning a TV studio into a shebeen.

I asked John Lynch to come over from Dublin to direct *The Hostage* and he certainly gave Behan's drama the sensitive balance between tragedy and comedy that it needed. Maurice Blake as Pat the caretaker, and Finola Keogh as his wife Meg, made appealing hosts at the prescribed Dublin brothel, and the company gave authenticity and style to the various comings and goings.

Unfortunately, it wasn't long before the tour got into difficulties. The main problem revolved around James Donnelly. My initial hopes that he'd perform the part well were subsiding. He was struggling with the demands of playing Old Doyle and became irascible in the process. It was a good leading role and I think he saw it as a springboard to revive his stumbling career. At times he

Jack Doyle – The Man Who Boxed like John McCormack! by
Ian MacPherson. Green Fields and Far Away tour, 1979-1980.
Luke Hayden as Young Doyle and James Donnelly as Old Doyle.

was powerful and commanding in the part, but his drink problems
had made him 'ring rusty'. He dropped lines, lost his temper, ac-
cused others and then hit the bottle. Unfortunately, a disaster was
unfolding.

After a very nervy opening at the Warwick Arts Centre, things
came to a head in the southeast section of the tour. After the end of

the show, the towering, six foot five, ex-Irish Guard Donnelly was asked by our Company Stage Manager, Sandra Wynne, to hurry up and do the get out. Donnelly felt demeaned. As far as he was concerned, he was being talked down to in a bossy, abrupt fashion by a young person with insufficient experience. Suddenly he made aggressive physical attempts to attack her but was pulled away by some of the company. This was seriously unacceptable behaviour and several committed regulars of the company voiced their concerns privately and told me that some actors wanted to leave. When your friends warn you of such threats, you know you've got a serious problem.

The future of the tour became in doubt and a company meeting was assembled in a huge cavernous, echoing hall. It was like a scene out of 1984, as I stood on the stage justifying myself to the mutinous throng. Some of the company had already been complaining about other matters, and in some cases I felt that they were using the situation to accelerate their agitation. However, understandably everybody was appalled that a man could attack a young woman at her place of work in such a way. Certainly, there was a strong demand to sack Donnelly, but I warned the company that would seriously threaten the whole tour. To recast such a part quickly was going to be impossible. Not only did we have little time to rehearse on the road but, more importantly, we had immediate dates to fulfill and if we didn't do them our funding could be cut.

While accepting the seriousness of the situation, I proposed that we worked together to find a compromise. I suggested a two-point plan. One, that Donnelly should come out of *The Hostage*, in which for some bizarre reason he was struggling to mime playing the bagpipes, and concentrate just on *Jack Doyle*, thus reducing his workload. Two, that those who still wanted to leave should do so and I'll recast. After further discussion, the company accepted this and departed from the eerie hall in silence. Of course, Sandra understandably left with two other actors – the likely moaning suspects. The tour and the company were saved but it was a close shave.

After the departures, the company was rejuvenated. Ags Irwin became our Company Stage Manager. Fair-haired, intelligent, and amiable, she was temperamentally suited to dealing with the difficult, volatile Donnelly. Bill Rourke, a solid Northern actor, took over the English roles and integrated well. The role of Monsewer, an Anglo-Irish landlord, in *The Hostage* was taken over by me. This had been Donnelly's part but we couldn't get another actor in time. I had no desire to act but given the lack of time and money, it seemed the best option. I managed to do a Rex Harrison to Monsewer's musical numbers, which could be semi-spoken to music rather than fully sung. I also played the part of Jack Peterson, Doyle's opponent in the staging of the seminal British Heavyweight Championship fight, which was a bit ridiculous considering I had a slim, unmuscular build. Let's say the fight was, in this case, metaphorical. I suppose some enjoyed the sight of the director being beaten up each night. It was a strange experience and one I did out of necessity rather than enjoyment. One side of my brain was always the director, wondering about the development of the play as a whole rather than just my part, which isn't where an actor should be. Things reached a climax when the Arts Council came to see *The Hostage*, only to discover that the director was now on stage in a kilt with bagpipes! Naturally, I was apprehensive, but Ruth Marks didn't say anything derogatory so I assume we must have got away with it.

Donnelly still lurked in the background but the problems were less once the changes were made. Or should I say they were less public. Michael Loughnan was in a more difficult situation. He had all his scenes with Donnelly, playing the journalist who interviewed Old Doyle throughout the play. Donnelly confided personally in Michael and told him how he was worried about his girlfriend, who was a drug addict. There was obviously a lot I didn't know about even though I got a sense of Donnelly's inner turbulence. Michael had the patience to deal with such a mercurial character, but he suffered unnecessarily because of it. Donnelly could be charming, witty and insightful, but like many alcoholics he was also selfish and mean. When he forgot lines, he blamed Michael, never himself. He never considered Michael's feelings or had much consideration for his part. It was all about his character and his performance. If you have such an egotist in a company make sure he is good and delivers a well above average performance so the suffering is worth it. Unfortunately, Donnelly never reached such heights. He was very good in sections of the play, but seemed incapable of listening with sufficient concentration to unite these moments into a complete characterisation. It was as if he couldn't override the chaos in his own life.

Despite such problems, the tour still had its lighter, bizarre moments. For instance, while in Sittingbourne Kent, Patch Connolly, our bearded beanpole of a man from Warrenpoint, and Michael Loughnan, were stopped by the police while driving the three-ton

Jack Doyle – The Man Who Boxed like John McCormack! by Ian MacPherson, designed by John Hallé, Green Fields and Far Away tour, 1979-80. James Donnelly as Old Doyle and Luke Hayden as Young Doyle (front) Michael Loughnan as Page, Jessica Swift as Judith Allen (his first wife), Maurice Blake as Dosser, Finola Keogh as Sister Eucalyptus, Hilary Field as Groupie (behind Sister Eucalyptus), Moira Fitzgerald as Mrs Godde, Patch Connolly as Referee, John Quinn as Manager, Jacinta Martin as Movita and Paul O'Keeffe as Newsboy (left to right behind the Doyles).

van. Now Patch, an actor of rare comic gusto, was playing a variety of character parts in *Jack Doyle*, not least a Marxist policeman. Thank goodness he didn't joke about his part with the men in blue, as at the time bombs were still going off regularly. However, after the police had looked in the back of the van and discovered dummy rifles, they emerged confused. When Patch answered questions in his Northern Ireland accent, it wasn't an exactly auspicious start to the proceedings. 'We're doing a play,' said Patch. 'Right, okay,' said the disconcerted bobby, before cautiously departing with no greater enlightenment than when he and his mate started their investigation.

Jack Doyle toured for a long time, including performances at the Theatre Royal Stratford East, the Olympia Theatre Dublin, the Cork Opera House and as part of the 'A Sense of Ireland Festival 1980' at the Lyric Hammersmith. Ian MacPherson's play was funny and had moments of pathos, but it tried to do too many things. It had around ten musical numbers, some of which were brilliant like the memorable 'Coal Dust and Whisky' about Jack's early upbringing. However, it fell between being a musical, a satirical comedy and the core of a quirky straight drama. Producing a biographical play is a big challenge because you're usually overloaded with information. I discovered that you have to edit down to the essence. You can't include every event in the person's life, however entertaining. While there was a wonderful sense of devilry in the play, which certainly caught Doyle's character, I think if we'd been more ruthlessly economic we would have produced a tighter, more focused production. It was a fun show but a bloated one. Still, it was a very good start for Ian's writing career, audiences seemed to enjoy it and it served its purpose in widening our audience and getting a Dublin and London showing.

After completing his *Hostage* production, John Lynch made a documentary for RTÉ on the *Jack Doyle* tour. Amidst the various dates, cameramen followed us in hotels, down streets, unloading vans and getting in and out of several theatres. The film John produced is one of the best about being on the road during the late seventies and early eighties: it really gets to the grime of touring, the sheer hard work of it all. In it, I look skeletal, undernourished, pale and ghostly. Nonetheless, the good humour and commitment of the company comes across very well. The second half of the film partly consists of individual interviews, which try a bit too hard to get into the psyche of the actors and how they really felt. The Donnelly incident is mentioned somewhat obscurely, which was a relief to me, but at times it makes for some confusing viewing. Nonetheless, for an insight into the touring process of the day it's excellent.

22 – Chasing the Whale

AFTER *JACK DOYLE* AND *THE HOSTAGE*, Green Fields presented one of its more off beat productions. Believing that the company needed to develop its repertoire and not sit in its comfort zone, I accepted designer John Hallé's adaptation of *Moby Dick*. While I couldn't make a case for the author, Herman Melville, being Irish, I could see that the book had affinities with Irish drama, mainly in pitting man's fate against the sea and nature, something for instance Synge explored in *Riders to the Sea*. In any case, I always think Irish actors tend to be good in American drama, being very much part of the US diaspora. Poetically and temperamentally, there's an affinity there and unsurprisingly there were several Irish actors in John Huston's film of the novel, including none other than that bearded *Irish Times* Drama Critic, Seamus Kelly!

I later heard that some thought my reasoning spurious but I don't accept that a company should rigidly adhere to its most obvious parameters. In fact, Irish theatre generally has been bedevilled by the monoculture of only doing Irish plays. The Gate might provide a certain corrective to this, but a quite narrow one. The great plays from continental Europe are too often missing from Irish programming, the American repertoire produced is narrow and many good English plays are rarely produced. I was therefore keen for the company to take such opportunities and illuminate a non-Irish classic. Normally, I avoid adaptations. I much prefer a play to be originally for the stage rather than ciphered through another medium. However, the challenge of realising a whale on stage was too tempting.

John's adaptation was spare and economic, like his design style. While this had visual advantages, the text was too faithful and could have been filled out a bit more dramatically. The production was aided by some imaginative movement by choreographer Judy Gridley, and supplemented by sound that evoked the approaching danger of the whale. A vast mast, a bridged platform and benches conjured up the various settings and the diverse cast created a distinctive community.

David Blake Kelly, the most civilised and genial of men, played Ahab. He was certainly nautical and believeable, but lacked that sense of danger and charisma that would propel the crew to go to such inordinate lengths for him. Only a few middle aged actors have the latter qualities and such luminaries were unlikely to tour. Consequently, David held the centre of the play without dominating it. He was brilliantly supported by Des McAleer as his second in command, Starbuck, a menacing, sinister, austere presence. There were also two black actors in Moby Dick: Errol Shaker and Robert Phillips. Errol is big man from Brixton who is built like an American footballer. He had a great sense of humour and a lot of energy. I remember him rapping on about soul music when we were travelling in the van. 'I don't want to be racist about it but when white singers sing about love, I just don't believe them, man. Not like Esther Phillips. When Esther sings, man, I believe that love.' Robert was more taciturn and less forthright but a sensitive actor who fitted in well.

Then there was Vernon Nurse, a Scot who looked like a moustachioed South American barman. Vernon was a bit of a womaniser and I remember his irate Scottish wife ringing our office demanding to know where her 'fucking husband' was. Naturally, I kicked for touch there!

The rest of the company consisted of more regular Green Fields actors: John Quinn, a small stocky Dubliner who had been

Moby Dick adapted and designed by John Hallé, Green Fields and Far Away
tour, 1980. Errol Shaker as Queequeg, William Rourke as Stubb
and Michael Loughnan as Ishmael.

very sharp as Jack Doyle's grasping manager, the colourful Maurice
Blake, who with his grey-haired pony tail and booming voice was
an imposing Father Mapple, the prelate who gives a stern, prophetic sermon before the sailors go to sea. Michael Loughnan was
Ishmael, the only survivor of the voyage. He had both the presence
and vocal clarity to link the action and tell Ishmael's own story,
to be both engaged and disengaged. His mellifluous singing voice
was used yet again to carry the ballads which were sung between
scenes.

After a shaky start in Coleraine, *Moby Dick* gathered momentum without ever attracting large audiences. This was probably because, although it was a known title, it was the most experimental
show we'd done. It was more a dramatised poem than a conventional play. It was an attempt to use movement, sound and design
in a more freewheeling, less lineal narrative form, and to get an

Irish company to translate their own culture into a universal classic. It was a development both for me and the company.

23 – Hogan's Way

HAVING STRETCHED OUR ARTISTIC muscles by embracing a foreign project, we now presented the premiere of a new play, Desmond Hogan's adaptation of his novel *The Ikon Maker*. The play centres around Susan Conlon, a dressmaker in Ballinasloe, and her relationship with her son Diarmaid, who had left to go to England after the suicide of a close friend, just as his father left Mary to go to Chicago. Susan is lonely and bereft by these departures, and goes searching for her son around England. In the process, she comes to terms with his gay sexuality and a new sense of herself. The play was beautifully written, if not fully escaping its literary origins. Des is a writer of great sensitivity and imagination, and he was well served by two lead performances of considerable quality. Mary Duddy and Liam Halligan played together with a wonderful intimacy which was incestuously dangerous and widely praised ('heartfelt performances', *The Guardian*; 'played to perfection', *The Stage*). A fine ensemble was completed by Lisa Cook, now a successful agent, Isolde Cazelet, Ulster actress Frances Quinn and Michael Loughnan.

The tour was mainly played in small venues which were suitable for the intimate tone of the material. At the end of the tour, we also presented the play for a season at the Gate, Notting Hill. The production was performed against an abstract white set, with minimalist furniture and lighting creating the various settings. There were no props and various activities were mimed. James Fenton, the *Sunday Times* critic, gave the play a respectful review but did comment on the way various 'glasses' were miraculously altering position! Despite the disappearing glasses, I think the stylisation worked well, especially for touring. It was clean, clear and economic, which helped the fluidity of the production and gave strong focus to the story. It also meant that choreographer Judy Gridley had the space to develop the physical work we did on *Moby Dick*.

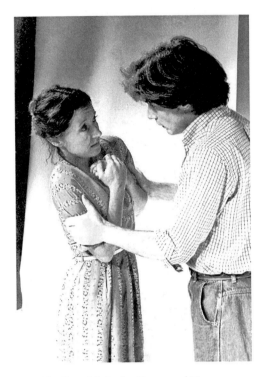

The Ikon Maker by Desmond Hogan.
Green Fields and Far Away tour, 1980.
Mary Duddy as Susan O'Hanrahan and
Liam Halligan as her son Diarmaid.

Des Hogan was an intense, eccentric, monastic-looking figure who went around London on a bike. He was generous and supportive. At the time he was with one of the hottest literary agents in London, Deborah Rogers, who had great admiration for him. Yet, Des seemed to be above the greasy career pole. His personal and artistic journey seemed to be beyond recognition and certainly fame. I remember he used to keep a lot of his work in a satchel on his bike. At the time, he was working on a new novel. One day in rehearsal, he revealed that he had lost his latest draft in a pub and that when he went back to try to recover it, it wasn't there. He concluded that the cleaner must have thrown away the hand-written manuscript mistakenly thinking it to be rubbish.

When I questioned his serenity in proclaiming this news, he told me that he didn't think the draft was up to scratch and that he needed to rewrite it anyway. Des was supremely confident that it was all there in his head. This was something I remembered when many years later I inadvertently erased something from my computer. Instead of raging around in frustration, I recalled Des's relaxed approach to the missing manuscript and tried to immediately remember and improve the content.

While working on the play, Des invited us all to one of his freewheeling parties. We sat on the bed and floor of his north London flat as we drank wine and ate sandwiches. There was an interesting cross section of guests, including a fair smattering of the London literary scene. Des was certainly liked and respected by some illustrious colleagues. Then, later, he disappeared off the scene both in London and Ireland, with very little work being published. More recently, he has resurfaced in Ballybunion, County Kerry with some new short stories. His absence has been our loss. A fine writer, I think Des could write a major Irish novel. Who knows, maybe it's in his satchel? Let's hope he doesn't lose it this time. Or if he does, I'm sure he'll still retain it in his head.

Financially, Green Fields was beginning to struggle. We weren't extravagant but possibly a bit naive. We needed more administrative input and should have pursued a harder business approach to secure the stability of the company. The trouble was that all our energies were being consumed with managing the current tour and putting in applications for a new one. This certainly didn't help long-term strategic planning. It was also difficult to keep a per-

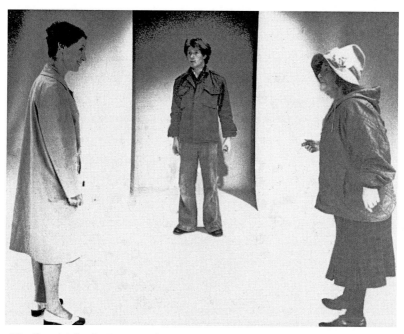

The Ikon Maker by Desmond Hogan, designed by John Hallé. Green Fields and Far Away tour, 1980. Mary Duddy as Susan O'Hanrahan, Liam Halligan as her son Diarmaid and Isolde Cazelet as her neighbour Mrs Conlon.

manent administrator, given the gaps between tours. Mick Walsh left after *The Scatterin'* and was followed by a succession of other administrators who stayed for the run of the tour, while money was available. This wasn't good for either continuity or financial stability.

The most colourful of these was Patrick Newley. Patrick was the son of the Cork playwright Patrick Galvin. Tall, with owlish brown glasses and extremely camp, he was great fun, with a real love of theatre. Working for Green Fields was only one of Patrick's many activities. He was also a show businesss journalist and manager of Mrs Shufflewick, a struggling drag act. Shuff, or Rex Jameson, which was his real name, came out of the tail end of the music hall. He was probably a bit too smutty for the wider audience that Cork-born Danny La Rue had conquered, but he continued to appear in north London pubs and other such venues. Patrick was a big fan and was doing his best to both stabilise his personal life and resurrect his career. Rex was a heavy drinker and I think it was a bit of a struggle keeping him away from the sauce. However, Patrick did succeed to some extent, getting him publicised to a new generation as a cult figure.

Patrick's client list was eclectic and included Douglas Byng, another more 'posh' music hall drag act; Quentin Crisp, the flamboyant gay raconteur; Tommy Trinder, comedian and former chairman of Fulham Football club; 'Mad' Frankie Fraser, notorious criminal; and Robin Maugham, author of *The Servant* and nephew of Somerset Maugham, the distinguished best selling writer. In fact, during *The Ikon Maker* tour, Patrick invited me to lunch with Robin at his house in Brighton. The dining room was laid out as if for royalty. The guests were all formally and elegantly dressed men. No women were present apart from those serving the meal. Various scents wafted in the air. It had the air of a prelude to gay bacchanalia. There was wit and merriment but I gradually felt a sense of claustrophobic imprisonment, like being forced to join a club when I didn't want to become a member. After a couple of hours, I'd had enough. Fortunately, Patrick had already told Robin that I had to return to the venue, so I had a convenient exit strategy. However, the meal was first class and Patrick as ever was an entertaining companion. Sadly, in 2009, I heard that Patrick had died from cancer. It was ironic that he should pass away in his fifties while writing obituaries for *The Stage*. Patrick had a genuine love of entertainment and showed particular commitment to Irish theatre. His rare warmth and dedication is missed.

24 – Taking On O'Neill

PATRICK WAS FOLLOWED BY LUKE DIXON who became our third administrator. I think Luke, who often dressed in elegant white suits, was more interested in experimental work. Nonetheless, he oversaw our next production, Eugene O'Neill's *A Touch of the Poet*, with competence if not enthusiasm. One of the greatest American playwrights, O'Neill is a writer of strong Irish heritage. After seeing *The Iceman Cometh* at the Abbey, I was confident that Irish actors would bring something unique to O'Neill. They fully embraced the temperament of a foreign voice, vital when acting the work of a different culture. In any case, didn't O'Neill himself say that the first thing you had to understand about him and his work was that he was Irish?

O'Neill is one of those playwrights who doesn't read well but plays brilliantly. Initially, you think his dramas are overwritten, melodramatic, hollow and repetitive. However when performed, his work springs to life. I think this is because O'Neill, like O'Casey, wrote from the depths of personal experience. It is this sense of truth that inspires actors quite often to go to places they haven't been before. One of the particular qualities that Irish actors bring to O'Neill's plays is humour, quite often expressed by the gap between fantasy and reality – man's insistence on clinging to his delusions.

A Touch of the Poet is set in 1828. Con Melody, the central character, keeps romanticising about his days as a gentleman officer in Wellington's army and showing disdain for his fellow Irish workers, whom he serves in his Massachussetts tavern. He is challenged

A Touch of the Poet by Eugene O'Neill.
Green Fields and Far Away tour, 1981.
Ann O'Connor (seated) as Nora Melody
and Niamh Mahon as her daughter Sara.

by his headstrong daughter Sara, who is looking to marry the patrician Simon Harford. Sara ruthlessly attacks her father's pride and his constant romanticisation of the past. Melody eventually succumbs to her persistence, despite the support of his loyal wife. He is forced to face the nature of his own identity and kills the horse he rode as a soldier. Although Sara knows that she's now freer to marry Simon without the burden of her pretentious father, she also realises that she's helped him destroy an innate sense of his gentlemanly self.

Con Melody is a part for a star – Jason Robards or Peter O'Toole – however there's a danger that the play becomes a vehicle for only one performance. Our production had the advantage of being an ensemble. RSC actor Bill McGuirk was still a charismatic presence, with his neatly set grey hair, trim figure and piercing blue eyes. Maybe he didn't have the full emotional unpredictabilty that such a part demands, but he was sensitive, self-deprecatingly humorous and passionate.

O'Neill seems to be the godfather of the American theatre of accusation, with a lineage right up to Albee's *Who's Afraid of Virginia Woolf* and later Mamet's *Oleanna*. Sara, the main accuser in the play, is a challenging part for a young actor. I chose Niamh Mahon, who trained at the Focus Theatre in Dublin. Committed and dedicated, with attractively dark Celtic looks, Niamh brought energy and sexiness to the part. Her exchanges with Melody had all the intensity of a love affair. This highlighted the possibility that by so earnestly wanting her father to reform, she was not only destroying part of him but also part of herself. The other main part of the mother was played by another Focus Theatre alumni, Ann O'Connor. Well cast, she brought an inner strength to the ritualistic drudgery she went through to satisfy her ego-fuelled, fantasist husband.

One of the themes of the play is class. Melody wants to be accepted as a gentleman not as an Irish peasant. Our designer, Jan Cholawo, managed to segregate the different bars imaginatively, so the gauze-like construction at the back gave you an opportunity to see the Irish workers drinking in the public bar while Con preened proudly in the saloon. It was as if his unruly compatriots were hovering over his dreams and aspirations like intruding ghosts. The other side of the play is the Yankee side. Less interesting and dramatic, it contrasts with the more Irish section of the drama. It centres around Simon's mother and her patrician concern for her son and family. The play is long and ambitious, especially for touring. It got its best houses in university towns like Cambridge and Aberyswyth. Despite getting good reviews ('warmth, sensitivity in well-observed O'Neill', *Liverpool Echo*; 'I enjoyed it thoroughly', *Guardian*), it struggled in other venues.

It was at the end of the tour that one of those incidents that every director dreads occurred. All the company went to a restaurant in Liverpool at the end of the last performance. Things seemed to be proceeding happily enough. There was laughter and some good food. We had finished our desserts and were dealing with dividing the bill, when suddenly there was an outpouring of invective against me from one of the actors playing a Yankee. 'You shit, you fuckin' shit, you never cared a fuck' and so on ad infinitum. I didn't understand where this bile came from. In fact, it took everybody by surprise. I was angry and moved to confront our exhibitionistic agitator. Fortunately, Maurice Blake, like a good policeman stopping traffic, once more intervened. 'Take no notice, Roly, he's pissed.' I took Maurice's advice and avoided my ranting protagonist. It was a pity as it was a depressing end to a happy tour.

A Touch of the Poet by Eugene O'Neill, designed by Jan Cholawo and Paul Lanham. Green Fields and Far Away tour, 1981. Noel Slattery as Mickey Maloy, Niamh Mahon as Sara Melody, Michael Loughnan as Jamie Cregan, Bill McGuirk as Cornelius Melody, Bernard Collins as Paddy O'Dowd, Patrick Horne as Nicholas Gadsby and Maurice Blake as Dan Roche.

Later, I heard that the actor in question didn't think that I gave him sufficient attention. He had a small part and felt marginalised. I think that was more due to his insecurity. If he had a problem he never told me. I don't respect those who indulge in histrionics without dialogue. In fact, one celebrated director once told me that he never attended last night parties to avoid potential violent overspill. I've learnt that sometimes being a director can be physically hazardous.

25 – The Riddle of Erskine Childers

IRONICALLY, GREEN FIELDS'S LAST TOUR in 1981 was one of its best. For some years I'd been interested in the life of Erskine

Childers, the author of *The Riddle of the Sands.* I was curious to know how an English public schoolboy, adventurer, writer and MP could end up as Director of Publicity for Sinn Féin, shaking the hands of his executioners during the Irish Civil War. It was an amazing story and one which I thought could be shared by English and Irish audiences alike. To write a play on such a subject, I needed a writer of style who could not only get to the emotional heart of a complex man but would also be able to have a sense of the period, be comfortable with Irish and English dialogue, and dramatise seminal political events. I immediately thought of Leigh Jackson. I first met Leigh in the early seventies at the Overground Kingston, one of the bigger fringe theatres. He had written several plays for that venue including one about Bob Dylan and another very impressive drama about former British Prime Minister Anthony Eden, in which Alan Devlin played the part of Eden's Irish butler. After seeing *Eden*, Alan told me that he didn't have to change a word, such was Leigh's ear for dialect. Unsurprisingly, Leigh went on to write plays for the Royal Court. I always found his work full of humanity and humour. He was an underrated playwright, less fashionable than many more politically modish ones. He didn't go in for seventies sloganising, although he was as committed as anyone. His writing was more subtle and contradictory than many other writers, but at that stage he hadn't had a breakthrough work. His plays were thoughtful and well written, but maybe they lacked both a theatrical energy and a fashionable subject to find the big audience he deserved. Leigh was interested in history, its protagonists and its effects on people. He was perfect for writing the Childers story and duly presented a very good script.

Bookended by the making of Childers's coffin and the last hours in his death cell, the play charts his rise to prominence within the British establishment, his gradual disillusionment with the Empire and his commitment to Irish independence, which precipitated his death. At the centre of the play is a love story. Childers had married the disabled Bostonian, Molly Osgood, who was a great inspiration to him. It was Molly who saw Britain making the same mistakes in Ireland that she had made in America. Her moral persistence drove him on. Childers was initially an adventurer and a Tory but he became a Liberal who supported Home Rule and after 1916, through his cousin Robert Barton, he became a member of Sinn Féin. He seemed to have a sense of moral duty to make his life meaningful. In that sense, he had a similar Edwardian attitude to Churchill, who ironically bitterly chastised Childers's final 'treachery'. Far from treacherous, Childers's moral duty was to liberty. It was a genuine tragedy that he got executed by those whom he wanted to free.

Childers was played by Robert O'Mahoney who was excellent in the part and exuded authority. Robert had been at the RSC and had the hallmarks of a fine leading classical actor: a great voice, a finely-honed, controlled technique and graceful movement. If Robert had a fault it's one that some English actors often have – of allowing technique to become too self-conscious and undermine the emotional exposure of feeling and vulnerability. Nonetheless, he was a very good, complex and committed Childers. David Haig portrayed his friend Basil Williams. David has that great ability of good actors to make the mundane interesting. He can convince you that the most ordinary person is fascinating. It's not surprising that he went on to play leads in the West End. The other key part of Childers's wife Molly was played by Sharon Lee Holm, a young American actor based in London. She brought an intelligence and passion to Molly that helped give the play an emotional centre.

A Flag Unfurled, as the Childers play was called, covers a lot of historical ground and complex events. John Hallé's set was framed by a screen that projected the time changes and settings in a simple, clear way. This was supplemented by a basic abstract structure, simple changes of furniture and imaginative focusing of directional light. Getting across information to audiences in such a play without being portentous isn't easy. In the predigital, slower world of seventies theatre, it was particularly challenging. However, Leigh's elegant dialogue managed to cleverly integrate information naturally without the characters merely becoming mouthpieces of ideas. There was also a helpful thread of wit in the play which contrasted well with the serious events and the eventual tragic outcome.

After a succesful opening of the play at the Venn Street Arts Centre in Huddersfield, I got on a train with Leigh to go to London. After sitting in my seat, I heard rumblings in my stomach. The local Indian takeaway wasn't agreeing with me. Suddenly I felt unwell and ran towards the lavatory. As I moved down the aisle of the train, I started being sick. Passengers veered away from me as if they were being approached by Frankenstein, or perhaps more appropriately, The Flying Puke! In desperation, I was forced to open a window. I unloaded the Indian meal but as the train was travelling so fast, the blistering wind ripped my glasses off my ears, and propelled them into the Yorkshire air, never to be seen again. Later, something more pleasant but equally surprising took place.

One of our most interesting performances was at Tunbridge Wells, home of the fictional Aunt Edna, a kind of Mary Whitehouse character, who would react extremely to permissive controversy. The play was received in this conservative bastion with rapt attention and given an excellent reception. As the audience made its way out of the theatre, I heard somebody say that he never knew that Erskine Childers was connected with the IRA. There was a sense of bewilderment and shock at such misinformation. In Britain, Childers had just been remembered as the writer of *The Riddle of the Sands*, the classic First World War thriller. The other side of his life was unknown to the wider public. It was certainly good to hear that we had managed to illuminate preconceptions. I was particularly pleased as I got the original idea for the play after meeting Erskine Childers's son at the Abbey, when he was President of Ireland. It made me realise that the wheel of history can turn very dramatically.

A Flag Unfurled toured in repertoire with the Restoration play *The Recruiting Officer* by George Farquhar. The Derry dramatist's play is the most earthy of Restoration Comedies. It's not just a satire on manners but about the real issue of enlisting gullible men for war. Our touring production directed by Terry Palmer had a roughness about it that worked in its favour. It also had some imaginative doubling, so there was a sense of improvisation and freedom that was in contrast to more traditionally staid, polished productions. This fitted well with the use of disguise in the plot. Robert O'Mahoney, a flamboyant Capt Plume, and Michael Loughnan, an amusing Kite, were the main recruiters, while the androgynous Michelle Copsey brought amusing mischief to Sylvia's change of sex to get Plume recruited to marriage. The production caught a good balance between the seriousness of the theme and the comedy, the world of recruiting and the desire to find a partner. Unfortunately, venues grabbed the chance to take a known title at the expense of booking the new play. My idea of doing each play in the same venue was becoming harder. By the end of the tour the Restoration play had done many more performances than the new one. This wasn't what was intended, but it became a harsh reality. Thankfully, later in 1998, I produced Leigh's rewritten radio version of *A Flag Unfurled* for Radio 3, so at least his play finally reached that wider audience.

The tour had been successful artistically but our debts were catching up with us. Elizabeth Jones was our Administrator for these final productions. She was an efficient practitioner who always had the rather stern look of an angry schoolmistress. Looking at our accounts didn't do anything to improve her demeanour. The losses over some other tours were becoming increasingly hard to sustain.

Unfortunately, for four years we were surviving on an ad hoc basis and it was catching up with us. Now, to make some tours work logistically, we had to take a few percentage deals that didn't help us meet our income target. Getting an itinerary together is a very arduous task. Particularly during the early tours, we were often zig zagging across the country like a motorcyclist manically racing over hill and down dale. Sometimes there was geographical incompatibility and within a week we were travelling from one side of the country to another. Of course, this can lead to tiredness, irritability, bad morale and performance. It was much to the credit of everyone involved that they managed to put up with some of our failings with good humour. They knew we were on a learning curve and gave us the benefit of the doubt. Unfortunately, I discovered that the structure for such an apprenticeship wasn't the best model to nurture long-term viability.

26 – Green Fields Coda

THE CLOSURE OF GREEN FIELDS IN 1981 was a sad moment for me. I felt I'd failed in establishing an Irish company permanently in the UK and of handing it on to the next generation. However we did manage one final London production at that centre of eccentricity, the Irish Club, Eaton Square – *The Other Side* by James Pettifer, which was about the Irish in a London branch of the Labour Party. Based on Shakespeare's *Measure for Measure,* it dramatised ideological, internal strife. Although it was a 'friendly entertainment from an exceptionally benign company' (*The Times*), it lacked the power of its source and a sufficiently tough political edge. It was rushed on to take advantage of available funding and keep the company alive. Consequently, James wasn't given the time to fully develop the piece.

Sadly, the strain of trying to survive caught up with us. I gambled that by continuing we could raise further income and manage our debts. In the end, it became too difficult. Unfortunately, we didn't make the breakthrough to revenue funding which could have stabilised the situation. Now we were entering a different era for the arts. Margaret Thatcher had been elected in 1979 and the full force of her government's cuts were soon to take place.

The Arts Council had put a lot of faith in me and I appreciated their trust. I remember when I told Ruth Marks about our difficulties, she looked at me sympathetically and said, 'unfortunately every company has its own lifespan'. Within that context of project touring Ruth was probably right: our time had probably run out and given the changing political climate we were even less likely to get revenue funding. In reality, very few small-scale touring companies last a long time, Field Day being an honourable exception. I can only admire the tireless work Stephen Rea did playing around the country in diverse venues for so many years. It showed fantastic commitment, especially when practitioners so often talk about taking theatre to the people but don't actually do it. Green Fields had a shorter history but it wasn't long after our own demise that many other excellent revenue-funded companies dissolved. Sadly this is inevitable, as not only do political times and tastes change but everybody gets older with more commitments, energies dilute and people need to earn more money.

Although I didn't leave the legacy I hoped for, Green Fields was one of the most significant periods of my working life. Careers are made in capital cities before middle class liberal audiences. Consequently, the plays performed are usually a case of preaching to the converted. Although Green Fields wasn't a radical company, I do believe that at a time when few Irish plays were being produced in the UK, and political tension was high, it did make a significant contribution in laying the groundwork for future Irish work to be more readily accepted. For four arduous years, Green Fields went on the road and travelled the length and breadth of these islands, presenting thirteen Irish plays to a wide-ranging, diverse audience. In forging links with those communities, we managed to entertain and hopefully enlighten our audience during 'the Troubles'. We may not have got an Oscar but the *Irish Post's* Award in 1981 for our work for the Irish community means more to me than Hollywood glitz.

LYRIC THEATRE BELFAST

27 – My Days in the North

SEVEN YEARS LATER I RETURNED to Irish theatre when I went to work at the Lyric Theatre Belfast. In fact, I'd already worked on several productions there and developed an eccentric relationship with the theatre since 1970, when I directed Wesley Burrowes's play, *The Becauseway*.

In those days, Mary O'Malley, the founder of the theatre, ruled it like a powerful potentate. She was a Catholic and a Nationalist with an obsession for the plays of Yeats. The theatre started in her back garden in Derryvolgie Avenue. Mary was a brilliant pioneer who worked tirelessly to get a major repertory theatre established in Belfast. Against the odds, she succeeded and created a non-sectarian environment to bring a whole cross section of good plays to Belfast. However, founders don't necessarily make good Artistic Directors. In the early years, she ran the theatre like her own personal fiefdom. She was like a mother who wouldn't let her child grow up. The theatre was run like a prison. It was always locked and inaccessible, and Mary's administrator, Winifred Bell, a sturdy, formidable Protestant woman, seemed more like a jailer than a theatre employee. Mary certainly encouraged some good local actors but by constantly casting them in too many plays, she put a strain on their talents while undermining opportunities for others. She certainly was brave and bold in her ambition, and her repertoire was often more wide-ranging than most theatres in Ireland, not least in producing continental writers like Büchner, Wedekind and Brecht. There was also certainly nothing wrong in having a quote from Yeats above the entrance door, but to insist on the production of one Yeats play each season was a millstone around every Artistic Director's neck. Yeats is undoubtedly a great poet, but he isn't a brilliant dramatist. He is also a rarified taste, a playwright more suitable to the lounge of Derryvolgie Avenue than the 304 seats in the new theatre in Ridgeway Street. No wonder Mary was called 'Hail Mary Full of Yeats'!

Consequently, when Abbey playwright Wesley Burrowes and I made our way up from Dublin to start rehearsals for the Lyric production of his absurdist play, we found ourselves up against intransigency. *The Becauseway* is a comic drama that needs to move quickly. It's about a young couple, George and Dolly, who find themselves lost in their marriage and decide to go on a journey to further their illusions, rather than wither and die. They meet others even more deeply steeped in illusion and end up confronting a character who had become an automaton, so far had he departed from reality. The scenes are episodic and needed to fade into each other like a film. Our designer, Rowel Friers, the celebrated Belfast cartoonist, had designed a revolve to accommodate this. Initially Mary seemed happy, but when she discovered that it needed motoring she deemed it too expensive and insisted that it should be pulled manually by the stage crew. Given that there were often several people left on the revolve, it meant that its movement was very sluggish like a heavy steamer carrying huge cargo. This hardly helped the light, fanciful, Alice in Wonderland-like atmosphere we were trying to conjure up. There were arguments but Mrs Bell, Mary's Enforcer, was insistent and prevailed. We already had an actor backing out a week into rehearsal so our work was cut out to get the production ready in time. We got there but no thanks to the management.

As a result of this fracas, I was surprised to be asked back to the Lyric. However, in 1977, I was offered a new play about an Irish actor struggling in London. It didn't sound inspiring as plays about artists usually have a self-inflated importance and this one sounded positively incestuous. I think they thought that I was the man for a play with a few actors, one set and a long text. However, Frank Dunne's play, *The Rise and Fall of Barney Kerrigan*, had a core of reality and 'a fine ear for language and a fine touch of humour' (*The Guardian*). In addition, we had assembled a very good cast: Stella McCusker, one of Ulster's best actors, Des McAleeer, later to be so good in *Moby Dick*, Louis Rolston, a middle-aged actor with a great sense of truth and charm, and the young, charismatic Liam Neeson. Liam carried the play and at this point in his career he was inexperienced and raw. However, he had a terrific appetite for rehearsing and we worked well together, not least on the several monologues. I think this helped to make his delivery more varied, which in turn led to his movement being more relaxed and less stilted. I also believe that by playing such a large part when so young – he was on stage the whole time – helped Liam learn how to shape a part, how to lead an audience into a character and story.

He was certainly a dominating presence and *The Sunday News* referred to his 'outstanding acting'. Given that his friends and relations were played by such a strong ensemble, we had a decent show. It was somewhat prophetic that the production's opening music was David Essex's 'Gonna Be a Star' as that's what Liam eventually became.

However, the good work in the production didn't stop fracas number two emerging. At the end of the first night, I was suddenly apprehended by Mary's husband, Dr Pearse O'Malley, a respected psychiatrist, bounding down the stairs before I could get away to the exit.

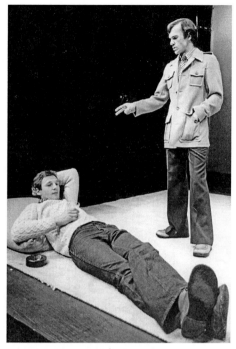

The Rise and Fall of Barney Kerrigan by Frank Dunne. Lyric Theatre Belfast, 1977. Liam Neeson as Barney and Desmond McAleer as Mike.

'How dare you! How dare you! How dare you cut plays! We're a literary theatre, we don't cut plays.'

'It was too long, Pearse', I retaliated. 'I got in touch with Frank and he agreed to the changes.'

'It's not your job to cut plays,' he replied.

'But I'm the director who's getting the script on stage.'

'Yes, exactly, you're the director. You're not the playwright.'

In fact, at that stage of my career, I wasn't a particularly good editor. I'd seen other directors in Dublin like Barry Cassin and Tomás MacAnna do it really well. It wasn't until I was in radio and had a time limit that I became better at this skill. The irony was that while travelling back home I read the *Belfast Telegraph* review and what did it say? That the play needed cutting. The critic was right; I should have been bolder. So having gone through fracas

The Rise and Fall of Barney Kerrigan by Frank Dunne.
Lyric Theatre Belfast, 1977. Liam Neeson as Barney.

number two, I surely wasn't going to be asked back again was I?
Oh yes I was.

Lo and behold, a few years later, Valerie Osborne, the new administrator, the redoubtable Winifred Bell having now departed, asked me if I was interested in directing Dominic Behan's *Európé*. This time I had a clause in my contract saying that I couldn't change the script. Nonetheless, I accepted the offer as I wanted to work in Irish theatre and I needed the money. Dominic's play centred around a series of adventures in the Európé Hotel featuring typical larger-than-life Behanesque characters (Prod barman, Catholic waiter, Brit officer, American shrink), arguing about 'the Troubles', climaxing with a visiting pop star getting shot by both the IRA and UVF for showing no allegiance to either side. It was a very undeveloped piece, a first draft that should have been a starting point not an end.

Európé by Dominic Behan, designed by Gerard Crossan. Lyric Theatre
Belfast, 1978. David Curbishley as Eddie Reubens, Ken Stott as Danny Blake,
Terry Adams as Steve Jordan, Peter Turner as Hippie, Cecil Allen as Dr
Foster, Louis Rolston as Mr Hogan and Desmond McAleer as Billy Perry.

Although Dominic didn't have the dramatic talent of his brother, he had a great ear for a ballad and sang very well. When he came
over to Belfast, he was in anarchic form. He invited me for a chat
in the York Hotel bar in Botanic Avenue. This was a place where
several sectarian murders had been committed but that didn't
stop Dominic going on about Protestants, their ridiculous sashes
and stupid marches. As he was getting more and more tanked, I
was getting increasingly alarmed. However, the irony was, that far
from confronting him and chucking him out, the staff seemed to
embrace him as a celebrity, as if to say, 'he's a Behan, sure aren't
they all mad?' I may have survived the lunch, but back in the freez-
ing rehearsal room in Cromwell Road the strong cast, including
Des McAleer, Louis Rolston, American Cecil Allen and talented
Scottish actor Ken Stott, were awaiting our presence. After having
refuelled during lunch, Dominic was ready for take off and blasted
the cast for their lousy singing. He then proceeded to sing very
well himself, in his own unique, heartfelt way. It all was a bit ex-

hausting but it was only a short visit and within forty-eight hours Dominic had thankfully disappeared back home to Glasgow.

After two weeks rehearsal, we had a run-through and I discovered that the play only lasted one hour, ten minutes. So much for not being able to change the script. When I told Valerie of the duration, I was asked by the board, Mary O'Malley now eating humble pie, if I could contact Dominic and add a couple of songs. I then mentioned that I was contracted not to change the script. 'Oh forget about all that! It needs to be longer.' I was now in the absurd situation of listening to Dominic sing on the phone, while at the same time getting his songs transcribed by musically-minded cast members in Belfast. In fact, even after having added the new numbers, the play was only marginally longer. At the end of the first night performance, Dominic came on stage and gave a theatrical, rambling speech which I found a bit embarrassing but nobody seemed to mind. He was a Behan, after all.

I worked more quietly on *When the Wind Blows*, Raymond Briggs's darkly comic drama about a nuclear attack. By then a *coup d'état* Lyric-style had forced Mary O'Malley to reliquish her post, take an honorary title and move to Dublin. Sadly, it was the right thing to do. The theatre needed to modernise and get somebody younger at the helm. In 1984, Artistic Director Patrick Sandford was part of that process and the Briggs play was a contribution to it. Raymond Briggs had something to say about our naivety and unpreparedness for nuclear attack, but he was more of a cartoonist than a dramatist and the play was one-dimensional. Even though Monica Frawley's design embraced the suburban surrealism of the original book, the characters didn't seem to develop very much when dramatised. Despite the play's limitations, there was an ominous tension hanging over the couple's inadequate preparations for a doomsday scenario, and John Hewitt and Brigid Erin Bates, as the fateful couple, skilfully humanised Briggs's caricatures.

During this visit, I was staying at a guest house off the Malone Road run by a delightful man, Reggie, and his volatile Scottish wife. A diverse group of guests were staying there including various students. One of the regulars was George from Ballymena. I was never quite sure what he was doing but I think he worked in Belfast during the week and went back home at the weekend. George was dark, slim, polite and smartly but conservatively dressed. He usually had an open-necked shirt with a dark pullover and greyish trousers. He seemed the convivial bachelor type. He was usually there dead on at 6.00 pm for his tea. I always joined him at his table in the downstairs dining room. George liked football and was convinced that the only way that England could win games and stop the fancy skill of the continentals was by choosing a half back of line of the hardest men in the league. 'That'll stop 'em,' said George with ringing certainty. Pity it never happened. Reggie, the landlord, had a full-time job. He ran his own business. His Scottish wife, who came from the Highlands, dealt with the the guests, aided by Reggie at meal times. His wife was generally warm and hospitable, but once in the middle of the night she went beserk. I think she might have had one or two drinks but she was furious and gave Reggie both barrels:

'I'm sick to death of these bloody students. I told him not to do it and he did.'

'No he didn't,' said Reggie, quietly placating her.

'Oh yes, he did Reggie.'

'No he didn't,' replied her husband, detached self-contained and unemotional, which made her even more angry.

'Oh yes, he bloody did, Reggie and you know it!' and on it went ad infinitum until she digressed into political matters.

'And I'm sick to bloody death of the IRA, the UVF and the whole bloody lot!'

I cowered under my bedclothes as if in an air-raid shelter, while this bombardment continued to rain down upon me. Eventually, it just became a domestic soundtrack and I managed to get to sleep. In the morning, I greeted my hostess with a cheery 'Good Morning!' as if nothing had happened. She acknowledged it with a weary response, looking decidedly the worse for wear.

It was during this period that another more virulent attack took place. A UDA man had pumped bullets into Gerry Adams's back and he was rushed to the Royal Victoria Hospital, where he managed to survive. Suddenly, from nowhere, on my way to the theatre, fully armed soldiers appeared on the pavement. Undoubtedly, tension was in the air. It was shortly after these events that outside the BBC in Ormeau Avenue I met up with Jack Holland, a student friend of mine. Jack invited me to come to dinner to meet his American wife. He'd become a journalist and was on a writing assignment. Later, when I looked more carefully at his address, I discovered it was in Andersontown. Given the current situation, I suddenly became increasingly nervous. This was a Republican stronghold and I was going there unaccompanied, displaying a blatantly English accent. After all, some English people had gone into such areas and not returned. I wanted to see Jack. He was a likeable, interesting person, who had been living in the States. We were both at Magee and Trinity together. Anyway, I couldn't refuse now. My fate was already sealed. I didn't talk much when the taxi driver drove me there and all through the meal, I was wondering who in the hell is going to take me back? I pretended to be relaxed and social. I heard that Jack was writing book on 'the Troubles' and that was why he was based in Anderstown. He and his wife Mary seemed to be very happy, which was more than I was. All through the meal, I looked surreptisiously at my watch, making sure that I didn't leave too late. Eventually, I politely made my excuses and said goodbye. When the cab came, I decided I'd talk in a southern accent. After working on so many Irish plays, this was something I thought that I could do. This wasn't 'top of the morning' stuff but a light Dublin brogue. I think I sort of got away with it, absurd though the disguise was. Thankfully when I returned to the guest house the Scotish landlady didn't go into orbit again.

28 – Northern Return

IT WAS THEN, FOUR YEARS LATER, in 1988, that I received a phone call from Ciaran McKeown, Secretary of the the Lyric Board, asking me if I'd like to come and meet them with a view to becoming Artistic Director. I'd been previously interviewed for the post and had missed out, but now they were looking again for a new appointment. I accepted their offer and this led to my three-year tenure. The Lyric had been getting reasonable houses but the board felt the standard of productions wasn't high enough. When I went to see *Da* by Hugh Leonard I understood what they meant. Some decent performances but low production values. After accepting the post, I met a previous Artistic Director in a north London pub. Although I knew many of the personnel at the Lyric, I'd only worked with them as a freelance, not as a staff member. Amidst the sounds of snooker balls, slot machines and with a pint in hand, I asked my colleague in whom I could confide over there. He looked at me dead between the eyes. 'Nobody', he replied. It was good advice. There were a lot of people with narrow agendas in Belfast. As Artistic Director of such a theatre it was imperative to be seen to be objective as possible. In fact, not coming from the town gave me a unique position. I didn't have a local axe to grind, yet I had previously lived in Northern Ireland, worked at the theatre three times under different directors and knew the Irish repertoire well. It was the perfect job for me. Other directors in the past, particularly English ones, were seriously undermined by their lack of such experience.

However, these advantages wouldn't guarantee me success. I realised that I needed to plan carefully, make major decisions early and consult with the existing artistic community. The board had already informed me that because they were under pressure to schedule, John Boyd, the Literary Advisor, had chosen the initial plays of the season. Members of the board choosing plays would normally raise alarm bells, but in this case John had made good solid decisions which would buy me important time. In the meantime, I'd decided to talk privately to nearly everyone involved with the Lyric over the previous year and get a good idea of what was needed. I then talked publicly to the staff and told them what I intended to do and what was expected of them. I think it's vital that from the start of any tenure that everybody is clear about policy and their part in it.

I wanted to produce world drama from an Irish perspective. This would consist of new Irish plays, Irish classics, American drama, European plays and a Christmas show. I was also determined to extend and reinvigorate the repertoire. This can only be done gradually if you want to keep the core audience on board. Audiences by nature are conservative and can easily leave you in droves if you move into the unknown too quickly. At least in Belfast this is balanced by the chance to reach an audience with new plays. A new play is an experiment in itself and is always a risk, especially if it's by an unknown author. Some directors have no interest in new work as it's seen as a bad career move. I come from the sixties generation where new work was at the centre of dramatic culture. New plays are the bloodstream of theatre and must be an essential part of any repertory company's *raison d'être*. One of the responsibilities of subsidised companies is to give the opportunity to new work and talent which isn't always possible in the commercial sector. New plays were a far greater risk during my tenure as there was no studio theatre. Nonetheless, that wasn't going to stop me from presenting at least one each year.

I discovered that having established an ethos, seasons need to have a narrative that makes the audience both intrigued and comfortable. For instance, as I developed policy, I always put an American classic in January, after the Christmas show. My theory was that by the new year the public were sick to death of all the festivities, and that after being driven mad by their family they were ready for a good challenging, serious play. Equally, it's better not to put on a dark tragedy in the early summer months, a good comedy being more suitable. I also think it's advisable that your first play of the season should bring the core audience back immediately after a break. Another factor is that a good Christmas show is a priority as it's not only a big money spinner but has the biggest family audience. During this time, kids are probably coming to the theatre for the first time, which can make an indelible impression. I therefore discovered that it was very important to up one's game here, especially as this wasn't my greatest area of expertise. Consequently, I looked to delegate such work to those more experienced in this domain.

Delegation is very important. Some good play directors aren't good Artistic Directors because they don't have much interest beyond their own work and want to do everything themselves. Being an AD, you should certainly lead from the front. Those who can't direct a play well are certainly in a weak position. However, you also have a responsibility to bring on the work of others by giving opportunities to emerging talents. Of course, you have to have a little luck in who's available. It was my fortune that my stewardship coincided with the emergence of some fine young actors, including Conleth Hill, Patrick O'Kane, Dan Gordon, Lynda Steadman, Stuart Graham, Brendan Coyle, Ali White and Sean Kearns, all of whom went on to give some terrific performances and, in Conleth's case, win two Olivier Awards as well. However, I discovered that the options for older actors were more limited. Those available were talented but worn down by the local scene and usually took refuge in drink. I was determined to establish a standard beyond which you wouldn't drop. Casting is an act of trust. I was certainly going to support and develop local actors, but I wasn't going to put them into a part just because they were in Belfast, when I knew they wouldn't meet the requisite demands. Mostly, I got the casting balance right, sometimes I was wrong, but I was always in pursuit of the highest possible standard. The Lyric's core identity certainly needed to be protected, but it needed to be developed as well.

I also found out that the visual side of the Lyric's productions needed upgrading. There were very few designers in Belfast and the better ones were overworked. Initially, I needed to hit the ground running and bring in designers I knew and trusted, who could quickly put a marker down for higher production values. This would be allied with how the plays are marketed. There needed to be a connection between what's seen on stage and how the poster and programme look. I remember when I was an Assistant Director to Lindsay Anderson at the Royal Court, burning the midnight oil at Sloane Square discussing the colour of the programme. Initially, I thought Lindsay was going too far and that as he didn't have a family, he wanted us to keep chatting about the play to give him a sense of domesticity. Then the penny dropped. Everything comes from the play and its production: the set, the programme, the marketing. If you have that unity of connection, the status of the production is increased and it can communicate much more clearly and effectively with the public.

29 – Battling with Shaw, Glendinning and O'Casey

THE FIRST PRODUCTION FOR A new Artistic Director sets the tone for a new regime. Peter Ling, my chosen designer, was central to helping me establish this. We'd previously worked well together. He was committed, personable and, unlike some designers, very good on content. Most importantly, he had an excellent sense of period and architectural construction. Bernard Shaw's *Mrs Warren's Profession*, has four acts and is set in two different gardens, the interior of a cottage and the chambers of a London solicitor. Peter managed to unite these disparate locations into a fluid theatrical whole. Elements were common to each while every scene had its own distinct sense of place. The interiors oozed respectability, gentility and class, while the exteriors in the Surrey countryside created a contrasting sense of space and freedom. Both were surrounded by a crescent of classical columns, set starkly against a white cyclorama. These pompous artifacts proclaimed the hypocritical high moral values of Imperial Victorian society. We also worked on the scene changes so the various units of the set and its accompanying furniture could be moved quickly and imaginatively. Scene changes shouldn't just be a stop in the action but a way of adjusting the audience's eye to the next scene. Given that such a play could be very cumbersome, we managed to make it relatively dynamic, aided and abetted by Ben Ormerod's subtle lighting and Paul Mottram's attractive period musical score.

Acting Shaw is difficult. There are long speeches, the dialogue is often very rhetorical and the ideas are complex. The actor is often juggling a lot of balls in the air at the same time. It is therefore vital to cast actors who have good technical control, otherwise the dialogue can either drag or be rushed by a speedy, unthinking delivery. At the core of my production, I had three good leads: Veronica Roberts was very authoritative as Vivie Warren, the feminist maths scholar who discovers that her education was paid for by her mother running a brothel. As Mrs Warren, Trudy Kelly combined blowsy sensuality with bourgeois refinement, and Brendan Barry as Sir George Crofts, her capitalist partner in the brothel business, was in turn charming, seductive and menacing. With Wesley Murphy as an idealistic romantic poet, Mark Mulholland as a hypocritical, fussy parson and Dan Gordon as Frank, Vivie's energetic, naive boyfriend, we had a range of good performances, which helped me set up my artistic stall. Most importantly, the play itself still had something to say and resonated to a modern audience. At a time when woman's role in society was changing radically, it brought out the struggle of of one woman to find freedom and independence, while her relationships with her mother and boyfriend crashed around her. In the end, Vivie is left alone. She bravely decides to make her own way and her own money.

The season moved on apace with Robin Glendinning's *Culture Vultures*. Robin is a sophisticated writer, and while some of his plays have done well in England they've not always attracted the audiences in Ireland that they deserve. He didn't fit into the sectarian scenario of 'Troubles' plays and the angry, often working class scenarios that they produced. A former schoolteacher, he is more literary, middle class and reflective. A prominent member of the Alliance party for several years, he's an underrated writer with a wide hinterland and a genuine vision. As an admirer of Chekhov, it wasn't surprising that he wrote a play about Roly, a young Protestant graduate coming back from Trinity with his Catholic friend Fergus, to put on his own Ulster version of *The Cherry Orchard* – *The Brambly Orchard* – in his rural town. This is counterpointed by the sectarian tensions surrounding the actual sale of his father's house. The idea of Roly's amateur production is to promote harmony but it soon runs into problems with the local participants because of conflicting political views. A fruitful comic contrast is made between Roly's ideals and the reality, culminating with his family's hotel bar being blown up, an effect so realistic with its shattering explosion, dust and collapsing walls, that one feared the audience might leave the building. Although Roly's play goes on it seems to remain doubtful whether art can change people's minds, even though you feel he wont stop trying.

The play lends itself to a whole gallery of Ulster views and types, and was well played by a strong local cast. Dan Gordon as Roly moved into a leading part with ease and aplomb. Eleanor Methven was excellent as his challenging friend Deirdre, despite giving the detached impression that she was above the proceedings, so I never enjoyed directing her. At one point in rehearsal, senior actress Margaret D'Arcy, as *The Brambly Orchard's* director, was all over the place with her lines, which became frustrating because

Culture Vultures by Robin Glendinning, designed by Peter Ling.
Lyric Theatre Belfast, 1988. Dan Gordon as Roly and
Eleanor Methven as Deirdre.

she was the central character in certain scenes. When I criticised her, she didn't like it. It was as if I was breaking some covenant of the Ulster theatre's pecking order. In fact, when I moved to radio many years later, I got the impression that she still held a grudge. After my Abbey experience that was one thing I wasn't going to do. If I had a disagreement, I'd voice it and then forget it. However, like those embittered Abbey actors, there are always some who prefer to harbour their wounds. It was a pity because ever since I'd seen her with the Ulster Theatre Company as a student I'd admired Margaret's work. Still, it didn't stop Irving Wardle, the distinguished critic of *The Times*, noting that her performance as the director was 'played to fatuous perfection' and that the aloof Ms Methven along with Dan Gordon were 'stunning'.

The season had opened well with solid work. It continued to do so with O'Casey's *The Plough and the Stars*. Initially, I asked Danny Boyle to direct it, as he was then working for BBC Northern Ireland as a television producer. I'd particularly liked his work at the Royal Court and the RSC and thought he'd give the play imaginative re-valuation. He was very interested but unfortunately unavailable. 'I've been here for some time but you're the first person to ask me to do anything', he responded frustratedly. Thankfully, I then managed to persuade Polish director Helena Kaut-Howson to blow the dust off the Irish classic. Helena is Jewish and her mother had miraculously survived a concentration camp. She was charming, lively and imaginative. She had a marvellous sense of the visceral sweep of a play, even if sometimes her sense of textual detail was lacking. Maybe that was due to her working in a second language. Her visual storytelling was particularly strong. The opening of her production was magical. The whole cast wandered on to a dark street with only a piercing shaft of light, like a lost tribe wandering through the maze of history. It was like something out of a Polish film.

Like the Irish, the Poles have been invaded many times and struggled to maintain their national identity. Therefore nationalism became connected to liberation. Helena's opening was like entering into a dream of lost souls. After this magnificent start, maybe the production didn't manage to continue at such a level but it did still maintain a sense of fragmented time, particularly in the subtle, muted lighting of Gerry Jenkinson, which created both sinister shadows and tragic beauty through various crevices, and through James Helps's magisterial set with its various flexible trucks creating fragile exterior and interior landscapes. *Plough* is probably O' Casey's greatest play because the tension between ordinary people's lives and historical events coelesces so completely. Helena certainly got a strong sense of that community into the play, one that seemed to be underpinned by a sense of tragic fate and destiny. It was an unusual production which did great business.

30 – Arthur Miller's Marilyn Play

AFTER A SUCCESSFUL FESTIVE PRODUCTION of John Boyd's adaptation of *A Christmas Carol*, which fully engaged our family audience, I needed lift off. So far I had produced plays chosen by someone else. I had made a good start, and through the introduction of strong visiting talent I'd managed to raise the production standards. Having done decent business and wanting to expand the repertoire, it was time to push the boat out. I managed to get the rights to *After the Fall* by Arthur Miller. The play hadn't been done in Ireland since the sixties, when I saw Ray McAnally and Maureen Toal in a production at the Dublin Theatre Festival. As director, Ray had sacked the original lead and took over himself, something it was rumoured he'd always wanted to do. I was captivated by the play. Not because it was perfect, it wasn't, but because it was daringly experimental and asked searing public and personal questions. It takes place in the mind of the leading character, Quentin, and oscillates between the public events of the Depression, McCarthyism and the Holocaust and the private world of three marriages, including one based on Miller's with Marilyn Monroe. The play moves around the different areas of Quentin's life like a dream, as he tries to make sense of his life. This was expressed in James

Helps's imposing multi-tier grey set, which reflected both the cells of the mind as well as the ashes of the holocaust, and was overseen by the restrained brutalist beauty of a macabre watchtower.

The Lyric board were certainly brave in allowing me to do the play. They had a reputation for being notoriously difficult, and at times this was so, however nobody could accuse them of not wanting to do ambitious plays. They were certainly upholding the Lyric tradition to produce writing of the highest quality. Once it had been green lit, I now had the onerous task of casting the play. The first half of the drama was virtually a monologue by Quentin. At that time, I couldn't see anybody in Ireland carrying such a difficult, long part. Consequently, I cast Tim Woodward, son of Edward, the celebrated TV star. Tim and I were good friends and had worked on projects in London. I could trust him to deliver. He had the cha-

After the Fall by Arthur Miller, designed by James Helps. Lyric Theatre Belfast, 1988. Michael Gormley as Father, Alan Craig as Dan, Claire Hackett as Maggie, Tim Woodward as Quentin and Fay Howard as Louise.

After the Fall by Arthur Miller, designed by James Helps. Lyric Theatre Belfast, 1988. Claire Hackett as Maggie, surrounded by Alan Craig, B.J. Hogg, Joseph Crilly and Noel McGee as her minders.

risma and technique to both sustain the role and take the audience with him. Now l needed to find the female lead, Maggie, the 'Marilyn' part. After extensive auditions, I discovered Claire Hackett, who had recently been in Kenneth Branagh's production of *Twelfth Night*. Sometimes, casting turns to gold. Well on this occasion, it certainly did. I remember on the first reading in Cromwell Road, the whole cast realising they would have to be good if they were to match up with these two actors. You're in business when your leads set a high bar for a production. Others can only respond or wither.

It's very rare that everything comes together in theatre. I remember having a drink at the Abbey bar and Irish actor and RSC luminary Norman Rodway sighing somewhat forlornly, 'there's always somebody'. However, this wasn't the case with *After the Fall*. We had a great script, the interpretation worked well, the reviews were good ('this fine production' – *The Times*; 'the production is playing to full houses in Belfast, it's grip on the play is very sure'

126

– *The Observer*), everybody got on to the point of socialising a lot and amazingly we played to 86 per cent capacity. It was a very difficult, challenging play and we'd pulled it off.

The reason for our success was total company commitment and two terrific leads. Tim succeeded in one of the biggest parts in modern drama. Quentin never stops talking. It was as if Miller was letting go of everything from this period in his life. For him the 'Marilyn' years were artistically barren. The only work he produced then was *The Misfits* screenplay. Miller may have been detached, arrogant and cerebral, but Marilyn was mentally fragile, volatile and high maintenance. In the play, Quentin's quest becomes similar to trying to put all the pieces of a jigsaw in the right position. The first half of the play deals with his early years: his parents' struggle, the effects of the Depression ('college men are jumping out of windows'), his anaemic first marriage, his infidelity, and the baleful McCarthy witchhunt during which a friend commits suicide. Surrounding all this is his current relationship with Holga, a Jew, who survived the Holocaust and manages to draw strength and dignity out of the experience.

Miller was influenced by Hannah Arendt and her theory about the banality of evil – that it was too easy to just pick out the villains like Eichmann and that we were all complicit in allowing such evil as the Holocaust to happen. Tim Woodward gave a brilliant performance because he was able to hold all these strands together and take the audience through the turmoil of Quentin's life. He did it with skill and charm. He perfectly set up the wonderful street meeting scene with Maggie at the end of act one when things become more obviously dramatic. Setting up a scene is a much harder acting task than actually playing a scene with established tension. Tim's triumph was helped by some excellent support: Fay Howard brought a wonderful, frosty suburban authority to Louise, Quentin's first wife, and B.J. Hogg, one of Ireland's most underrated actors, was suitably slippery as Mickey, a part based on the legendary director Elia Kazan, who named names.

After the Fall by Arthur Miller, designed by James Helps. Lyric Theatre Belfast, 1988.
Tim Woodward as Quentin and
Catherine Brennan as Felice.

I always thought that McCarthyism had a devastating effect on American cultural life because it led to fear and conformity. In the thirties Miller had watched the Group Theatre perform the political plays of Clifford Odets with actors like John Garfield, Lee J. Cobb, Frances Farmer and Elia Kazan. They set forth a theatrical agenda more politically radical than either the Abbey or the Royal Court. Even though the Group closed in 1941, the House of Unamerican Activities ruined several of them. However despite its theatrical demise, the legacy of the Group continued in the teaching of Lee Strasberg, Sanford Meisner and Uta Hagen, as well as the film work of Kazan, Odets, Garfield and Cobb. Their influence determined how American acting developed and led to Marlon Brando and James Dean. In fact, Miller wrote the original screenplay for what was to become Kazan's film *On the Waterfront,* but backed down, leaving Budd Schulberg, like Kazan an informer on colleagues to the House of Unamerican Activities, to write a script which was ostensibly about corruption in the New Jersey docks, but in reality was his and Kazan's apologia for naming names. The American premiere of *After the Fall* in 1964 was the first time Kazan and Miller had worked together since their falling out in the fifties. Kazan thought Miller was avoiding the Maggie-as-Marilyn issue. Always one for exhuming personal histories, Kazan wanted the play to be unapologetically about Marilyn. He believed that anything less diluted its emotional force. Miller saw the play in more universal terms so his relationship with Kazan was an uneasy truce which never resurrected the harmonious creativity of their earlier collaborations. The ghost of betrayal lingered as it did with so many about that period. Even when Kazan received a Lifetime Achievement Award at the Oscar ceremony many years later in 1999, half the audience refused to stand up and applaud.

I never thought Maggie was totally Marilyn, and we certainly didn't want an impersonation. What Claire Hackett portrayed was the essence of that spirit and how it captivated Quentin. From her opening entrance, she brought zest, spontaneity and sexuality to the part. Not only did she get to the depth of Maggie's vulnerability, rooted in her traumatic childhood, but also the ambitious narcissistic, volatile film star. If Tim prevented Quentin from being a prig, Claire stopped Maggie from being just a little girl lost in a man's world. In her own way, she was fighting against it.

After a few rehearsals with Claire, Tim took me aside and said, 'where did you find her, Roland, she's terrific'. Tim and Claire had an exciting relationship on stage. It was unpredictable and sexy. Both were alluring and highly talented. More importantly, they complimented each other beautifully. In the rows between Quentin and Maggie they both gave as good as they got. It was brutal, painful and exciting to watch as exemplified by Quentin's despairing plea: 'A suicide kills two people, Maggie. That is what it's for.' They produced some of the best acting I've seen in a production of mine. There was an exciting sense of danger and passion. I particularly remember during one performance when they were playing one of their more intimate scenes, a gentleman in the middle of the stalls heaved a public sigh of sensual satisfaction. It was clear that they had a very special chemistry. This was certainly one of the reasons for the production's success.

Another, apart from the good ensemble playing, was that the play gave a rare opportunity for big production in a visceral, visual way. Actors would appear at different levels on James Helps's arresting multi-tiered set, which vividly embraced the play's emotional landscape. For the opening, the whole cast flitted around a dimly-lit Quentin to a soundtrack embracing the music and politics of the different periods of his life, ending with JFK's inaugaration speech. It immediately grabbed the audience and made them enter a vivid imaginative world. Then the rest of the cast entered at a variety of levels, at odd angles, sometimes behind gauzes as Quentin struggled with his thoughts and memories.

At the heart of the play, like most Miller dramas, was the tension between the public and private world. Quentin's pain and guilt regarding Maggie's disintegration and tragic death are contrasted with his admiration for his third wife Helga's sense of hope after surviving Nazism. She has seen the breakdown of civilisation and managed to retain a sense of cautious optimism.We were performing the play at time when 'the Troubles' were still unresolved. In fact, when a bomb went off in the distance it reverberated on the huge set. Even though most people weren't actively involved, I think everybody in Belfast felt some responsibility for the breakdown of their society and the carnage it wrought. I'd like to think that Quentin's ultimate tentative plea for redemption resonated deeply with the local audience.

During *After the Fall* the whole cast often had parties. One of these was at Rugby Road near Queens University at the home of an absent academic. Thankfully, the walls were very solid and the shenanigans didn't wake up the whole street. Tim was very much a night person and so he not only led the company on to the stage but he seemed to be self-appointed social secretary as well. Rugby Road became a centre of hedonistic activity. The atmosphere was lively and fun; there was music, drink, cavortings and experimentation. At the end of this revelry, the place was a mess and an elegant carpet full of stains. Our academic friend was due to return shortly and we needed to act. Thankfully, Joe Crilly, who was giving a good performance as Lou, Quentin's communist friend, had an idea. Now, Joe is a charming, laid-back character and very laconically, he stated that he had a mate who was a carpet cleaner. Only trouble was he came from Lurgan, Joe's home town, about twenty-five miles outside Belfast. After Joe, in his inimitable way, convinced his friend to take on the job, we had a quick whip round to pay the cost. Fortunately, Joe's friend got the job done in time and the carpet was spotless. It now looked as if we had been partaking of tea and cumber sandwiches not sex, drugs and rock 'n' roll! In contrast, we had a quieter idyllic time during this period when, one Sunday afternoon, the company went to Fay Howard's family home at Rostrevor, County Down. I remember having a relaxed meal in their garden amidst beautiful rolling hills and Carlingford Lough. 'The Troubles' seemed to be in another world.

Earlier I had invited Arthur Miller to see the production. During the run, I received the following letter:

> Dear Mr Jaquarello,
>
> I have your letter of October 18th, and was unable to answer you because I wasn't sure of my schedule, but I see now that it would be impossible for me to get to Belfast.
>
> I know that you have opened *After the Fall*, and I hope it all went well.
>
> Yours Sincerely,
>
> Arthur Miller
>
> P.S. [written in his own hand, not typed] I've since learned of your success, and the idea of going to Dublin. Good luck!

Unfortunately, we never got to Dublin but we did have a considerable success with Miller's challenging play.

31 – The Lyric Board and Other Players

THE HOUSES WERE FULL WITH an aspirational, landmark production. We were taking the intiative, not copying others. However, this didn't lessen a certain wariness from the board. Their main players were: Dr Colm Kelly, the chairman, pleasant but deaf and somewhat jesuitical, he wasn't authoritative, which is vital for an Artistic Director; Denis Nichol, the treasurer, an accountant, an able pragmatist who seemed to relish repeating the word 'firefighting'; and Ciaran McKeown, secretary, seer and idealist, formerly a leading light of the peace movement. Ciaran had good ideas and certainly showed a sense of vision. But rather like a flawed Ibsen hero, you got the sense that he might lead you excitedly to the top of the hill, only to drop you off the top of it. I got on best with Professor Desmond Maxwell, an insightful academic from Derry, who had joined the board after recently retiring from a Canadian university. Des had written good books on Irish drama. He had worked in Africa and in England and had now returned home after retiring. On occasions, we went for meals together. A close friend of Brian Friel, he went out with Nora Ann Simmons, sister of the poet James Simmons. They were excellent company, and after a few drinks Nora Ann would excoriate Des about the parochial politics of the board.

John Boyd was also a prominent board member. Being Literary Advisor, other members looked to him for an assessment of the proposed plays. This gave him a significant position of power. He was the board's artistic *éminence grise*. Later, he was joined by his friend Louis Muinzer, an American academic working at Queen's University. Louis was a friendly, laid-back character but when it came to the crunch, he wasn't going to go against John's judgement. There were few female board members, despite its founder having been a woman. Edna Larmour was the one exception. She was an amiable, supportive and friendly person who later suffered dreadfully from Alzheimer's. Her friend Frank McQuoid, another board member, had been an actor in the days of Derryvolgie Avenue. He was a lesser influence but an encouraging one.

The board were certainly brave artistically. They had a good sense of the roots and ambitions of the theatre. However, some members in particular seemed more concerned about their own status. During the run of *After the Fall*, when the houses were full, the reviews from British and Irish papers were glowing and the theatre was buzzing, you got the impression that they felt marginalised. In fact later, at another interminable board meeting, when John Boyd disagreed with me about a particular play he asserted his authority by suddenly pounding his fists on a table like a demented Robespierre. 'Artistic Directors come and go. We run the theatre. We know the audience. We know the history. We have to make the decisions.' Paisley couldn't have done a better job imposing his dictates. I felt like saying, 'Why bother having an Artistic Director if you think you should run the place?' However, I decided to keep my cool and let Boyd's mania exhaust itself. Later, Des Maxwell rang me and apologised for John's behaviour, which he thought was unacceptable. I liked John and respected his views. We even talked about other subjects – like the merits of George Best. Nonetheless, I was annoyed that he was using his position to get his plays performed, when he should have accepted a level playing field for all writers. I also discovered that he was working on a version of Ibsen's *Ghosts* with Louis Muinzer and that apparently the theatre had an obligation to produce it. There was obviously going to be more conflict later.

Charles Fitzgerald, the genial, rotund, egotistical critic of *Newsletter* was a bon viveur of the highest order. It was he who in one of his articles amusingly described the board as 'the politburo.' I think the phrase was coined as a result of the board's invisible profile. From the start, I had been quite good with the press. I gave my first interview to Mike Nesbitt (now leader of the Ulster Unionist Party) of *Good Morning Ulster*. He went into a Paxman-like attack but I wasn't going to let him control the agenda as I had a clear idea of where I was going to take the theatre. I managed to stem the flow and get the listener thinking about the exciting things I was going to do, not a litany of past grievances. As for Charlie Fitz, he sometimes got his reviews completed so quickly down the phone that he was at the bar by the time the cast had arrived for a drink. Charlie was a warm man with a loud voice, who was usually accompanied by a weary female companion. He certainly had flair and got space in a fairly philistine paper. He loved the arts and managed to convey an energy and excitement that transmitted to his Protestant readers, who tended to be more interested in making money and going to church than attending theatre. So Charlie was very good at waking them up. He was probably a better arts journalist than a critic, but he made a significant contribution to the Belfast arts scene. Inevitably, being opinionated with an extravagant manner, he was living dangerously. One day he was fired, apparently for some form of inappropriate conduct. Then suddenly he disappeared off the scene. A pity, as his energy was missed.

32 – Beckett and Comedians

MY FIRST SEASON CONTINUED with a good production of *Waiting for Godot* with Ian McElhinney and Mark Drewry, directed by Tim Webb. Tim is director of the excellent children's company, Oily Carte. His production was simple, funny and effective, and brought an unpretentious simplicity to Beckett's classic. Ian and Mark were wonderfully contrasted as Vladimir and Estragon. Ian is the most intelligent and professional of actors, and his light Ulster tones contrasted most amusingly with Mark's gruff, earthy Doncaster ones. Sadly, Mark died tragically young after being critically injured in an accident in London. A brave talent, and a warm man, he left us far too early. *Godot* did remarkably well, considering that Belfast isn't a natural location for the esoteric.

Godot was followed by one of the best modern English plays, *Comedians* by Trevor Griffiths. The play had been performed on the fringe in Dublin in the seventies but never in Belfast or in mainstream Irish theatre until this production. *Comedians* is about the nature of humour and explores gender, class and racism. It's set in a seventies Manchester classroom, an imposing Victorian structure with a radiator, blackboard and overarching clock. Outside you could hear the intermittent sound of rain.

The play is about a school for apprentice comics and pits an old idealistic teacher, Eddie Waters, against Bert Challenor, a commercial pragmatist who proclaims that 'we're not missionaries, we're suppliers of laughter'. Most of the students adapt their material to the marketplace, which leads to their presentation of various comic styles being wrapped in racial and sexual stereotypes. Only one, Price, a van driver with ambitions, remains weirdly intransigent and presents a mime of class hatred, almost too honest to be funny. Challenor leaves after choosing two commercially viable candidates, and finding Price 'aggressively unfunny'. Waters then admits privately to Price that he was brilliant but worries that his act was 'drowning in hate'. He recalls that during a post-war tour in Germany, he visited the death camps and shamefully admits to having got aroused. He concludes that 'hate's no help', tolerance is better. Price thinks Waters is avoiding the harsh realities of his working class roots. He believes that only hardness will bring meaningful revolutionary change and he'll 'wait for it to happen'. After Price departs, Waters enrolls a Pakistani into his class, who tells a joke in keeping with his own liberal values. We're left to ponder the future as Waters and the Pakistani leave. Then the caretaker, after being disgusted by Price's provocative limerick being left on the blackboard, plunges the room into darkness. We finally see Waters and his new pupil receding in a fading street light through the windows.

Given the nature of prejudice in the North, the play was certainly relevant to a Belfast audience, but one attendee seriously

Comedians by Trevor Griffiths, directed by Brian Croucher and designed by James Helps. Lyric Theatre Belfast, 1989. Dan Gordon as Phil Murray and Sean Kearns as Ged Murray.

misunderstood it. One morning, my secretary Lorraine Boyce told me that a gentleman insisted on talking to me. When I finally took the call, he started ranting on the phone about 'the awful goings on last night in *Comedians*. They were making jokes about "the Troubles" in a disgusting way.'

When I tried to say that the middle act contains purposefully stereotypical jokes, he rebuffed me vehemently.

'What absolute rubbish. Now, Mr Jaquarello, I've been attending the Lyric since the days of Derryvolgie Avenue and I've never heard such awful language. Quite frankly, it was a disgrace.'

I tried to argue that the play wasn't supporting such language but dramatising it to show its limitations.

'You can argue until the cows come home, Mr Jaquarello, but that won't stop me from deploring what I saw on the Lyric stage last night.'

After politely agreeing to disagree, the angry punter abruptly put the phone down.

Comedians was well done but it was always going to be a hard sell. To counter this, I got ex-*Coronation Street* star Peter Adamson to play the pivotal role of Eddie Waters. Most of the time, Peter gave a good performance. His experience gave the production its anchor. He was strong in argument and commanding in presence. Unfortunately, he was a troubled man and on some nights he was very erratic indeed. It wasn't so long since he had been on trial for assaulting a child in a Lancashire swimming pool. He was defended by the formidable lawyer George Carman and judged innocent. Nonetheless, the press coverage was salacious and as Len Fairclough, a celebrated Corrie character, he was good copy. Sadly, a cloud still hung over him. When he went with John Hewitt to visit some firms to support Comic Relief's 'Red Nose Day', he was jeered by a posse of women. Later, at his digs, he told me that he had received a threatening letter from the IRA and wanted to leave the production. I appealed to him not to be a quitter, reassuring him that he was doing a good job and was in a terrific, rarely performed play. Finally, I looked at him and appealed to his sense of northern defiance.

'Peter. You're not really going to allow people to stop you doing a play are you?'

He paused and then agreed. 'You're right. Of course you bloody are. I'll go on playing the part.'

After our conversation, his old confidence returned, he became more focused and his hesitancy disappeared. It was certainly a terrifying example of how the tabloids can make you guilty in the eyes of the public, even though you have been

Comedians by Trevor Griffiths. Lyric Theatre Belfast, 1989. Peter Adamson as Eddie Waters.

proved innocent in a court of law. Unfortunately, I underestimated the public's reaction as I think the scandal surrounding Peter badly affected box office. A pity as a good, largely Irish cast under Brian Croucher's direction had done the play proud. More importantly, it was the first time for years that the Lyric had produced such an obviously political play.

33 – Glasnost Meets Belfast

THE SEASON'S NEXT PRODUCTION was to be another landmark occasion, which was to fulfill my European slot in the repertoire. Given developments in the Soviet Union, I chose a 'Glasnost' play, *Threshold*, by Alexei Dudarev, which I got adapted by the poet Derek Mahon. I was keen to harness the Lyric to an international experience and managed to get a team from Minsk to present a new work by a young Belorussian writer. At the centre of the play is alcoholism, a subject not exactly unknown in Ireland. Buslai, the main character in the play, is a drunkard. His supposedly dead body is brought to a town apartment, where the owner, *Godot*-style, is mysteriously absent, even though others talk inspiringly of him. Buslai is identified as dead but in fact he isn't, and in a wonderfully comic scene he pursues an alcoholic grave digger who made money out of his burial. On his reappearance his mother doesn't recognise him, his wife's new husband is bitter and he ends up reading a story to a young boy, who remembers him from only being in his coffin. The play has a poetic, mystical quality about alienated lives under communism, hovering on the border of death. The Belorussian team had a deep understanding of the play and gave us a very distinctive slavonic production which illuminated themes well described by Robert Dunbar, the *Times Literary Supplement* critic as, 'hallucination and dream, sophistication and naiveté, death and resurrection and the perilously fragile threshold which links them'.

The director, Valery Raevsky, proved to be genial and talented. His demonstration in rehearsal of how drink went through Buslai's body was a master class in physical absorption. He got himself into amazing contortions as he felt the drink descend into his uttermost recesses. Actor B.J. Hogg then wryly observed, 'you don't take a drink yourself do you?' Valery laughed, nervously non-committal. In fact, to play the part of the venal grave digger I'd cast Alan Devlin, who was an alcoholic but apparently was now abstinent. I mentioned this to Valery, describing Alan as a talented character actor worth the risk as he would be excellent in the role. Unfortunately, Valery was unimpressed. 'I don't like alcoholics playing alcoholics', he replied mournfully. Of course, he was right but I just thought Alan could do the part better than anyone else. Nonetheless, I didn't trust him. Alan's walk out in the middle of a scene in the Gaiety production of *The Pirates of Penzance* was legendary. He ended up having a drink in nearby Nearys dressed in Gilbert and Sullivan regalia, while the play was still running. Funny in retrospect, but a nightmare for those working with him. He'd also messed up playing Seamus Shields in *The Shadow of a Gunman* at the Abbey, and a regular role in RTÉ's *Fair City*. Why would it be any different with me? I suppose I gambled that the part was small and that after regular visits to AA he wasn't drinking. However, I was under no illusions. Sadly, Alan had always been an alcoholic – admittedly a charming, perceptive and very funny one, but an alcoholic nonetheless. Consequently, my answer to the Alan problem was to make sure that he had an understudy.

I contracted Sean Kearns, a talented young actor, to perform this task. Everything was fine until the final performance. Half an hour before the start, there was no sign of Alan. I was furious. True to form, Alan was going to let another friend and colleague down. I went and told Sean to get ready to play the part. His face went deep red and I could tell he was very nervous. I felt dreadful putting him in this position, even though I'd covered myself for such an eventuality. Time was ticking away and then suddenly who comes rolling down Ridgeway Street but your man himself, very much the worse for wear, mumbling like Marlon Brando on speed. Nervous about him getting through the performance, I followed him into the green room. Coffee at the ready, the assembled throng did their best to sober him up. The mumbling gradually departed and some sense of articulacy emerged.

Given he was playing a rough alcoholic, I decided to take the risk and to continue with Alan. Mightily relieved, Sean's nervous red face gradually turned white, I left the company to prepare and went to the front of house. While I was in the foyer, I was shocked to discover the presence of several board members. They usually didn't come to last nights but this time they wanted to say goodbye to the cast. If Alan didn't get through this, I was going to be for the high jump. I could hear the vitriol in my head. 'Why did you employ this crazy, alcoholic Dubliner? You knew he was a lush yet you went ahead and here's the result. A jibbering idiot on stage with nobody understanding a word he says. It's appalling amateurism. Truly appalling.'

In fact, at times Alan was incomprehensible but when he started veering from the script with inappropriate ad libs, our two resident veterans, Trudy Kelly and Birdy Sweeney, cut him off before he could start any meandering improvisation. Even though he was playing an alcoholic, and we might get away with it, the

Threshold by Alexei Dudarev, adapted by Derek Mahon from a translation
by Nina Froud, directed by Valery Raevsky and designed by Boris Gerlovan.
Lyric Theatre Belfast, 1989. Marianne March as Alina and B.J. Hogg as Buslai.

fact remained that Alan was drunk and I was worried about the
repercussions. At the interval, I hid from the board by going to the
lavatory and walking up and down a cold Ridgeway Street, trying
to give the illusion of being occupied. When, at the end of the play,
I went to the foyer, Ciaran McKeown was initially complimentary,
but then observed that Alan was a bit 'different' tonight. Well,
that's one way of describing it.

Then, suddenly from the top of the stairs, Alan descended
with staggeringly uneven steps, helped by Dan Gordon. When he
beheld the bearded Ciaran, he yelled, 'Christ. Why do so many
people in the North have bleedin' beards?' We tried to calm Alan
down but he got more insistent and only reiterated. 'No. I want to
know why do so many people in the North, have bleedin beards?'
Much to his credit, Ciaran remained amused. Whether he and
chairman Dr Kelly, who was also present, were liable to have the
same attitude now that they knew Alan was really drunk, I'd only
discover at the forthcoming board meeting.

Dan, who was brilliantly juggling the roles of nurse, companion
and mentor, steered Alan out of the theatre and ushered him into

a waiting taxi, Alan still wailing, 'Is it because they're evangelicals or something? No tell me. Why do they...' While Alan's voice faded into the Belfast night, back at the foyer, I talked gingerly to the board members, said goodbye to the cast and went home. What a night, but thankfully I survived the board meeting!

Threshold wasn't a great success commercially but it was an artistic one ('well served by its cast' – TLS). It was the first time that a director of the Soviet Union had ever worked in Belfast and was described as 'a coup' by *The Times*. It gave Irish actors a unique opportunity to work with international artists and to explore their own culture with them. We were very fortunate to have the services of Ludmilla, our excellent interpreter, who was married to a Belfast teacher. She was pivotal to the success of the production. Thankfully, she kept things moving at a brisk pace. Only during the technical rehearsals did things become more complicated. However, when they were explained visually, it was amazing how clarity emerged and the universal language of theatre took over. Our Lighting Designer, Roger Simonsz, who was in the front line of such discussions, dealt with the Belorussian demands admirably. His father was a senior Dutch diplomat so he was well trained. However, even Roger wanted to evaporate into thin air when during previews he was sitting next to Valery, who on the failure of a sound cue would rail loudly at our able sound operator, Patrick Dalgety, shaking his fists at the booth, shouting with full slavonic venom, 'Patrickum!'

However, overall the Belorussian team were very relaxed being in Belfast. They had worked on the play before, so that gave them confidence. So much so that after a couple of weeks they cut a rehearsal short to go on a shopping spree. I suppose due to the debilitated Soviet economy they couldn't wait to get their hands on some western consumer goodies. In fact, I began to get a bit alarmed that they might be seeing their visit as a working holiday. When I spoke to Valery and reminded him that we only had three weeks rehearsal, not the usual ten to twelve that were allotted in the Soviet Union, he insisted that it was okay. 'I understand. I understand', he remonstrated insistently. Thankfully, he was as good as his word.

Valery's close colleague, the designer Boris Gervolan, was a quiet, small man with greying hair, who produced an imaginative, economic set comprising of four wooden panels which pivoted at the centre. When lit, characters appeared out of dark shafts of expressionistic light like figures in an elegant painting. It gave the play an unworldly, soulful quality. The third member of the Belorussian team was Alexei the writer. He was a fair, tall, intelligent man in his thirties, full of good humour and with a propensity for always wearing polo neck sweaters.

From an acting perspective, the production was a triumph for its lead, B.J. Hogg. B.J. had been a very able performer for many years who had mainly played supporting parts. This was the moment when he became a leading actor, somebody who could hold a play together. It was an excellent performance, full of power, humour and pathos In fact, B.J. got so committed that he spent several nights sleeping in the Cromwell Road rehearsal room, both to get the feel of living rough and to escape from his family, while learning the lines of such a big part. Maybe we should call this approach the Belfast Method. At the end of the first performance, the audience rose as one to give the company, particularly the Belorussian team, a standing ovation. I don't think this was just about the play, but also 'glasnost' and the movement towards freedom. Sometimes theatre goes beyond the play itself and this was one such moving, unforgettable occasion.

Later, Valery asked B.J. to perform the play in Minsk for several performances, which he did, replying to Russian cues in English. As the play was widely known, sharing their culture was warmly appreciated. B.J. was given flowers and hugs everywhere he went. As we discovered in Belfast, Belorussian theatre can be more stylised than ours and B.J. was often trailed on stage by a follow spot and primary coloured, symbolic lighting changes. Lights weren't the only things following him as there were always three or four policemen around the theatre precincts. Unfortunately, Belarus, as it's now called, is currently ruled by 'Europe's last dictator'. However, in those days vodka was cheap and many citizens took refuge in drink. Like in O'Casey's dramas, women seemed to rule the house, propping up male inadequacies. B.J. met many well read, erudite people, but also too many who were living on scraps. Maybe because there were insufficient outlets for their creative energy, the Belorussians embraced a more declamatory style of acting. What couldn't be doubted was that Valery and his team were a group of talented, imaginative people who gave us a unique insight into a culture which had become remote for so many years.

34 – The Belle and Female Playwrights

MY FIRST SEASON DREW TO A CLOSE with Christina Reid's *The Belle of Belfast City*. Christina was one of the few women writers from Northern Ireland. Her plays are rooted in the Protestant working class and show particular insight into women and families. Set in a Belfast corner shop against a background of protests to the Anglo Irish agreement, *Belfast City* is dominated by a matriarch, Dolly, an ex-music hall star who rules the family and keeps her daughters Rose and Vi in line. When Rose comes back home with a mixed-race daughter it brings out the political tensions within the family, particularly with staunch unionist cousin Jack. Vi and Jack were played by two of Ulster's best actors, Stella McCusker and John Hewitt. They always brought a sense of detail to Ulster parts that I found very enlightening, both in terms of accent and attitude. It was almost as if they'd pinpointed the characters' exact Northern Irish location. Watching them made me realise how broadbrush some Ulster interpretations are.

Belfast City communicated well. Tim Luscombe gave it a fluent production and its political background ensured a contemporary edge which fully engaged its audience. It was also refreshing to see a new play getting good houses. Of course, by this stage of her career, Christina had already built up her own audience so that was a huge advantage. Northern Irish writers sometimes drew support along sectarian lines. I call it the Rangers–Celtic factor. Protes-

The Belle of Belfast City by Christina Reid, directed by Tim Luscombe
and designed by James Helps. Lyric Theatre Belfast, 1989.
Suzette Llewellyn as Belle and Sheila McGibbon as Dolly.

tants went to Protestant plays and Catholics went to Republican
dramas. There was a certain depressing truth to that during 'the
Troubles', but I like to think it's not so prevalent now. In Christina's
case, I think she had already broken down that taboo as women
across the divide came to her plays. Later, Marie Jones brilliantly
extended that franchise. As the play ended, I wondered why in the
past there were so few female Irish playwrights? Even allowing for
the historical injustice of women's position in society, there seems
to be an incredible lack of Irish female writers, with only the patrician Lady Gregory and the underrated Teresa Deevy springing to
mind. It's good to see that changing, albeit slowly.

I was enjoying my time at the Lyric. It was good to have a home.
While freelance work has its own excitement, visiting different
places and working with a variety of people, there's something
unique about developing the artistic policy of a theatre. Thankfully, I'd initiated a successful first season, established a standard
and expanded the repertoire with flagship productions like *After
the Fall* and *Threshold*, while maintaining good houses. This laid a
decent foundation to develop the work in the second season. Hav-

ing earned the audience's trust, I wanted to extend the repertoire further and take the audience on another distinctive journey. Artistic Directors just governed by box office create dull seasons. I judge those at the helm not only on box office percentages but by whether he or she takes you to places you haven't been before and moves audiences on. Those who dare nothing lack vision and produce deadly theatre.

35 – Ulster Journeys with Stewart and J.D.

To INITIATE THE NEW SEASON I produced Stewart Parker's modern classic play, *Spokesong*, which interweaves the history of a bicycle repair shop with that of Ulster. I was fortunate to meet Stewart when I was directing a freelance production in the eighties and went for tea at his Belfast flat. A highly intelligent, amiable man, who even when slumped in an armchair with a crumbling cake was bristling with energy and ideas. It was tragic that he should die of cancer at the age of forty-seven. His plays combine two sides of the Irish coin: charm and articulacy with violence and darkness. He came from a Protestant working class background but seemed objective and perceptive. He was writing at the height of 'the Troubles' so it's no surprise that his characters seemed to be ensnared by history. The simple, charming lovers of the bicycle in *Spokesong* were no exception.

Helena Kaut-Howson directed the play. The bicycle shop setting was contained within a circus framework with a sawdust floor and hanging bicycle parts, framed within a false proscenium painted as a sky. I was hoping that Helena might bring a new insight into a local play and recoin the material. However, although the production achieved a perfectly decent balance between humour and menace, it never really took off. This was probably because it wasn't brave enough with its circus concept so that the macabre 'Troubles' intrusions didn't bring us down to earth with a big enough bump. Also, even though it was well written and had an attractive sense of invention, Belfast audiences were beginning to become tired of any play that explored 'the Troubles'. Unfortunately, there was a disappointing attendance.

I thought we would do much better with Stewart Parker's best known play. Sadly, this wasn't the case. When I mentioned this to a colleague he said, 'Belfast don't like their own being too much of a clever dick'. The implication was that Stewart was too intellectual a playwright to have a wide appeal, that the local audience would prefer a less calculated, stylised play with more direct accessibility. Later, I discovered that even a Brian Friel play wasn't a guarantee of box office success. Some would be, others certainly wouldn't. These revelations were useful but alarming. My hope that *After the Fall's* success would usher in good attendance for a wider repertoire was only being partially realised.

The next play in the season, *Tartuffe Today*, was certainly more direct. Unfortunately, both writers were dead: Jean Baptiste Poquelin (Molière) and John D. Stewart (the modern adapter). Stewart's idea of making the preacher hypocrite a Paisley-like figure who undermines the moral rectitude of a modern bourgeois Protestant family was a good one but, on reflection, it needed a bolder, updated version to follow through the central conceit. Unfortunately, the writer, a journalist who was prominent in the civil rights movement, wasn't around to do that. In retrospect, I should have got another playwright to develop and refine the material. The production by Jonathan Myerson did its best to compensate for such deficiencies, and it was certainly funny, not least at one point when Tartuffe's control over the family was accentuated by him snapping his fingers and a golden ray of light miraculously appeared like a halo on his head, comically accentuating his bogus pious nature. The production was full of such fun, but it just lacked that cutting edge to make it really resonant.

36 – Taming the Gorilla

AFTER *TARTUFFE*, I THEN EMBARKED on directing a new play, *Charlie Gorilla* by John McClelland, a young, pipe-smoking oyster farmer from Whitehead. John had a strong central idea about a

Tartuffe Today by John D. Stewart after Molière, directed by Jonathan
Myerson and designed by Jane Green. Lyric Theatre Belfast, 1989.
Sean Caffrey as Rev Dr Tartaraghan and Fay Howard as Eleanor McCluless.

gorilla in captivity and how he's abused not only by human beings but by a scientific experiment that finally murders him. Casting somebody to play a gorilla wasn't easy. I finally plumped for a
young London actor, Terry Bird, who had the necessary physique
and became an Englishman humilated by the Irish. The cage in a
zoo was ably designed by Alison Böckh, successfully combining
elements of a prison and a laboratory. We also changed the con-
figuration of the seating and put some of the audience on the stage.
This helped to create a voyeuristic, claustrophobic atmosphere.
The yobs aggressively bating the animal were vigorously played by
Dan Gordon and Sean Kearns. I energised them in rehearsal by
getting them to run down Cromwell Road like demented thieves
before taking out their frustration on the bemused gorilla. Pedes-
trians looked on bewildered and somewhat fearful, suspecting a
nearby robbery. Birdy Sweeney played the sympathetic zoo keeper.
In fact, I'd asked Birdy to be in *Waiting for Godot* but he wasn't
available. That was a pity as I think like a lot of variety performers
he would have been perfect for Beckett.

I always loved the music hall. I remember playing recordings of the celebrated cockney comic Max Miller to my Dublin friends, who loved him. In fact, I'm still waiting for some of Maxie's LPs to be returned from South Dublin, so he must have gone down all right there. John Osborne and Harold Pinter were both influenced by such comics. You get a sense of that influence in the rhythms of their dialogue. Osborne, most noticeably in *The Entertainer* with such *bon mots* as, 'Don't clap, it's a very old building!' During *Charlie Gorilla*, it emerged that Birdy knew none other than the controversial comic Bernard Manning from his stand-up days. In fact, unbelievably I was once regaled by a Dublin taxi driver about the virtues of Bernard Manning's racist humour, which he described as 'very funny, mate!'

To help with the physicality in *Charlie Gorilla*, we were aided considerably by Jane Gibson from the National Theatre as Movement Director. She helped us develop a sense of humans as animals and animals as humans. This really gave us further insights

Charlie Gorilla by John McClelland, designed by Alison Böckh.
Lyric Theatre Belfast, 1989. Anthony Finigan as Fred, Terry Bird
as Charlie and Birdy Sweeney as George.

into physical possibilities. In fact, as well as its comments on animal cruelty, *Charlie Gorilla* was unusual in being so physically
and visually distinctive. Nonetheless, during a free preview, when
a group of young people from West Belfast came, they laughed
throughout the play. An atmosphere of delirium invaded the theatre. I think they were hysterical not because the play was bad but
because the whole experience was foreign to them. They'd never
seen a live play before, let alone one where the leading character
was a gorilla!

Despite the derision, I don't regret trying to initiate a new access policy of free previews, hoping to break through boundaries
and give greater access to disadvantaged communities. Unfortunately, budgets were very tight and after discussions with the
board about loss of income, the policy was scrapped. This was a
great mistake and I should have fought harder against it. Price of
tickets and what deals you can sell are a seminal part of theatre
policy. The only way you can change theatre from being exclusive
is by having radical price offers, for even if people with less money
would like to attend, they just can't afford it. The problem in those
days was that the theatre had a very limited number of seats. Now
that the capacity is bigger and the Lyric has more sources of revenue from their new facilities, there's greater opportunity for such
initiatives. Theatres should be more inventive in finding deals to
get houses full. Although pay-what-you-can-afford has had an effect in some places, a more consistently progressive approach is
needed. Subscription doesn't seem to take off in these islands, but
attractive bargains need to be better marketed and integrated into
policy. After all, an empty seat is a useless seat.

Charlie Gorilla didn't play to big houses nor did we expect a
first play by an unknown writer to do so. However, it would have
played to capacity if it had been in a studio theatre where it belonged. In those days we either gave new writers an opportunity
on the Lyric stage or not at all. I was keen to introduce first-time
writers not just recycle those who'd already established themselves. In that context, *Charlie Gorilla* did well and the theatre

made progress. When the play was grounded in observable reality, it was very effective. There was a real sense of menace and cruelty in man's Darwinian practices. In the second act, the play started going into the realms of science fiction with its rather overblown Frankenstein-like proceedings. In fact, lighting designer, Roger Simonsz had obtained a Svoboda light (named after the celebrated Czech designer), which not only gave appropriately tight beams from a hanging batten to provide harsh illumination for Charlie's operation, but also sunlight for his flashbacks in the jungle. Roger had to bring the light from London and although it looked like a Katyusha rocket, it went through two checkpoints without anybody blinking an eye. Hardly an endorsement for security.

Although *Charlie Gorilla* was unusual, engaging and imaginative, it seemed that the concept came first, instead of the characters organically shaping the ideas. However, despite such reservations, it was highly original first play and we'd given a talented new writer a chance in the hope that he'd go on from there, which he did.

37 – Time for Show Business

Every Artistic Director needs showmanship in their locker. I wanted to demonstrate this by bringing a bit of oomph into the season, and when a chorus of long-legged, attractive asian and black women appeared for the opening number of *Little Shop of Horrors*, I got it and how! You could sense the shock and surprise that here was a different Christmas show. So far the season had produced some interesting work but only average attendance, so we needed to retrench and engage that wider audience.

I've always enjoyed musicals from an early age; they are the fairy tales of theatre. *Little Shop* is a particularly bizarre one in the New York camp tradition. It centres around a flower shop and the quirky romance between nerdish Seymour and kookie Audrey, the flower seller who escapes the clutches of a crazy, sadistic dentist. The romance is finally destroyed by a villainous flower, Audrey 2, who finally grows to alarming heights, eats both of them and then sets its sights on the audience! Conleth Hill was an excellent Sey-

Little Shop of Horrors. Book and lyrics by Howard Ashman.
Music by Alan Menken. Directed by Vanessa Fielding and designed
by Eve Stewart. Lyric Theatre Belfast, 1989. Conleth Hill as Seymour
and Deirdre Harrison as Audrey.

mour: stylish, comedic, with an engaging singing voice. He was
ably partnered by Deirdre Harrison, a versatile, blonde American
with a good voice and a bubbly presence. Kenny McDowall, a grav-
elly voiced Belfast blues singer, brought menace and gravitas to
the vicious flower, despite being unseen. Director Vanessa Fielding
gave the bizarre proceedings an underlying reality, and Eve Stewart (later to design many Mike Leigh films) created a colourful,
whacky, fantasy world. Two local talents, choreographer Ann-
Marie Brady and inventive Musical Director Brian Connor, also
made excellent contributions. Most important of all was the sense
of moving the Christmas slot on from more obvious, saccharine
material and giving our core audience the sense of wider theatrical
possibilities.

38 – What's in a Title?

AROUND THIS TIME, I HAD A good conversation with John Boyd.
I had given him a copy of a play produced by the RSC called *Prin-*

cipia Scriptoriae, a play about the subjugation of writers in a South American state. When he came to my office, he plumped himself down in an inviting armchair and told me that it was a decent play but a bad title. It was too academic. He then proclaimed that 'a title has to grab the imagination of the audience'. One of his litmus tests was the reaction of his sister. 'My sister isn't going to go to a play called *Principia Scriptoriae* but she will certainly come to one entitled *A Streetcar Named Desire*, *Cat on a Hot Tin Roof* or *The Playboy of the Western World*. Titles, they're really important. Some writers are lazy about them.' It was good advice. If you're taking an audience on a journey, then you need the signposts to be clear. Boyd also made another interesting observation, saying that 'the more plays move away from your own culture, the more the box office decreases'. I found this a bit depressing but there was a truth there as as well. Audiences like to be in their comfort zone, but producing the same plays incessantly isn't the way to move a theatre forward. One of my best contributions was to gradually take up the challenge of extending the repertoire and bring the likes of John Boyd's sister with me.

39 – The Challenge of the Iceman

THE BOARD WAS VERY BRAVE to allow me to direct *The Iceman Cometh*. I had fallen in love with the play ever since seeing the Abbey production in 1972. I'd also been to the RSC production which precipitated Ian Holm's nervous breakdown and led to him locking himself in his dressing room in the middle of a performance and not coming back on stage. Holm may well have been an excellent Hickey, the righteous salesman who looks to erase the 'pipe dreams' of his erstwhile drinking friends, but I saw his understudy. I remember preferring the Abbey production despite its faults. The RSC actors were too clean and self-conscious. Patrick Stewart and Co. didn't give a feeling of a group who'd drunk a lot. The Abbey company certainly did. O'Neill said that he wrote *Long Day's Journey into Night* in 'tears and blood', and while *Iceman* isn't about a family, it's no less personal.

O'Neill was a drinker himself and he knew all the characters in Harry Hope's bar. His play isn't theoretical but wrought out of human experience. In *Iceman* there are sixteen different stories, which is why it's a long play. Space is needed to give air to the characters and their individual narratives. This presented a practical problem. The play was going to run for four and a half hours. After much discussion with the board, the play started at 7.30 pm, not the usual 8.00 pm. I had argued for a 7.00 pm start with the offer of food at the interval. I wanted it to be an event. In Belfast you needed to present something extraordinary beyond theatre, so that the punter would be grabbed by a unique one off. Although we provided some food, we couldn't get a suitable service provider for more extensive provision, and the board were nervous about the start being too early because they didn't think it gave people time to get back from work. So 7.30 pm became the compromise solution, which was a pity. Of course, getting a known leading ac-

The Iceman Cometh by Eugene O'Neill, designed by Alison Böckh. Lyric Theatre Belfast, 1990. Peter Marinker as Theodore Hickman (Hickey), (standing), Rebecca Bartlett as Cora, Eugene Scott as Joe Mott, Don Foley as Piet Wetjohn, Anthony Finigan as Cecil Lewis, Eric Loren as Rocky Pioggi, Deirdre Harrison as Pearl, Eileen McCluskey as Margie, Liam O'Callaghan as Larry Slade, Paddy Scully as Hugo Kalmar, Noel McGee as Chuck Morello, Gerard O'Hare as Don Parritt, Conleth Hill as Willie Oban, John Hewitt as James Cameron, Maurice Blake as Ed Mosher, Martin Dempsey as Pat McGloin and Ray Callaghan as Harry Hope.

tor to play Hickey would have helped, and I pursued various luminaries without success. However, I was happy to have the Canadian actor Peter Marinker accept the part. I had worked with Peter in the 1960s when he played the satanic hippie murderer, Charles Manson, in a play about an imaginary meeting with Lt Calley of Mai Lai Massacre fame. So he had certainly done his audition for mesmeric figures.

I'd learned from *A Touch of the Poet* that Irish actors can bring out O'Neill's humour particularly well. Certainly, the gap between the fantasies of the characters' 'pipe dreams' and the basic reality of their everyday life was ripe for humour. This was particularly true of bar owner Harry Hope and his sentimental adoration of his late wife, whom the other characters regarded as an ogre. When Harry makes a speech on his birthday, he goes into euphoric hyperbole about his love for Bess, while the others make cynical asides. Harry becomes suspicious of his fellow pipe dreamers and he has

The Iceman Cometh by Eugene O'Neill, designed by Alison Böckh. Lyric Theatre Belfast, 1990. John Hewitt as James Cameron, Maurice Blake as Ed Mosher, Ray Callaghan as Harry Hope, Conleth Hill as Willie Oban, Martin Dempsey as Pat McGloin, Eugene Scott as Joe Mott, Eric Loren as Rocky Pioggi, Anthony Finigan as Cecil Lewis, Noel McGee as Chuck Morello and Rebecca Bartlett as Cora.

to be flattered and assuaged in order to continue his absurd reverie. Ray Callaghan, a small wiry Mayo man, who left Ireland in his teens, was excellent as Harry. A committed actor, he is also a huge admirer of Gustav Mahler. In fact, he puts a rose on his grave in Vienna every year. Ray had worked for the RSC but I first met him when he was driving a minicab in West London. Ray was enthusiastic and intense. At one rehearsal, when he saw me ensconced in the text, he shouted out. 'Don't read, watch me.' Although I was concerned that the text was accurately spoken, and that the characters' contrasting rhythms were realised, Ray had a point.

Sometimes, a director can be so buried in his own way of working that he or she can become oblivious to what the actor is offering. I remember Jim Fitzgerald, that very talented Irish director of *Stephen D*, saying, 'always watch carefully what they come back with'. The relationship with an actor is a conversation, and I was caught that afternoon being a bit deaf to one side of it. I was just very aware of the paraphrasing in the Abbey production which I wanted to avoid at all costs. There's one thing to be too reverent to a good playwright, but there's another to be totally disrespectful and careless. Too much paraphrasing leads to a loss of rhythm and dramatic focus. The result is general acting. Good acting is particular. For an actor to 'nail it', he or she needs to take pride in polishing the text as jewellers do silver. From such detailed work, physicality and emotion will emerge organically. Not by running around generally imposing a layer of meaning without thought.

We only had four weeks rehearsal for *Iceman*, admittedly a week longer than usual but there was still a lot to absorb in that time. It wasn't only the learning of the lines but the listening to the whole story. Listening is an underrated art in acting. Everybody concentrates on the spoken side of the play but what about the non-spoken story? Talking for the actor is giving, listening receiving. In *Iceman*, there are times when the characters are so drunk that they wouldn't hear anything. However, as actors they must listen and decide how they awaken and what energy they bring to their next speech. This in turn opens up the physical story, their posture and movement. Given the static nature of the play, energy was vital, but it needed to be a controlled organic energy that gradually moved the play forward. Not just a spewing out of lines, but a momentum that came from the genuine, believeable thought that absorbed what was said. Also, every character needed to relish their own 'pipe dream' and have a compulsion to 'sell it' to everybody else. Working on such a mammoth text, I was very aware that directors can sometimes talk too cerebrally about their views, instead of solving theatrical problems. I always remember the warning of a fellow director early in my career: 'ten minutes bad rehearsal talk is two minutes bad production time.'

One of the big successes of *The Iceman Cometh* was Liam O'Callaghan. Liam was a recovering alcoholic who had been estranged from his son, which had echoes with his part. Thankfully, his son reunited with him when he came to see the play. Liam started at the Lyric in the early days. Mary O'Malley recognised that with his rich, deep voice and commandingly good looking stature, he was made for classical drama, and in particular the verse drama she loved. After his initial success in Belfast, Liam went to Dublin, then played leading parts in Wales for Theatr Clwyd and had a spell at the National Theatre. He used to entertain us about his conversations with Sir John Gielgud in the National canteen regarding Sir John's tax problems. Apparently, his accountant had told him that the only solution was for him to work outside the country!

Liam was very authorititive in the pivotal part of Larry Slade, the most cynical of the characters, who sees that Hickey is not just selling redemption but death. Larry supposedly accepts his fate as he has lost faith in both the labour movement and life. He's waiting for death and doesn't want to be interrupted, but that's his particular 'pipe dream'. When Don Parritt, the son of his fellow anarchist ex-girlfriend, stalks him in Harry Hope's saloon, he becomes increasingly challenged. Guilt hangs over the play, not least in Parritt, who's looking for redemption from the father figure of Larry. After initially telling Larry that he betrayed his mother to the cops as a patriotic act, Parritt finally reveals that he did it for personal reasons, because he hated her selfishness and neglect. I particularly remember Liam creating a memorable moment when Larry's wry detachment snapped and he decided to release Parritt's tortured, suicidal soul by passionately telling him to leave this life before he strangles him himself. One of the highlights of the production was Liam's ensuing look of despair when he heard the body of Parritt fall from a fire escape.

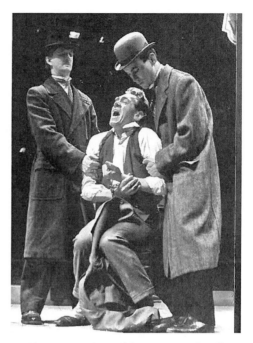

The Iceman Cometh by Eugene O'Neill, designed by Alison Böckh. Lyric Theatre Belfast, 1990. Brian MacGabhan as Moran, Peter Marinker as Theodore Hickman (Hickey) and Fintan Brady as Lieb .

Iceman depends on a good Hickey. It's a mammoth part, a feat of learning in itself. It was a credit to Peter Marinker's ability that he managed such a rounded performance. Unlike Godot, Hickey is the 'saviour' that appears. His mates, the roomers in Harry Hope's last chance saloon, are waiting for one of Hickey's intermittent visits when he entertains the multitude with his tales about the road and gets them to believe in their delusions. They think that he's bound to come as it's Harry's birthday. However when Hickey does arrive, he wants all the roomers to throw away their 'pipe dreams' and restart their lives.

A lot of American plays are about selling and buying. Not surprising in a country where 'the deal' is at the heart of its commercial culture. Peter understood this and managed to keep the tension of the seller as preacher. He wouldn't let his targets off the hook, but challenged them to face the truth with maniacal fervour.

In doing so, he managed variety by particularising his victims, so that the tone was different to each of the roomers. The delivery was in turn charming, humorous and ruthless, which made them feel increasingly insecure. The roomers were hoping that Hickey would confirm their delusions. The fact that he had changed so profoundly disturbs them all. Gradually they find out how this change emerged.

At first, Hickey tells them that his wife had died, then he admits that she was in fact murdered. Finally, in a speech lasting twenty minutes, Hickey confesses to murdering his wife because he couldn't live with his guilt when she kept forgiving him. He was living a lot on the road and wanted to free his wife from his adultery. He laughs crazily before he recalls killing Evelyn and telling her what she can do with her 'pipe dream'. The roomers think he went insane and want this to be used as a plea at his trial. Hickey refutes such support and wants to die. He now realises that a man stripped of his delusions is left naked to his fate.

During the latter stages of rehearsal, Peter and I went over his mammoth speech several times in the evening in the cold confines of the Cromwell Road rehearsal room. He would always come to rehearsal very well prepared so we were able to use the time well. Given that we were rehearsing all day this was just as well. A lot of the key to directing *Iceman* lies in how you orchestrate the text. Each character has musical solos, plus there are interactive, tense duets as well as choruses of relief and celebration. Hickey's big speech is an aria which needs particular variety of pace and tone. It's a confessional, full of unburdening and accusation. It's also suspenseful storytelling.

At the core of the speech was emotional revelation. Hickey has a volatility of mood swing towards his wife, Evelyn. There's a celebration of their love (they were young sweethearts) and Hickey recalls the way she adored him as well as his hatred of her 'pipe dream', her insufferable goodness and inability to face the truth, which finally leads to the revelation of her murder. We therefore needed to find dynamic mood changes that would surprise the audience with their intensity and also create danger. Such demands are always difficult but Peter made great strides in both surprising us and revealing depths of emotion. As a director you hope you are creating the conditions for an actor to have the confidence to use him or herself. O'Neill sets big emotional demands. Taking refuge in the refinement of technique won't fully answer those challenges.

The Iceman Cometh became a community play. To see sixteen characters on stage was both unique and exciting, especially as the whole company rose to the occasion magnificently. Amidst the 'pipe dreams', there's a persistent, intermittent cry of a call for radical change. It comes from the former editor of anarchist periodicals, Hugo Kalmar. Patrick Scully, a Dublin Jew living in Belfast, showed a wonderful comic understanding of this desperate man. After Hickey leaves at the end of the play, the whole cast

The Iceman Cometh by Eugene O'Neill, designed by Alison Böckh. Lyric Theatre Belfast, 1990. At left table: John Hewitt as James Cameron, Maurice Blake as Ed Mosher, Conleth Hill as Willie Oban, Martin Dempsey as Pat McGloin, Ray Callaghan as Harry Hope (hidden). Standing: Peter Marinker as Theodore Hickman (Hickey). At right table: Anthony Finigan as Cecil Lewis, Don Foley as Piet Wetjohn, Eugene Scott as Joe Mott, Eileen McCluskey as Margie and Noel McGee as Chuck Morello.

are so relieved that they celebrate by reinstating their 'pipe dreams' with a cacophony of different songs, which are all sung at the same time. It's a wonderful chorus of chaos only topped by Hugo's final defiant cry for freedom. It was a fitting conclusion to the work of the company, which the *Times* critic described as 'a distinguished ensemble.'

The Iceman isn't a play for a director to self-consciously advertise his skills. In any case, I dislike that kind of fashionable high concept production which draws attention to itself. If a director has a concept he or she should make sure a consistent world is created. However, too often concepts work for some scenes but not for the whole play. The result is that the actors are left to act in scenes that don't make any sense, that are dishonest and untruthful, even though they may look great and dazzle audiences with their shimmering superficiality. It's good to reinterpret and be brave, but you need to do so with a finely honed theatrical logic. It's foolish for directors to think that they're more important than the writer and impose meaning that is flashy, insincere and trite.

In *Iceman* we avoided such ostentation. Alison Böckh, our designer, is a minimalist, subtle designer. The edges of her set were designed like those of a ship, based on O'Neill 's references to the sea. He had, after all, been a sailor. As the actors first entered, accompanied by a dim backlight and Debra Salem's haunting score, it was as if they were about to take a seat on a journey to destiny. The action in O'Neill's play is condensed into three days. Before each act, we looked to have a different tableau both physically and visually to interpret the time change. The increasing weariness and fear of the characters was expressed through a different posture and position. Roger Simonsz's lighting design created a living sepia photograph, the cues were slow, subtle and unnoticed so that the eye was naturally drawn to where the next part of the action would occur. For instance, as Hickey was looking to convert the roomers (disciples), there was a slight celestial glow to Harry's birthday party, similar to the Last Supper as the roomers gathered in a line around the tables. However, only minimal light seeped through blind covered windows. This was a hermetic, sealed world looking away the from the cold glare of reality.

The Iceman was certainly a landmark production. It signalled ambition and intent, but despite its length it wasn't an overtly erudite or intellectual piece, remote from the average punter. This was substantiated by a middle-aged couple who couldn't stop laughing at the deluded antics of the pipe dreamers, in particular those of Harry Hope trying to keep his customers in order. They were obviously only too familiar with such a publican. I also heard a young man from West Belfast revealing say, 'the people in that bar are just like my Dad.' Considering its length, *Iceman* did good business. Not only did it show the Lyric to be one of the more ambitious theatres in Ireland, but it also continued the narrative I was developing of producing a new American play every year after Christmas. It was a clear signpost in the journey I wanted to take with the audience. The season had built up to such an epic production, and it had given the theatre a very high profile.

40 – Ghosts and Consequences

HOWEVER THERE WAS A PRICE to pay. I now had to present Ibsen's *Ghosts* translated by two board members, John Boyd and Louis Muinzer. I wasn't against doing *Ghosts*; after all, I'd directed it. However, I certainly didn't want it to be programmed to follow *The Iceman Cometh*. After such an expensive production, we shouldn't have immediately produced another classic with limited appeal. It should have been presented at a later date. Unfortunately, this was an argument I wasn't going to win, and the board insisted that it had to be produced after *Iceman* as there was a likelihood of the play going to an International Ibsen Festival in Oslo later in the year. Louis Muinzer was a Scandanavian drama specialist and had paved the way for such a deal. I was all in favour of the Lyric going abroad and getting a European profile. I just didn't agree with the timing and the way two board members were using their position to their own advantage. Unfortunately, John Boyd seemed to think that I didn't want it produced at all. This view corroded my relationship with both him and the board.

The production itself was sensitively directed by Danish director Kim Dambaek and had a strong sense of a society in its dying embers. Stella McCusker was effective as a vulnerable, respectable Mrs Alving, struggling to stop the ravages of the past from resurfacing in her son Oswald's fatal illness. Joe Crilly, anaemic and wan, gave a strong feeling of Oswald's lost potential, caught in the pincers of time. Peter Ling's imaginative set complimented such themes: a grand circular garden room with neglected, decaying walls, an upstage window shaped like a Christian cross, and a surrounding gauze which opened and closed as appropriate. This was effectively complimented by the sound of consistent rain which claustrophobically shielded a view of the surrounding estate and the Fjord beyond. The production was well received and played to decent houses, but it didn't get the wider audience back to the theatre which I felt was essential.

As tension mounted with the board the season continued with *Observe the Sons of Ulster Marching Towards the Somme* by Frank McGuinness. McGuinness's play is one of the most important in modern Irish theatre history. Never before has a Catholic written about the Protestant experience in such depth. Some southern writers have tended to regard northern Protestants as just sash-wearing bigots. McGuinness humanised them and got to the heart of why they can be so defensive about their own culture. It isn't just because they are a minority in the island of Ireland, but also the legacy and scars of the huge psychological damage, inflicted when the Ulster Division was wiped out in the First World War. Although I found McGuinness's gay relationship in the play a rather imposed construct, ultimately I was very moved by the depiction of such tragic loss. It informed the wider Irish audience about a complex Unionist narrative, something hitherto insufficiently explored in Irish drama.

In fact, when I was living in Belfast, I found it very hard for southern friends to come and visit me. By 1991, the North was

Observe the Sons of Ulster Marching Towards the Somme by Frank McGuinness, directed by Noel McGee and designed by Kathy Strachan. Lyric Theatre Belfast, 1990. Michael McKnight as Nat McIlwaine, Gerry McGrath as William Moore, Andrew Roddy as George Anderson and Sean Kearns as John Miller.

relatively peaceful and moving gradually to the Good Friday Agreement. Nonetheless, I detected a reserve among those from the Republic to stay too long. I can understand that being so easily recognised by your accent and car number plate makes you an obvious target. However, it still surprises me that so many people in the South have never been to the North and don't really have a great knowledge of the place. During my time at Magee, with the B specials in their heyday, I was shocked at the political and religious sectarianism. However, as things began to change and a new generation took up the reins of authority, I made friends with a more diverse group of people in Belfast and began to appreciate the virtues of the Protestant community: their pragmatism, hard work and gritty sense of humour. All qualities which would certainly enrich a united Ireland.

Although Frank McGuinness's play had already been produced at Hampstead and at the Abbey, I think our production was the most important because it was the first indigenous one. *Observe* was directed by Noel McGee who had assisted me on *The Iceman Cometh* and had appeared as an actor in several productions. Noel comes from Dundalk but had lived in Belfast for many years. I wanted to bring through some home grown directors and I was delighted to see him take his opportunity. However, he'd cast a diverse crew with a few company members with chips on their shoulder. Once, when I went on a routine visit to the dressing rooms, one of the leading actors launched into a tirade of criticism. Much of it I found irrational and unjust, so I just stood there letting him burn himself out. I suppose Artistic Directors can always try to create better conditions and more support for a company, but there are times when actors are just using you as a punch ball to spew forth their general frustrations. More important than such outbursts was seeing such a relevant play in Belfast and Ulster actors Andrew Roddy, Sean Kearns, Patrick O'Kane, Gerry McGrath and Michael McKnight being very good in it.

It was at the end of the season that matters came to a head with the board. When I asked to go to Norway to represent the theatre, I was refused. The board thought it better that I stayed in Belfast. I explained that it was usual for the theatre to be represented by its Artistic Director and Chief Executive when engaging with other theatres. Their response was that the board would be able to do that as Messrs Kelly, Muinzer and Boyd would be flying to Norway themselves. This was totally and utterly unacceptable. I shared my concern with Mike Blair who was now our Administrator after the long serving Valerie Osborne went to work for the Ulster Orchestra. Mike, who had come to the Lyric from Irish National Ballet, was level-headed, personable and able. He agreed with me but thought that there was nothing I could do apart from resign. While it was definitely an issue, I wasn't going to take it that far. Given my previous experiences, I detected John Boyd's fingerprints all over this. Again, he was inveigling the board to get his own way. The idea that a theatre would go to an international event without its Artistic Director making an appearance contravened all known theatre practice and undermined my authority. In fact, Mike Blair told me later that the Artistic Director of the Norwegian National Theatre was asking where I was and seemed surprised that the only artistic representation for the Lyric were the old members of our beloved 'politburo'. Of course, previous Artistic Directors had suffered much more interference from this board and overall I had managed to keep them at bay. Now, though, they had crossed the line and it was a bad omen for the future.

41 – The Importance of Oscar and Playboy

DESPITE THIS SETBACK, IN AUTUMN 1990, I forged ahead with my third season. Given the large outlay on *Iceman* and *Ghosts* I started with two brilliant known plays before embarking on more adventurous fare. *The Importance of Being Earnest* went down very well indeed. Trudy Kelly was an imposing Lady Bracknell, Ali White an independent and enchanting Cecily, and Conleth Hill a brilliantly playful Algernon. Conleth proved to be a comic actor of style, timing and considerable technical accomplishment, and the evening was full of many laughs. One of the problems of playing *Importance* is that too many lines are funny. I think it was Noël Coward who said, 'don't have too many laughs in the first act so the audience can get to know the characters, have more in the second as the situation develops and accelerate the laughter in the third as the play races towards the denouement'.

With *Earnest's* abundance of wit, you have to know what to throw away in order to highlight the big comic moments to enable the narrative to proceed at a good pace. Conleth, aided by Stan Laurel look-alike Gordon Lovitt, as his friend John Worthing, dealt with such editing with the ease of a mature veteran. It was a prime example of how live theatre is so much about how an actor interprets a performance in a particular moment. In film, the editor does this in post-production, but in live theatre the actor is the editor, in terms of nuance, emphasis of interpretation and orchestration of response. Sometimes in theatre you can see a method-style performance with an excess of naturalistic detail, the actor misguidedly giving the same emphasis to every moment,

The Importance of Being Earnest by Oscar Wilde, designed by Jane Green. Lyric Theatre Belfast, 1990. Ali White as Cecily Cardew and Barbara Adair as Miss Prism.

with the consequence that the play becomes turgid and indulgent. This is because he or she hasn't edited their performance to get to the essence. Thankfully, this wasn't the case with our *Earnest* and the various contortions in trying to solve the mystery of Mr Worthing's parentage after he was found in a cloakroom at Victoria Station were resolved with comic style and observable truth. Jack married Gwendolen, Algy married Cecily and we had a hit, a palpable hit!

Earnest was followed by *The Playboy of the Western World*, possibly the best Irish play ever written. Although my production of *Earnest* wasn't radical, it communicated very well, not least to a younger audience less familiar with the play. *Earnest* is a delicate masterpiece and isn't a play that invites tampering. When I've seen self-conscious, post-modern interpretations, they've only confirmed one thing: that Wilde's sparkling dialogue is much better than any overloaded imposition which wishes to stress that the writer was gay or had an identity crisis. Nonetheless, I dreaded another run of the mill *Playboy*.

The play had been done to death in Ireland and although I did not want a production set in a swimming pool, I did want a sense of reappraisal and freshness. Therefore I looked for a director coming to the material from left field. I saw this quality in Jonathan Holloway of Red Shift, a company which specialised in innovative interpretations of classics. Holloway put a strong stress on the sexuality and loneliness of the women. Before the play started they were roaming Niall Rea's undulating set with subdued moans. This was a production with a strong feminine perspective where the women fully enjoyed wreaking revenge on Christy for telling them a lie.

Brendan Coyle, later to find TV fame in *Downton Abbey* as Mr Bates, was a handsome, virile Christy; Lynda Steadman, a powerful Pegeen, angered by the loss of her dreams; and Conleth Hill amusingly brought out the comic inadequacy of Shawn Keogh as a rival suitor. Supported by a strong supporting cast which included such experienced hands as Martin Dempsey (Old Mahon), Sean Caffrey (Michael James) and J.J. Murphy (Jimmy Farrell), we had a good ensemble. The production recoined the play for a modern audience with a different emphasis and some visual flair.

42 – An Emotional Journey with Sam

SAM THOMPSON IS A FAVOURITE Ulster playwright of mine and *Over the Bridge* is his most successful work. I was excited about directing it as the next production in the season. *Over the Bridge* is a play with an incendiary political history. In 1958, James Ellis, then Director of The Group after its celebrated founder Harold Goldblatt had resigned, met Sam in the Elbow Room, the appointed pub for Belfast actors. Sam challenged Jimmy Ellis by saying he had written a play but The Group wouldn't touch it. When Jimmy Ellis read it, he knew that he had discovered an exciting new talent. The Group's reading committee corroborated Ellis's view and the play went into production. Then, suddenly the board, which included Mr Harry McMullen, Head of Programmes of BBC Northern Ireland, then a considerable Unionist bastion, panicked and a statement was issued by its chairman Richie McKee, a Unionist estate agent:

> We are determined not to mount any play which would offend or affront the religious or political beliefs or sensitivities of the man in the street of any denomination or class in the community and which would give rise to political controversy of an extreme nature.

Sam's play was about sectarianism in the dockyards. He had worked there himself as an apprentice painter for Harland and Woolf. He knew the truth about what was happening. McKee was concerned about such revelations because he was not only Chairman of The Group, but also had fingers in all sorts of Unionist pies. He was Chairman of the grant awarding body (CEMA) and his brother was the Unionist Lord Mayor of Belfast. Nobody seemed to be too concerned about a conflict of interest in those days. Instead, McKee mouthed platitudes saying that 'plays with sectarian themes make it difficult for Lord Mayors who are anxious to give money to the arts'.

As a result of the ban in 1960, Ellis resigned and, with some outside help, formed a new company, Bridge Productions, to produce the play, not at The Group Theatre but at the old Empire Theatre in Victoria Square. The result was that a six week run played to packed houses and was followed by seasons in Dublin and London. Unfortunately, for various reasons, The Group company went into permanent decline and its actors went their separate ways. Sam went on to write two other stage plays (one unproduced) until he died prematurely at the age of 49. A lifelong socialist, he was a member of the Northern Ireland Labour Party, standing in the 1964 election. He was also an actor, and while I was at Magee I saw him in an Ulster Theatre Company touring production.

Directing *Over the Bridge* turned out to be an important moment in my career. Not because it is a perfect play but because it was a great all round theatrical experience. Sam's play is flawed – its construction is wobbly and some characters sketchy – but

Over the Bridge by Sam Thompson, designed by Houston Marshall. Lyric Theatre Belfast, 1990. Roma Tomelty as Martha White, Mark Mulholland as Rabbie White, Sean Caffrey as Mr Fox and Lalor Roddy as Warren Baxter.

what it has at its centre is the visceral passion of truth. Just take the speech of Rabbie, an experienced union man, talking to his younger colleague, Warren Baxter, at the end of Act 1.

> In the early twenties, Warren, they chased Catholics out of the shipyard and Jimmy Nugent was one of the ones too slow getting off his mark. When the mob caught up with him they threw him from the boat deck out of the boat he was working on into the tide. The cratur had to swim fully clothed fifty yards to get to the other side of the channel. But that wasn't the end of it, Warren. When he did get to the other side they had a reception party all lined up for him, and they made him a target for bolts, stones and rivets. He was a sorry sight when they had finished with him. Then we had the case of Bobby Owens. He was pointed out as an Orangeman in the wrong district. He was set upon by a gang of thugs who kicked him within an inch of his life. To this day Owens walks with a limp, and Nugent and he are steeped in hatred and revenge.

Over the Bridge dramatises a society riven by sectarianism. Framed by union politics, the play starts with an individual dispute and follows with a bomb explosion. This leads to the rise of a vengeful mob, violence and the death of a union leader trying to protect a Catholic's right to work in a predominantly Protestant shipyard. Although some of the union politics are dated, it still packs a very powerful punch. It's very much a community play with scenes at work, including a communal mob chorus of around ten workers, contrasting with those at home.

For the mob we involved people from the local community and rehearsed them separately. When directing extras it's important to make sure that they understand the discipline of professional theatre, while inspiring them to a strong sense of commitment. Consequently, I tried to make them think in detail about their character, so we didn't have 'rhubarb' acting when you get general shouts and murmurs. They needed to have a particular understanding as to why they were in a mob and what had driven them to become violent. Consequently, I encouraged them to make their own biography and back story so they brought a real sense of reality to the proceedings. It was especially good to share such a Belfast play with local people. Their response was excellent and aided by a menacing cacophany of banging on scaffolding, they helped to make their scenes particularly frightening.

At the centre of *Over the Bridge* was Mark Mulholland, who played Rabbie White, a union leader obsessed with the rule book. Mark was a good actor with a strong presence and a fine voice. Unfortunately, he drank too much but never enough to be classed as 'drunk'. He had a strong constitution and he needed it. He was well cast in *Over the Bridge* and his scenes with Lalor Roddy, as Warren Baxter, a young shop steward, were particularly well played.

One evening, just before the show started, I left the theatre, crossed the Lagan Bridge and made my way up Sunnyside Street, only to see a heavily built, grey-haired man swaying on the pavement. Suddenly I realised it was none other than my leading man in the current production, Mr Mark Mulholland. Mark hadn't seen me yet but when he did, he immediately got more sober like a drunken driver pulling up just in time before a red light. On approaching him, I told him that I thought he should have some coffee. 'Aye, I will. Don't worry Roland, I'll be fine,' he remonstrated as he departed treading gingerly across the bridge. I faded into the night and left him to it. What could I do? I had an understudy for Alan Devlin because he was a special case. Mark had never appeared drunk on stage, although sometimes he did look like a bloated beetroot which was usually at odds with the character he was playing. However, in most regards, Mark was very professional. He was committed, and studied hard. At his best, his characterisations were interesting. However, for those in the company, it could be difficult playing scenes with a man who was permanently smelling of drink. Nobody officially reported back to me about Mark, but I got the sense that others were fed up with that particular odour being an extra character in the play.

Over the Bridge was designed by local designer Houston Marshall who created an imposing scaffolding surround on which mob members could clamber like monkeys and emerge from a dark tunnel of hate. Office and exterior meetings were played within the surrounding space. There weren't many local designers, and during the previous regime Houston was asked to do too much. I think it wore him out and his work deteriorated. Now coming back refreshed he did a very good job.

We had a strong cast but maybe the person who most embodied the spirit of Sam Thompson was Louis Rolston. Louis had previously worked in the shipyards for over twenty-five years and sadly contracted asbestosis as a result. He was a serene, dignified man, who always rose above petty theatrical intrigue. Maybe being an actor seemed relatively pleasant after the hard world of the docks. Louis knew Sam well and he gave a reality and dignity to Davy, the pivotal character of the union boss. Although Louis' voice could be thin at times, his sheer understanding of the role gave the part a massive moral authority. Consequently, when Davy

Workmen in *Over the Bridge*, designed by Houston Marshall. Lyric Theatre Belfast, 1990.

died it was as if a light had gone out and that a dark chasm was left in the community.

The other important factor in the production was the audience who packed the Lyric. While this is always the case, in this particular instance it was especially so. There seemed to be an innate emotional bond with the material. Everybody who came to the play knew about sectarianism. Many people had experienced it personally, and while things were steadily improving, it still existed. The play was a siren warning about man's inhumanity to man and that a plague was still in our house. So despite a certain old-fashioned clunkiness, the play was emotionally very powerful, creating a unique sense of a shared experience. This is in stark contrast to performing Shakespeare in Stratford to an audience of photo snapping Japanese tourists who can't fully understand the language, or in the West End to corporate hotel bookings with no close affinity to the material. Art provided a much needed forum for 'the Troubles' and all its tensions because it offered a platform for artists to go into areas where politicians dared not tread. I remember a Belfast taxi driver telling me that he thought it was the only good thing to come out of the whole mess. Sam Thompson was a trailblazer for such courageous acts of the imagination.

Through an excellent review in the *Glasgow Herald* ('a gripping drama played with passionate conviction'), the production, with some necessary but unsuccessful recasting, was later invited to the

Glasgow Mayfest. Unfortunately, it was marooned in the cavernous spaces of the King's Theatre with its 1,785 seats. It was no longer an intimate community play and got lost in such grandiose surroundings. It was at the right event but in the wrong place. A pity, as there was a warm response from the audience. Nonetheless, the visit helped extend the Lyric's profile and overall the production was a memorable experience.

43 – Dickens and the Board

Following the Lyric production of Sam's play, I managed to develop the Christmas show with a new version of *Oliver Twist*. It was as if Lewis Carroll met Charles Dickens. What emerged in James Merryfield's audacious design was something more surrealistic and stylised, far removed from our earlier, more traditional production of *A Christmas Carol*. Even though we may have moved too fast for some of the audience, we still managed to get good attendance. Most importantly, family audiences weren't seeing what they already knew but the wider possibilities of visual and physical theatre.

It was around this time that I was talking to Mike Blair about the future. My contract was running out at the end of the season and I needed to clarify the situation. Mike had done a great job getting much needed sponsorship from various companies. He was supportive, reliable and encouraging about the work. He thought that given what I'd done at the Lyric, my contract was bound to be renewed for at least a couple of years. I wasn't so sure. Professor Desmond Maxwell, a great supporter of mine, had resigned over the *Ghosts* debacle and I wasn't convinced that certain board members didn't have long memories. On the other hand, I didn't want the situation to linger on. I needed time to plan my future.

On balance, I decided to ask the board whether they were interested in me staying. After a somewhat prolonged hiatus, I pushed them further for a response. Dr Colm Kelly, our Chairman, finally informed me that they were going to let me go. When I asked for a reason after producing some of the better productions in the theatre's recent history, getting good attendance, establishing end of season festivals and Sunday performances, giving the company a higher profile, let alone running the theatre on my own for a year when the previous Administrator was ill, he told me he thought that I would be better off in England. Instead of leaving it there, it got worse and he inexplicably elaborated on how my taste was too English.

Now Colm was basically a kindly man but this was unacceptable, somewhat racist language. This was absurd, as apart from the Dickens adaptations, one of which was programmed by the board, I'd only produced one English play, *Comedians* by Trevor Griffiths, which is widely regarded as a modern classic, so I certainly wasn't going to apologise for that. There was no mention of the way the repertoire had developed, how standards had improved, how a lot of good Irish actors emerged and what good reviews we'd received from both the Irish and English press. There was a feeling of, let's keep it in the parish and let's make it as small as possible. The irony was that I'd already worked for the National Theatre of Ireland, a company far more Irish than anything in Belfast. In any case, arguments about shades of green were puerile. After working for the Abbey, running my own Irish company and directing/producing over 50 Irish or Irish-related plays, I think I'd shown considerable commitment to Irish theatre. Ultimately, the board had once again showed that they were more interested in conserving power than artistic development

Now I was in a unhappy place. I didn't want to leave the Lyric. It was a home for me. I liked the people and enjoyed the work. Although that particular board never gave Artistic Directors longer than three years, until the *Ghosts* dispute I was hopeful that I might break the mould. Unfortunately, it didn't happen and I wasn't able to build on the work I'd done. While I didn't expect to stay in perpetuity, the three years went very quickly and I felt that I still had a lot more to offer the theatre. I was disappointed that I didn't have the opportunity to continue nurturing emerging Irish talents and develop ongoing schemes for the theatre's site. What increased my annoyance was that the board had already asked me for my plans for the next season before letting me go. I also realised that a decision about my future was probably reached without a full board being present. If rumour was to be believed, the vote was close so maybe those absent may have made a difference. On such slender margins does fate sometimes hang. On a personal level, I didn't have any problems with board members. However as the 'politburo', they could be manipulative and treacherous. I was naive to think that having usurped my authority once, that they were going to allow me to reassert it.

44 – Living with Tennessee

GOING INTO A PRODUCTION KNOWING your departure is imminent isn't easy for any Artistic Director. It's rather like continuing with a relationship when you've decided to split. Thank goodness I had a great play to direct and therefore could divert my mind from my departure. Tennessee Williams's *Cat on a Hot Tin Roof* became the third American play I directed. It's a drama about lies, greed, sex, money, power and death – just for starters! At the heart of the relationship between the central young couple, Margaret and Brick, is homosexuality. Brick has married the beautiful, ambitious Maggie but the marriage is a failure. Brick, an ex-football star, is ridden with guilt about his friend Skipper, who committed suicide after his feelings for Brick weren't reciprocated. Brick has become alcoholic and won't sleep with Maggie. Maggie, who escaped childhood poverty to marry into the Pollitt plantation family, is sexually frustrated but determined not to lose her newly acquired status. Meanwhile, the Pollitt family meet for Big Daddy's birthday and even though most of them are aware that he's dying of cancer, it doesn't stop them voraciously vying for his estate.

Cat on a Hot Tin Roof moves between Strindbergian feuds and social satire via long monologues and passionate duets. *Cat* isn't naturalistic; it evolves in a world of heightened reality, HR would be the shorthand. Actors need to be comfortable with vocal size, 'acting up' and what part of the play they're in. The characters are

Cat on a Hot Tin Roof by Tennessee Williams, designed by Alison Böckh. Lyric Theatre Belfast, 1991. Sara Stewart as Margaret and Patrick O'Kane as Brick.

truthful but larger than life. However the play isn't a melodrama, the characters are full of exaggerated vitality but not caricatures. They may be foul-mouthed like Big Daddy, ruthless like Maggie, foolish like Big Mamma or self-disgusted like Brick, but they also manage to embody other qualities which make them more contradictory and complex.

For instance, Big Daddy embodies the vitality of living, love for his son and courage in facing death, Maggie wants a baby to start life afresh and Big Mamma shows stoic dignity in the face of family greed. Even more humorous supporting characters like Mae, Gowper, Dr Baugh and Rev Tooker, who further embody the mendacity at the heart of the play, shouldn't be played too broadly. They all need to be allied to the writer's particular heightened poetic style. Williams expresses this visually in rather florid stage directions, but one understands the principle. He's looking for a universal truth that rises above the mere mundanity of naturalism and a social setting.

Although *Cat* takes place in one evening, Williams doesn't seem so interested in the classical unities of time and place. This is manifestly clear when he states that the set should be 'far less realistic than I have so far implied', and 'that it should be roofed to the sky'. Alison Böckh's design certainly created size with tall, wooden-slatted walls reaching for the stars while encircling the private traumas of a dysfunctional family. Supplemented by Gerry Jenkinson's warm, mellow lighting, it also radiated Mississippi heat and sex with its light pine colouring and enticing bed. This all corroborated the need for the actors to be expansive without resorting to indulgence.

I was fortunate to have leads who could match these demands and combine power with vulnerability. Sara Stewart was an alluring Maggie. Not only was she attractive but she was also able to

Cat on a Hot Tin Roof by Tennessee Williams, designed by Alison Böckh. Lyric Theatre Belfast, 1991. Patrick O'Kane as Brick and Ted Valentine as Big Daddy.

Cat on a Hot Tin Roof by Tennessee
Williams, Lyric Theatre Belfast, 1991.
Patrick O'Kane as Brick.

express Maggie's volatile mood changes from fear and frustration to utter ruthlessness. Patrick O'Kane was then a young Belfast actor not long out of Central School. He had a brooding, dangerous sexual quality, with a good physical command of Brick's impotence as he struggled around on crutches after a sports injury. Maybe at times I followed Williams's stage directions too literally, and while my staging was efficient I could have freed it up more and given a greater physical dynamic to the play's tensions.

Central to the success of *Cat* is the part of Big Daddy. Ted Valentine held the emotional centre of the part well. Despite being physically clumsy at times, he was excellent vocally and had a strong authorit) presence, vital for a patriarch. His wife was played by Trudy Kelly, who always brought a strong emotional quality to her work. It was unusual to have relations in the same production, but Susie Kelly, Trudy's daughter, played Mae, the supposedly respectable but inwardly grasping relation. *Cat* is about southern whites and there's only one, very small black part. It's inevitably a servant, played by Arnie Hewittt from Birmingham. Not Birmingham, Alabama but Brum, England. I felt a bit guilty about Arnie because he had so little to do. Mind you, his presence did remind one of the appalling racism in the south for so many years. Later, in 2008, there was a highly praised all-black production of the play on Broadway, so at least that interpretation acknowledged the omission.

Cat on a Hot Tin Roof played to very good houses and was well received ('Riveting' – *The Irish Times*); 'an excellent challeng-

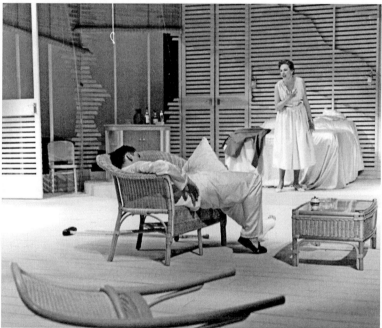

Cat on a Hot Tin Roof by Tennessee Williams, designed by Alison Böckh.
Lyric Theatre Belfast, 1991. Sara Stewart as Margaret and
Patrick O'Kane as Brick.

ing production' – *Anderstown News*; 'the best thing Jaquarello has done at the Lyric' – *The Stage*). However *Cat's* successful run was brought to an abrupt end by personal tragedy.

Sara Stewart 's mother died suddenly in the last week of the run, and after Sara saw a doctor she was advised not to work on such an intense play. After consulting the board, they decided to cancel the last three performances. It was a sensitive and considerate act that was much appreciated by Sara and her husband. Although everybody was gearing up for a final run of full houses, it was the right thing to do. Despite Colm Kelly taking the cast out to dinner, the run ended in a anti-climax and everybody dispersed their separate ways. However, overall I was very pleased with the way the American productions had gone. We had presented three of the best American writers – Miller, O'Neill and Williams. We had not only played to good houses (*Cat on a Hot Tin Roof* did 80 per cent before early closure), but had received great reviews and, most importantly, my intention of moving the repertoire forward had succeeded.

45 – Lorca and the Irish

However, programming European plays has always been difficult. We are meant to be part of the European Community but we seem to display little cultural acknowledgement of the fact. Of course, language plays a significant part in this, but nonetheless it's disappointing to discover that there's a rich seam of continental drama that is never performed. I was looking to correct this by producing at least one such play a year.

Frank McGuinness is one of those who has admirably led the charge in trying to extend the European repertoire in Irish theatre. Luckily, we had managed to get his translation of Frederico García Lorca's *The House of Bernarda Alba*. I had seen several English Lorca productions which I thought were awful. They were lacking passion and were far too studied and Protestant, as if they were set in an English boarding school. For instance, after a Lyric Hammersmith production with Glenda Jackson and Joan Plowright, I remember witnessing a woman in a very loud Home Counties voice declaring loudly to the emptying stalls, 'No. Not very convincing!' However, in Ireland, there was a more profound understanding of dogmatic Catholic culture. The audiences were familiar with the stories of what went on in schools and convents in the fifties and places like the Magdalen Laundries. *The House of Bernarda Alba* is about this form of oppression and how one matriarch ruthlessly rules.

After the death of her second husband, Bernarda Alba insists that, in accordance with family custom, her five daughters observe eight years of mourning without having any relationships with men. This inevitably leads to frustration and finally tragedy. Adele, the youngest daughter, hangs herself after mistakenly thinking that her lover had been shot by her mother. In fact, Romano, the lover, flees away on his pony and the play ends with Bernarda Alba proudly declaring that the whole town knows that her daughter died a virgin. When one thinks of how Lorca was murdered by Franco's forces for being gay, the play resonates beyond a mother and a family to the perverse fascism of the state. Peter Ling's set certainly reinforced this oppression. The whitewashed stone walls of the house were so high that no sky could be seen. Big gates, locked doors, tiny windows, and a cold, drab flagstone floor completed a powerful sense of incarceration. In addition, the women's mourning black dresses were vividly contrasted with the pale, shaded space. The lack of freedom was palpable.

Although there was a volatility about most of the acting that gave the play dramatic momentum, the central part of Bernarda Alba was miscast. Sheila Ballantine is a good actor, but she lacked the emotional power necessary for such a part. Helena Kaut-Howson had certainly managed to get an interesting Irish ensemble together, including Eileen Pollock, Trudy Kelly, Gerardine Hinds and Ethna Roddy as Adele, but we had no Irish mother. I remember we had trouble with the availability of some contenders for the part and Helena felt more comfortable with Sheila. Interfering with another director's casting is like telling an artist to paint their canvass in different colours, but in this case I should have done so. Sheila was in another play, and not a very good one. That very English prissiness that I had seen in other Lorca productions now invaded us like a plague blowing across the Irish sea. I took my eye off the ball here and was too trusting. I don't think that my forthcoming departure had anything to do with it. I like to think I remain professional whatever the circumstances. I should have insisted that we had an Irish actor rather than importing an unsuitable English one. Although it was a good production, it had a hole in its centre, where the mother fans the flames of destruction.

46 – The Struggles of Youth

MY LAST PRODUCTION AS Artistic Director was *Rough Beginnings* by Robert Ellison. This was the third new play that I had produced in three years. Like *Charlie Gorilla* this play would have normally been presented in a studio theatre. Ellison's drama has a marvel-

Rough Beginnings by Robert Ellison, designed by Alison Böckh. Lyric Theatre Belfast, 1991. Peter Ferris as Snazzer, Alan McKee as Anton and Stuart Graham as Jimmy.

lous sense of alienated youth – playing football, competing for girls and jobs and getting sucked into 'the Troubles'. There were a series of good performances from a company of young actors: Gerry Rooney, Peter Ferris, Alan McKee, Stuart Graham and two strongly contrasted women, the tall, leggy Laine Megaw and the diminutive, pert Helen Trew.

Alan McKee gave a particularly sensitive performance as the troubled, simple-minded Anton, who after unearthing an arms cache becomes violent, undermining his relationships with an increasingly fracturing gang. Alan went on to becoming a successful comedian. When later I saw him in another play, he seemed to have lost that finer sensibility, substituting it for the rougher art of aggression, which of course is necessary for stand-up.

The play is better in its excellent dialogue than its narrative, which becomes a little predictable as the boys get caught up in a murder and its retribution. That said, the acting was believable with a strong sense of ensemble ('a sizzling company of young Belfast players' – *Independent on Sunday*). Set on a green football playing surface, supplemented by trucks for oppressive interiors and with music from Madonna and other pop luminaries, the production had a compelling youthful energy ('bustling activity' – *The Times*). I may not have ended with a bang but I didn't go out with a whimper either.

47 – Final Rites

EVERY DIRECTOR NEEDS A HOME. Without one it's difficult to develop unless unless you're one of the select few who work consistently as a freelance. However, I was sad to leave the Lyric, not just because I was going to be out of work but because it was a special place to me. I felt part of a family there. During my three years we'd made considerable progress together. Of course, like all Artistic Directors, I made mistakes and there are some things I would now do differently. Nonetheless, overall, given the resources available, I believe I extended the repertoire, improved standards and moved the theatre forward. After the announcement of my departure,

Grania McFadden, in a very generous tribute in *The Belfast Telegraph*, said:

> The Lyric Theatre will be bidding farewell to its Artistic Director this summer. The combined cast at Ridgeway St will sorely miss the talents and enthusiasm of the latest in a long line of directors at the theatre.
>
> Roland extended the brief in many ways, bringing his enthusiasm for European plays to the stage with productions such as the Russian *Threshold* and the local adaptation of *Ghosts* which was warmly received in its native Norway.
>
> During his time with the Lyric the theatre has also performed some memorable revivals, none more successful than *After the Fall* – one of the high points at Ridgeway St for many years.
>
> This was followed last year by *The Iceman Cometh*, Eugene O'Neill's epic play which was performed to large audiences during its run at the Lyric.
>
> This season sees the final in a trilogy of American classics, when Tennessee Williams's *Cat on a Hot Tin Roof* takes the stage this month.
>
> There is little doubt that Jaquarello has gambled with the fate of the Lyric. But his gambles in the main have paid off, attracting wider audiences to the theatre and earning it a name for daring not predictabilty.
>
> Roland has pressed for the theatre to be opened for Sunday evening entertainment and has attracted some fine actors from outside Northern Ireland to appear on stage (notably those seen in one man shows during last year's May Festival).
>
> He has encouraged new local writers to bring their work to the Lyric, which courageously performed *Charlie Gorilla* last year and hopes to produce another play this season.

Other plays have been revived with much success, in particular Sam Thompson's *Over the Bridge*, which played to packed houses during its Festival run at the Lyric.

It is to be hoped that Roland's brave endeavours will be recognised, if not here, at least elsewhere.

And we must hope that his successor comes armed with equally brave plans and high ideals, prepared to take the Lyric into the 1990s.

Although many of the actors during my tenure deservedly went on to great things, I wish I could say the same about the theatre. It was depressing for me to observe that the first play after my departure was *Rebecca*, a great story but miles away from what I was doing. While the Lyric has continued to produce some good productions over the many years following my departure, I haven't seen any consistency. The theatre seems to lurch from pillar to post, rather than display a vision of what it wants to do.

There's been insufficient development of the repertoire, artists and the audience. The choice of plays has often been predictable and the tone too insular. The programming has been risk-averse. When an English consultant was brought in to advise about the new building, it was just a blueprint of what was done across the water: do less, have more visiting companies, bring in amateur societies, musical events and give a new name to an administrator, thus enhancing his authority. This isn't the best policy for the Lyric.

At the centre of the theatre should be ethos of the Lyric Theatre company. During my tenure, we did too much with too little money and we certainly needed more time to develop productions. Now the focus seems to have been blurred and the Lyric company season is just one of the theatre's many activities. In my time, financial restrictions meant we had to have through casting (an actor going through into the next production). However, this did have advantages because if cast properly it not only built up opportunities for actors to stretch themselves in different roles, but also created a form of ensemble with a distinct Ulster profile.

Today casting is freestanding. This has advantages but it lessens company identity, especially if the gap between productions is too big. With such a hiatus, the audience doesn't get the necessary continuity to build up a relationship with an artistic narrative, especially if there are so many other diverse activities.

Given the theatre's small size, the Lyric had a unique opportunity to continue developing a dynamic play culture, not a patchwork of rootless co-productions, diluting the Lyric Theatre Company's standing. Despite some excellent work in developing a good new theatre building, the artistic side has lost focus. Mary O'Malley was brilliant at getting the building together, less so at running it; nonetheless, she understood the importance of an artistic mission. More recently, the theatre seems to have succumbed to the generalised world of entertainment, the modern artistic shopping mall. It seems to be more governed by business and political considerations than a commitment to an artistic vision. For too long there has been a lack of a core company ethos with a clear path of travel. Only recently has the repertoire seemed to recover some sense of impetus. However I remain concerned when the senior person in the theatre isn't an Artistic Director but an Executive Producer. Good theatre isn't made by those with such titles. When you think of the Moscow Arts, the Berliner Ensemble and the Abbey, you think of Stanislavski, Brecht and Yeats, not administrators.

Prior to my departure from the Lyric, I was going about in a bit of a daze like a punch-drunk boxer. I didn't want to leave and I hadn't really thought of where I was going to go. I made a few applications and got an interview at the Northcott Theatre Exeter. I travelled somewhat blindly all the way to the west coast of England only to discover that I got the wrong time. The interviews had finished and there could be no recall. I was late because my heart wasn't in it. I still wanted to be at the Lyric and therefore endured a long, rather desolate journey back to Belfast. When you've managed to find a theatrical base it's always a wrench to leave. On the other hand, theatre is basically freelance and those who permanently move from one full-time theatre job to another are very few. However, as a freelance you are in the hands of others and you either accept their choice of material or you don't. At least as an Artistic Director you have some control over the repertoire. The other alternative is to form your own company. This is always an exciting prospect but difficult to maintain unless you have accessible funding. Whatever way one looked at it, I'd be back in the brutality of the marketplace. After three years with a salary while thoroughly enjoying my work, it was a daunting prospect. However, it was no different to what I'd been doing previously. Even though I'd recently had a more regular life, I was used to being on the street.

So after a lively leaving party during which I was given very generous presents, I made my way up the incline of Ridgeway Street and departed into the summer night. Although I was no longer Artistic Director, I was determined this wouldn't be my last Irish appearance. Like the general said, 'I will return!'

MOVING TO RADIO

48 – Radio Induction

IN FACT, MY RETURN TO BELFAST was in 1996 as Senior Radio Drama Producer for BBC Northern Ireland. I'd grown up with BBC radio in the 1950s and the voices of those who performed *Winnie the Pooh* and *Listen with Mother* are indelibly etched in my consciousness. It was wonderful creating characters in your imagination just from voices and soundscapes. *Journey into Space* was another gem of radio, which introduced me to science fiction. For a young boy, it was an insecure and unnerving experience listening to the threat of Martians, indicative of post-war uncertainties. No wonder Orson Welles scared the hell out of his fellow Americans with his celebrated *War of the Worlds* broadcast in 1940. Through this radio hinterland I became a regular listener. However, I still had a lot to learn about the medium.

Unfortunately, just before I went on a BBC training course my mother died. It was a difficult time for me but I got sensitive support from my colleagues at BBC Northern Ireland, particularly my PA, the elegant, dark-haired Myrtle Johnston. My mother adored radio. One of my last conversations with her was about a direct opera relay from the New York Met. She talked about it with all the excitement of a youthful teenager. When her body was discovered in her Fulham house, the radio was on and the sheet music of Brahms's 'Four Ballads Opus No. 10' was on her piano rest. Right to the end, my mother was still practising. She had given herself to teaching music to young people with a commitment and dedication that was unique. When I returned to her house, a father brought his young daughter for her piano lesson. When I told them of my mother's death, the child got very distressed and her cherubic face disintegrated into tears. She was so upset that she wasn't going to see her piano teacher again. I later saw this family amidst a very large attendance at the funeral sevice. The last time I saw my mother, I was helping her tidy up (something I wasn't renowned for doing) before going to Belfast. She was so pleased that I'd just got a job at the BBC, so it was sad that she never heard one production of mine.

The BBC training course was rigorous. It took place in London at Great Portland Street in the former flat of Jeremy Thorpe, the colourful but disgraced former Liberal leader. We had to go out and do vox ops and create a package. I used mine to explore the potential demise of Fulham FC, whose ground, Craven Cottage, was about to be sold. When I made enquiries about getting an interview from somebody at the club, I was curtly refused by the suspicious club secretary. 'Nah, we can't do that. Sorry.' It was a long way from the refined PR machine that was going to emerge from the spin doctors of the Premier League. Rejected by the club, I managed to record an interesting interview with Melvin Tenner, leader of the Fulham 2000 group, who were looking to keep the club at Craven Cottage. When I asked him if the current manager was intelligent, he replied that wouldn't be the word he'd use.

Another part of the course was editing a tape (this being well before digital, so it was razor blade time) of a *World at One* pack-

RJ in BBC recording studio, Ormeau Avenue, Belfast, 1996.

age on the arrest of Gorbachev. Listening to the outtakes was fascinating. Things were happening very quickly and BBC Radio 4 were desperate to break the news first. The problem was that that they couldn't find the correspondents to do so. You heard the Producer constantly saying, 'where's Bridget?', 'any news on Kevin?', followed by the mutterings of the PA. Finally, just a few minutes before going on air, they managed to contact them and get their reports down the line. It was a close shave. 'Thank God for that,' exhaled the relieved Producer. At the end of the transmission, I heard him give his debrief which started by categorically and honestly stating, 'that was a cock up.' I admired such frankness. Too often, Producers and Directors hide behind the mask of their position when sometimes you need to be open and share the problem.

Later, my drama piece for the course was a section of *The Man with the Flower in His Mouth* by Luigi Pirandello, a play I'd directed in a London fringe theatre, where it had been very well received, but it didn't make particularly good modern radio. Thankfully, in the debrief Producer Eoin O'Callaghan gave some helpful pointers. After years in theatre, I was about to work in a much more intimate, conversational medium. Therefore, I needed a radical reappraisal of my approach to direction.

I remember being in studio during my first production thinking everything was going well, when Myrtle whispered in my ear. 'We've been working for an hour and we've only done five pages, you need to move faster.' It was a salient reminder. In the current culture you're working to the clock. You need to manage the play within the time. Like a rowing boat being called back to the shore by a park official when 'your time is up', it's the end – somebody else is coming into studio or going on air.

Twenty-four hour radio just rolls on and waits for no one. The days of rehearsing for a long time, then recording, all at a leisurely pace, had gone. All those clubbable sojourns at London's Broadcasting House when the George pub, or in Belfast's case, the Elbow Room, were virtually the green room, had disappeared. You needed to rehearse and record to strict time limits. For instance, a 45-minute play is just a day and a half's recording in studio. For somebody coming from a theatre background where things are much slower and organic it was quite a shock. Also, you wouldn't necessarily record in sequence. All exterior scenes would be in the 'dead room', so you'd do a lot of them together regardless of their position in the play, just as you'd record all voice-overs in a screened off studio or the trap, a small confined space, suitable for greater vocal intimacy. Fortunately, I shadowed a good radio director, Martin Jenkins. Martin seemed to have an excellent shorthand, very suitable for working quickly: 'take it off the page', 'tighten' etc. I used this and developed it to my own needs. In radio, you don't have the time for long discussions so you needed to tap into the actors' imagination quickly and clearly.

49 – Studio Firsts

ON MY FIRST PRODUCTION, I hadn't yet been able to do this. I was still a theatre director directing radio. I was fortunate that for my first job, *Beached* by Robin Glendinning, I was working with two actors I knew: Kevin Flood, from his London days, and Peadar Lamb who was an Abbey colleague. More importantly, I had a good script. In this case, it was about a whale sighting and the machinations of two ageing Irish politicians in which both whale and humans become finally ensnared. I was also aided by two talented and experienced technicians: Arthur McClintock, as Studio Manager, and John Simpson working the desk – recording, mixing and editing.

Arthur was a great fan of Tony Bennett; in fact, he was a leading light of his fan club. He also liked Sinatra. He was amenable and very good at guiding me through unchartered waters. During breaks, I used to catch him reading that trashy journal, *The Hollywood Reporter*. When I challenged him about buying such rubbish, he responded by saying that he only got it for the mother! Later, on another bizarre occasion, I came into the studio to discuss our preparation for a production, only to discover Arthur singing and swinging à la Tony Bennett and John recording him. Apparently they had finished early so there was a bit of 'creative space'. That reminded me of the underground tape somebody gave me years ago of Anthony Hopkins doing a send up of *Under Milk Wood*, only instead of going through the Welsh village, he went through the whole of the acting fraternity doing brilliant impersonations of Gielgud and Olivier etc. Apparently, Hopkins and his Producer had finished a radio play and also found some 'creative space'.

John Simpson was particularly good at getting a recording down quickly. This was extremely useful in such a hectic culture. More than once John got me out of holes. For instance, I remember working with him recording a fifteen minute book reading, when the contracted actor came into studio totally unprepared. In many ways, a reading is one of the hardest things for an actor to do and needs careful planning. This particular person was talented but it was clear that he'd come in for a 'wee reading' and thought that he'd just stroll through it. I was furious and embarrassed as he kept on repeatedly stumbling and going back on sections. Unlike theatre, I couldn't have a row as that would only lose me further studio time.

At the end of this stuttering nightmare, there were around seventy edits for a very short production. That was totally unacceptable. When our actor had departed, I looked round to John as if to say, 'over to you mate'. He relished the challenge of such demanding editing and in the remaining time completed the job. It was typical of both his expertise and commitment. Although there were times when I had to slow John down because we needed to be careful we didn't omit detail, it was always good to work with him because he is such a consummate professional. Pity the actor wasn't.

Funnily enough, one of the best actors in preparing for radio was Mark Mulholland. He might have had a quick one before performing but that wouldn't stop him being ready. Once Mark left his script in the studio and it was a revealing insight into the actor's radio world. It was marked neatly and carefully in different colours, highlighting certain words and particular sections. As an older actor he had grown up with pioneering Belfast Radio Producers like Ronald Mason and knew what was needed.

Belfast certainly had a pedigree with radio drama but it was a pity that some hadn't inherited Mark's professional habits. Radio needs as much work as other media, it's just a different type of work. It's about preparation and being ready for studio. For the actor, that means making decisions and being ready to present the Director with what you've done. For the Director/Producer, it's about getting the script prepared, knowing how the text should be heard, good casting, logical scheduling and making sure the actors are vocally in the same play.

50 – Colleagues and Culture

At Belfast we were in a small room on the ground floor of Broadcasting House, Ormeau Avenue, our bunker being away from most apparatchiks. Apart from Myrtle and myself there was Pam Brighton and her PA. I knew Pam from London where for a time we both worked at the Half Moon Theatre. Bradford-born, she was hefty, committed, opinionated and political with a good eye for spotting new writing talent. She lived in West Belfast and supported Sinn Féin, prompting one writer to say to me, 'Thatcher had given the left such a whack in England that they're all migrating over here to find a cause'.

Pam had discovered some good writers, not least Marie Jones and Gary Mitchell, who in fact were both working class Protestants, but too many of the plays she produced had the feeling of being about the suffering of the Catholic population. A perfectly legitimate subject but there needed to be more variety of output and I think this was reflected by research at the time. In fact, I remember reading a letter from a woman now living in the Home Counties but originally from a working class Catholic background who resented such victim culture. Pam's passions were certainly strong but so were her prejudices. She had a propensity to romanticise some working class actors and writers, and to be dismissive of good ones from a more middle class background. She was never very interested in the work of other directors and seemed just set on her agenda. There were times when Pam appeared more interested in politics than drama, whereas I believed politics should inform drama not govern it. Recently she'd stepped down from being Senior Producer, hence my appointment. As I later discovered this was a shrewd move. Within Broadcasting House, Pam seemed to have a reputation of being a bit of a handful. One of the camper presenters at the station cheekily asked me on arriving to work, 'how are you getting on with mein pamf?' Although there was a certain wariness between us, I respected Pam's commitment. She belonged to the Yorkshire awkward squad of the likes of Arthur Scargill and cricketer Geoff Boycott. She told it how she saw it, took risks with challenging subject matter and helped inexperienced writers with her good editing skills. I also certainly enjoyed her rumbustious sense of humour, not least when proclaiming loudly, in a broad Yorkshire accent, the latest BBC sex scandal.

During my tenure as Senior Producer, Pam's PA was Anne Simpson, John's wife, who was very committed to radio. Fair-haired, good humoured and bright, she knew radio drama like the back of her hand. In a later culture she became a good Manager of the department. My PA, Myrtle Johnston, was new to Drama having previously worked in Schools Broadcasting. Her husband was Neil Johnston, a well known journalist from the *Belfast Telegraph* who specialised in folk music. I found her both helpful and supportive. She wasn't a BBC clone like some and had the insight and wisdom of somebody who had brought up two children. In fact, it was Pam, in one of her wilder moments, who appeared to show bizarre judgement about Myrtle. When a sound effect was missing for a religious scene, she suggested that Myrtle should be asked for a rosary. I think Pam presumed that because Myrtle and Neil liked Irish folk music they were Catholics!

In my early years at Ormeau Avenue, despite our little spats, we were a good team with our own department. However, I wasn't finding it easy to deal with the new culture of the internal market and the offers system with its relentless synopses and constant changing of managerial targets. The old BBC was certainly elitist (I'd heard that some people at their interview were asked which Oxbridge college they attended) and too much of a closed shop. It was also probably true that some productions took too long and were indulgently produced. Nonetheless, the BBC had still managed to create a range of high quality programmes that were the envy of the world. However, times were changing. Mrs Thatcher's 1980s privatisation spree scared the corporation, especially after Director General Alastair Milne was sacked in 1987 over the legacy of the *Real Lives* programme about Martin McGuinness and Gregory Campbell. Thames TV were also highly criticised by the government for their film *Death on the Rock*, which was deemed critical of the execution of three IRA members by the SAS in Gibraltar, and duly lost their franchise. From these decisions, there was a real fear that the BBC wouldn't continue to exist as a public service. There seemed to be a sense of reform or die.

The result were the changes instigated by Sir John Birt. This in turn led to Producers being deskilled. Commissioning Editors would now inform Producers what they wanted, and Producers would bid for work by making a formal offer for a slot. No longer were they able to decide what was transmitted themselves. There would also be an internal market whereby you bought resources like a studio, and each department would survive by being paid for the number of offers they had accepted, without the safety net of quotas. Although this wasn't a solution I liked, there was certainly a problem with radio drama. Apparently, a departing Controller of BBC Radio 4 said at this time that he felt that radio drama was experiencing the equivalent of a theatre audience leaving at the interval, and that Producers were doing too many plays for their friends and not the wider public. Consequently, the BBC was paying a considerable sum of money for plays to which only a small audience fully listened. This may have been true in some cases, but the consequent changes were too extreme. The content often became banal in attempts to chase audiences, inappropriate writers were commissioned and 'stars' were indulged. Shorter play forms were instigated like the regular 45-minute afternoon slot. This might have been necessary but in its initial phases it was a dog fight and one I wasn't always winning. I had to learn how to pitch: to sum up a narrative in a few words, place it in both genre and a slot and sell it clearly and strongly.

This was completely different to theatre which still had a sense of a more gradual progression to develop complex ideas. In radio new offers were flying around and disappearing like so many birds in flight as we tried to impress various editors. It was mad and hectic. Another Senior Producer once told me that I'd joined the BBC at the worst time in its history. I think she was right. In the past, Directors had gone to the BBC and done good work with terrific writers and actors on the quiet road to retirement. Not any more. This was like working for a multinational. The sad thing was that too little time was spent about ethos and vision, and too much about accountability and ratings.

51 – Early Ventures

DESPITE THIS BAPTISM OF FIRE, I did manage to produce some varied and interesting work, which made me learn how to deal with different kinds of material. I was particularly pleased that John McClelland was able to develop his writing in radio with two plays: *Keep Out Private*, a withering satire on privatisation, and *The Boy Who Thought He Was an Elephant*, about a boy who resorts to strange behaviour when alienated at school. It was a good start for a new writer and I was delighted when James Boyle, the Controller of Radio 4, sent me an e-mail congratulating me on the former, which was ironic given the BBC's deregulatory policy.

My first serial was a two part version of *The Aran Islands* by J.M. Synge, imaginatively adapted by Shaun McCarthy. I soon learned that for serials you need to make sure each part is freestanding for the one-off listener, while moving the narrative forward for the regular one. What the Synge lacked in plot, it gained in atmosphere, so much so that one of my tutors on the BBC course

Keep Out Private by John McClelland. BBC Radio 4, 1998.
(back row) RJ, Myrtle Johnston (Production Assistant), Philip Jackson (middle row) Paddy Scully, Matt McArdle (front row) Brenda Winter, Brendan McNally, Roger Lloyd-Pack, Walter McMonagle and John McClelland.

thought it was recorded on location. This made me realise that in modern broadcasting, sound, especially as the digital revolution emerged, had become nearly as important as language. Plays need to be written for the medium, not imported from theatre. While one shouldn't swamp them with effects or music, how they are heard is integral to the story. They should have a variation of location, a clear point of view and different length of scenes. In such respects, radio has got closer to film.

An unusual comic piece with Dubliner Eamon Morrissey and Ulster comedian Jimmy Cricket was Sean Moffatt's *Only the Birds*, a short 30-minute play about the way a creaking floorboard brings spiralling chaos into a home. Later I was to be discouraged in producing such satirical and surrealistic dramas and told to concentrate on more naturalistic plays with 'peaks' and 'troughs' and a strong emotional core as the jargon proclaimed. A pity as I received very positive correspondence from listeners about the offbeat *Only the Birds*.

Another funny piece was Martin Lynch's play *Needles and Pinsa*, a topical comedy about a local Belfast community worker spending his redundancy money on reuniting the sixties pop group The Searchers, much to the chagrin of his wife. Martin is a popular Belfast writer with a political edge and it was good to get his pertinent work across to a wider audience. One of the best plays I produced during this period was *Raskolnikov's Axe* by Christopher Fitz-Simon. Christopher is one of the most professional writers I've worked with in broadcasting. His scripts are always immaculately presented (particularly important in radio), he writes well to time and he's adaptable in studio. His play was about an actor, Denzil Fitzgerald (Mario Rosenstock), joining a 1930s Dublin theatrical company to play Raskolnikov in an adaptation of Dostoevsky's *Crime and Punishment* and identifying too closely with the role. The theatrical politics which brings about Denzil's frustration was hilariously portrayed. Well acted by Stella McCusker, Michael Cochrane and Gate veteran Bill Golding, who mischievously based his character on none other than Micheál MacLiammóir, *Rasko-*

Only the Birds by Sean Moffatt. BBC Radio 4, 1997.
(back row) Eamon Morrissey, Mark Mulholland, RJ
(front row) Myrtle Johnston (Production Assistant),
Jimmy Cricket, Stella McCusker, Anthony Finigan and Paddy Scully.

linov's Axe was nominated for a Writers Guild Award in 1997. It didn't win but it was very good morale booster for Christopher, myself and the department.

I also developed more work with Robin Glendinning, who prior to my arrival had been unjustly cast aside and went through a fallow radio period. Robin's play *Emergency* covered a bizarre time when a German landed in Ireland during World War Two, or 'the Emergency' as it's called in the Republic. His intention was to recruit IRA members to invade Britain. Robin is brilliant at dramatising nuggets of history and this was no exception. The story was comic and offbeat. There was one scene which took place in the Irish house of a resident who had his property designed in the shape of a swastika. Apparently this was based on fact! Also, at one stage some of the protagonists get absurdly involved in the production of Laurence Olivier's *Henry V*, which was filming in Ireland at the time. However, Robin's most interesting revelations were in *Stopping the Rising*, which dramatised how many Irish volunteers saw the 1916 Rising as an act of folly and did their best to prevent it. If they'd succeeded, the course of Irish history might have been different. This was a long play covering a very important and relevant issue. Many parts were played by actors from the south, and it was revealing to discover that some of them didn't know about this division within the Irish Volunteers. It was certainly one of the biggest casts I've ever had in radio. Such long form radio isn't so frequent these days. This was the last of the radio epics from Belfast.

I also produced a short form drama, *Getting On* by Aodhan Madden, a 30-minute play about a middle-aged Dublin bachelor struggling to come to terms with the recent death of his father. This was an understated and well written piece. As the son went through his father's possessions, you sensed the emotion many have experienced with such rituals. Correspondence certainly confirmed the listeners' identification with the character, sensitively portrayed by Barry McGovern. It was good to work with Aodhan. He'd been a theatre critic for the old Dublin *Evening Press* and had seen my earlier theatre productions. This would have included the gay relationship in *When Did You Last See My Mother?* at Trinity. Aodhan was gay so that must have struck a chord with him. He went on to write an unusual screenplay, *Night Train*, about that rarity in cinema, a love affair between two older people. Sensitively directed by John Lynch and beautifully played by John Hurt and Brenda Blethyn, it was a real breakthrough for him. Although he struggled to follow it up, Aodhan continued to write eloquently, particularly about Irish homophobia. Despite being intelligent and articulate, he was a troubled man who became alcoholic and sadly died much too early.

Colum McCann's drama, *Flaherty's Window*, about an ex-boxer, his relationship with his Mexican wife and his past in the fight game was another of my early productions. Colum is a fine writer but perhaps he's more of a novelist than a dramatist. His well wrought prose shone through but dramatically the piece meandered a bit. There's such a difference between the personal

Flaherty's Window by Colum McCann. BBC Radio 4, 1997. Radio Times illustration.

interior world of a novel and the more public one of dramatised action.

Michael McLaverty was another novelist whose work I produced. He was also a school teacher who became the Principal of St Thomas's Secondary Intermediate School in Balllymurphy, Belfast. In the ensuing decade several of his pupils joined the IRA. For a period, Seamus Heaney was on his staff and admired his writing.

School for Hope was an adaptation of his novel set in 1950s Ulster. At the centre of the story is teacher Nora Byrne's love affair with an older local headmaster of a rural school. The play dramatises how a lie about her past overshadows their relationship and is used by the headmaster's bitter sister to try to destroy the seeds of their love. Nora hasn't admitted that her mother and sister died of TB and, in those days, TB was a plague in Ireland. Some people treated it in the same way as they did AIDS in the 1980s. McLaverty was a committed Catholic and his story is a crisis of conscience. Nora didn't want the revelation of her mother dying in a sanatorium to ruin her chances of marriage, and yet she felt guilty hiding the fact. McLaverty was a religious writer and although his views are different to mine, it was good to get away from materialistic modern dramas and be challenged by a writer with a strong sense of metaphysical, religious and moral values. The production was greatly aided by the fine central performance of Laura Hughes, as Nora, the outsider coming to take up a new job in a village and discovering herself suddenly entangled in a troubling romance. Damian Gorman, the Irish poet and dramatist, adapted the story with insight but maybe not enough was at stake dramatically to make it wholly satisfying to a modern audience. However, even though forgiveness and reconcilation were perhaps too easily earned, one couldn't deny the force of McLaverty's distinctive vision.

THE MAD WORLD OF DOCUMENTARIES

52 – Enter Van the Man

GIVEN THE NATURE OF THE bidding culture, Producers were encouraged to try to get commissions outside their specialist area. I gambled on Radio 2. I had an interest in music but I wasn't an expert so I just threw my hat into the ring more in hope than expectation. Much to my surprise, I discovered that my proposal for a 60-minute music documentary on Van Morrison, the most obdurate of interviewees, had been accepted. When I lined up possible contributors including Van himself, it wasn't long before Van's manager came back and said that Van wanted to know whom I was going to interview. Insecure about the project, I had consulted with music journalist Steve Turner after reading his book on the Belfast rebel. After sending the interview list to Van's manager, I then received a fax from Peter Carter-Ruck and Partners, one of the most ruthless litigant lawyers in London, threatening me with legal action if various people mentioned in Steve's book made the same comments in the programme. What an introduction to the world of radio documentary. Myrtle laughed and told me, 'not to worry, Roland, as they're now letting out lots of the "terrorists", there'll be plenty of room in prison and we can come out and visit you!' Despite the hassle and Van wanting to control my programme, I managed to get a perfectly good list of interviewees together, including several in America. This was certainly going to be an adventure.

After interviewing members of his old band, Them, in Belfast, I flew out to New York. I stayed at the Quality Hotel which was an ironic name as it was cheap and a bit of a dive. The idea that BBC producers were staying at the Plaza, swanning around with fashionable NY dignitaries, was pure fantasy. With such a small budget, I was a second class tourist. I was put on the top floor at the Quality and as I suffered from claustrophobia in lifts, I felt that my journey to breakfast everyday was a massive accomplishment. I also discovered that in the most capitalist country in the world, which trumpets the glories of the free market, you pay an awful lot of tax. When I got the final bill, there were quite a few extras that weren't advertised – federal tax, state tax etc. Given that unions have considerable power in cities like New York, the US is a lot more regulated than people think.

First I made contact with ace guitarist John Platania. John had played on Van's albums, *Moondance* and *It's Too Late to Stop Now*. He was also a member of Van's Caledonian Soul Orchestra that toured in 1973. I saw them at the Rainbow Theatre Finsbury Park, which is up there as one of my favourite all-time live gigs. I touched base with John in New York and remember him yelling on a public phone, 'can I talk to a real person please?' It was my introduction to the frustration of digital call systems. Via Amtrak, I later went out to his home. He picked me up at the station and drove me to his wooden porched house with its sedate balcony. Inside his sitting room, I'd just got out my massive digital recorder that I was hauling around, when it immediately started to pour down with rain, accompanied by occasional lightning. We both laughed and got on with it. I knew that we'd end up with small 'bites' of conversation so it wasn't going to be massively intrusive. In any case, we could always put music underneath it. John isn't your typical musician and I can understand why Van and Don McLean took him on the road. Not only did he have a great musical vibe but he was someone you could talk to about many other topics. Meeting such a person made me enjoy doing something different to drama and getting away from BBC politics. As I journeyed around talking to people the subject came more clearly into focus. By a strange osmosis, I began to feel I knew Van a bit, even though I'd never met him.

My next port of call was Jay Berliner, the guitarist on that esteemed album, *Astral Weeks*. Jay and his family lived on the West Side in a flat on the highest floor. The lift seemed more suitable for products than human beings. I stared at the tiny elevator with severe trepidation as if it was a prison cell. However, after pacing nervously up and down for a few minutes, I suddenly jumped in like a deep sea diver hoping for the best. After pressing the relevant button and closing my eyes, I finally surfaced at the top floor and was welcomed by a very warm family. I sat around their dining room table drinking tea while Jay proceeded to tell me about the way the industry was changing and how it affected him: computerisation meant that session work was getting more limited and even pit bands on Broadway were becoming smaller. Consequently, it was now more difficult to do such work as the creative jam of *Astral Weeks*. After completing the interview, I went out on to their roof to get a magnificent view of the Hudson River on a beautiful autumn day. Some years later, I was delighted to read that Jay was reunited with Van for his successful *Astral Weeks* concert in LA.

Next, I travelled to that most European of American cities, Boston. A relaxed train journey from New York's Grand Central Station gave me the opportunity to view the serenity of the East Coast. Eventually, I made my way from Boston Station to my hotel, Cambridge House on Massachusetts Avenue. It was the best of the trip, a stylish, nineteenth century building with a beautifully carpeted room and canopied double bed. I needed such comfort after my tatty NY accomodation. It was a bit remote from the centre of town but I was going to have to use taxis anyway. In any case, I enjoyed walking, getting a feel of a quiet, stylish residential area. I'd come to interview John Payne, a flautist, and Tom Kielbania, a bass player, who had both played with Van in coffee houses in his early years in the States. Payne also went on to play on *Astral Weeks*. Both were now involved in different activities. Payne was teaching; Kielbania, surrounded by a young family, was organising a music festival. Their days as regular performers were in the past but nonetheless their time with Van was a seminal part of their professional lives.

The next part of the trip was in Nashville where it was quite a shock to see guys walking around with huge cowboy hats, hard-edged boots and spurs. There was an energy to the town but also a tackiness as well, with its down market country and western museums and out of date beauty contests. The bars were certainly lively and the people friendly. I stayed in my first motel, Shoney's Inn on Demonbreun Street. No, I wasn't greeted by Norman Bates, but a business-like middle-aged woman. I was there to interview Mary Martin, an early manager of Van's. She was a former assistant to Albert Grossman, Bob Dylan's manager, and linked him up with The Band. She also signed Emmylou Harris and Leonard Cohen for Warners. Mary has a reputation of being a tough lady – allegedly, she once left hooked a rude patron in a New York nightclub – but to me she was more like a charming, meandering ex-hippie. Maybe that side attracted Van in those days as she seemed to give him the management support to get his career started.

My final destination was LA. I thought I was being clever staying in the centre of town. Little did I know that central LA is dead. It's just a place where there are offices and fitness clubs with little night life. I lodged at the Orchid Hotel on South Flower Street, which should be twinned with my beloved Quality Inn in NY. Only the Orchid was even more downmarket, cold and impersonal, a purgatorial, sparse place where nobody stayed long. One of Raymond Chandler's characters of yesteryear might have bunked down there for a night.

I was in LA to meet Joe Smith, a former Vice President of Warners with responsibility for artists and repertoire. I went to his home at in Malibu, so this meant a pleasant coastal taxi drive to his ornate, Spanish-styled house. As I descended down the pebbled drive, I was greeted by a lively, warm, loquacious personality. The trouble was that he was used to taking control and I couldn't get a word in edgeways. Fortuitously, while I was there, Joe received a call from Ted Templeman, one of Van's former producers, and got diverted into a conversation about Van's idiosyncrasies. Ted had just completed an album and was taking a break in the Hollywood Hills. 'Unfortunately he won't be able to meet up with you,' regaled Joe before continuing his ramblings. When he insisted on taking the microphone from me, I knew that we were into even more of a monologue and that I wasn't going to get anything of further interest. In fact, Joe was semi-retired, but once a recording exec always a recording exec. Mind you, it was a nice pad.

Back in Belfast I arranged a few further interviews: Tom Paulin to do the more literary slant, Harvey Goldsmith to cover Van's celebrated performance at The Band's final concert and Neil Drinkwater, his current MD, to bring me up to date with his latest work. Publicly, Paulin has a reputation for being a cantakerous and pugnacious intellectual, but at home in his Oxford study he was both friendly and accomodating. As a good poet himself, he showed considerable insight into Van's use of language and undoubted poetic sensibility. Harvey is an admirer of another side of Van's talent – his intuitive, creative spontaneity – and loved it when his live performances were a one-off riff. In fact, I'd heard that in Belfast, during their days at the Maritime Hotel, Them used to do a 40-minute version of 'Gloria'. That must have been something to behold.

When I went to Neil's home in east London, his partner, June Boyce, an experienced singer, looked at me pitifully as one might at a child whose expectations are about to be disappointed. 'I think you might have your work cut out,' she said, knowing Van's reputation for volatility. Neil then added, 'As you know, he does go through a lot of musicians.' He thought Van was brilliantly spontaneous but seemingly could drive musicians mad, particularly when he kept changing the running order. Apparently, Van rang Neil on Christmas Day wanting to discuss the gigs. When he was reminded of the day and that all Neil's family were present, it didn't seem to sink in.

Working for Radio 2 was a liberating experience. I was developing my skills as a producer working in a new area and recording all the interviews myself. I'd been to the USA, got interesting material and met some unusual people. There was one problem. I hadn't got an interview with the man myself, which was a bit of a hole in the programme. What's more, there didn't seem to be any suitable archive. Van rarely gave interviews, and when he did they weren't particularly illuminating. He seemed to be a shy and private man with an unusual talent. So this was rather like the writer who wrote a book on J.D. Salinger, the renowned literary recluse, and couldn't get him to contribute. Hopefully, it wouldn't matter. Van would be my Gatsby, the man at the party that no one initially sees or, in this case, hears. Maybe this would make the programme more interesting?

Of course, there were sightings and rumours; Ireland is a haven for conjecture. A friend of mine told me that he had a mate who saw Van in a cafe near Bangor. When the great man got up and departed, he discovered that he had left a piece of paper on a table. Immediately, his friend thought: did it contain exciting lyrics for his next album, a souvenir for posterity that might interest Christie's? However, when he went over and looked at the writing, the friend didn't discover neatly honed poetry but a mundane shopping list. I just hoped my programme didn't give listeners the same disappointment.

First, I had to get the links recorded. To do this I'd engaged Marianne Faithfull. When I travelled down on the train to Dublin to record her at RTÉ, I was apprehensive. Would she be there on time? Would she have looked at the script sufficiently? Would she do it in the allotted time? My fears were groundless.

Marianne was there in reception ready to go. Stylish and intelligent, I enjoyed working with her. She'd recorded a really good version of Van's song 'Madame George' and admired his work. On occasions, they met in Dublin where she was living. When she had to do several takes on one part of the script she said, 'I don't want to screw up on this otherwise I'm not going to be able to face Van!' Authorititively, she corrected me about some American pronunciation and within a few hours we were finished.

When the programme finally came out, I think the best part of it was the early section with Ulster musicians like Billy Harrison (now an electrician whom I interviewed on a motorboat) and Jim Armstrong of Them; it had the real smack of authenticity. The rest was fine but it didn't have the intimate detail of the early years. Nonetheless, I was pleased with my first effort. I'd managed to put a good listen together. Radio 2 had the highest ratings of any station in these islands, and therefore no work of mine had reached so many people.

Working for Radio 2 was always enjoyable. The Controller of the station was James Moir, assisted by Lesley Douglas. Jimmy was from the old school; he'd worked as Controller of Light Entertainment on TV and produced *The Generation Game* with Bruce Forsyth. In contrast to Radio 4, his meetings were always to the point and mercifully brief. Jimmy didn't tell producers how to produce, he just encouraged them to make better programmes. His notes were succinct and to the point: a little less of this, a little more of that. Sometimes his jokes were a bit inappropriate and when he came over to Belfast, he seemed to insist on showing off his bad Irish accent at some stage in the proceedings. However, despite his eccentricities, he was a warm, shrewd man. Probably the best Controller during my period at the BBC. You certainly left the room wanting to work for him. He didn't burden you with undue pressure. No wonder he managed to turn round Radio 2 from a fuddy duddy station to an energetic, modern, wide-ranging one. He brought the listening age down, widened the demographic and brought in new presenters to radicalise the station.

Jimmy was aided in his success by Lesley Douglas, who had a much better modern music knowledge. Jimmy sensibly listened to Lesley and made sure the play list widened. Lesley had been a producer and had a very good knowledge of the station. When Jimmy finally retired Lesley took over and rightly so. She continued and developed his good work A Geordie, knowledgeable with a good sense of fun and unlike the Oxbridge-educated execs of Radio 3 and 4, her regime was younger, audacious and less formal.

Unfortunately, Lesley's risk-taking came a cropper when she became obsessed with comedians, Russell Brand in particular. Brand was given too much leeway with insufficient oversight and this led to the notorious obscene phone call being made to Andrew Sachs. Lesley hadn't heard the material before it was broadcast. The ensuing public and press furore led to her resignation. She left the BBC after many years of good work. A pity that a distinguished BBC career was brought to a rather ignominious end.

53 – My Meeting With Joni

THE VAN MORRISON DOC WAS the first music one to be produced for Radio 2 by BBC Northern Ireland, so I'd managed to pave the way there. Much to my surprise, my following offer to produce a doc on Joni Mitchell was also accepted. Of course, I'd grown up with Joni Mitchell records but I wasn't a connoisseur of her work. However a journey of discovery can be a good starting point for the listener so I felt I had a chance of making an interesting programme. I proceeded to stay around late in my Belfast office for a few weeks while ringing Los Angeles. Unlike the Van Morrison trauma, the actual subject of the programme was willing to be interviewed and I was to meet Joni at LA's Bel Air Hotel.

This was one of the few times when the reality was the same as the advert. The hotel consisted of beautiful, extensive gardens, ornate, opulent furniture and smart restaurants. Recently there have been public protests against the owner, the Sultan of Brunei, because of his country's severe legislation against gays and adulterers. Back then, it was quieter. As I approached the hotel, on a hot sunny afternoon, a wedding was taking place on the approaching lawn. After meeting Joni's PA, who it later transpired later was interested in dog psychiatry, we went into a private room selected for the interview. There the furniture was so fragile and extravagant, I hardly dared sit down. Maybe it was just nervousness although Joni was perfectly friendly and accessible.

After carefully setting up the equipment, I proceeded with the interview. Joni likes talking, in fact in one of her songs there's an aside in which she sends herself up about this trait of her personality. We were getting on well and I was obtaining good copy. The only problem was that when my allotted 40 minutes were up, we'd only just got to the 1970s, the core of her career; I certainly didn't have enough material for a programme. Luckily, after pleading with her PA, who then consulted with Joni, we went into the restaurant and continued chatting. In the hotel's opulent dining room, Joni was treated like royalty. Over the next hour and a half, she talked very freely. It wasn't like speaking to a pop star. She was a highly intelligent woman with diverse interests who wasn't preoccupied with just talking about herself. In fact, I was enjoying the conversation so much that I had to be careful it didn't diverge into too many areas unsuitable for Radio 2.

One of the big things of her life at that time was her reunion with her daughter. Joni had married Chuck Mitchell, another folk singer, when she was very young. She got pregnant and was unable to deal with motherhood when they split up. The result was that she gave up her child for adoption. Apparently, a good relationship with the foster parents led to a reunion after many years. Although this was obviously a big emotional moment in her life, it didn't stop Joni being critical of young people's short attention spans and slavish adherence to technology. I think this particularly came to her attention when she was in a park with her daughter who seemed more interested in her headphones than the beauty around her.

We also touched on politics, jazz and art. Joni went to art school and is an accomplished painter. In fact, sometimes her conversation moves around rather like an errant brush on a canvass. Joni's eclectic approach manifested itself in her album celebrating the life of Charlie Mingus, the great jazz composer and bass player. Joni's homage to Charlie featured a lot of good musicians, but despite the result being distinctive and inventive it sold very badly. She then apparently asked Warners why they were keeping her on their books when she wasn't making them any money. To which the reply was, 'you're a prestige artist.' In any case, she told me that she now made more money from her writing than performing or making albums.

Joni certainly had a strong vision of what she wanted to do and she managed to realise it in the very male dominated world of the 1960s and 1970s. Ironically, she told me that she didn't get on that well with other women. She thought that may be because of her turbulent relationship with her puritanical Canadian mother, who wasn't at all impressed with her Hollywood friends. Nonetheless, a younger female artist like Natalie Merchant, whom I interviewed later in a Kensington hotel during her English tour, was considerably influenced by Joni and sees her as a trail blazer for female singer-songwriters like herself, Suzanne Vega and Sarah McLachlan.

During my conversation with Joni, I took advantage of the high quality wine offered to me. Unfortunately, this nearly made me forget that I was on a job not a social outing. Thankfully, the macabre presence of my monstrous DAT recorder reminded me that I still had work to complete. Despite Joni's seductive charm, I still managed to keep a grip on whether I had sufficient coverage to uphold an hour's narrative. Thank goodness she'd given me more time. I had a feeling that if she saw that you weren't stupid and not a parasitic journalist, she'd be happy to talk. So maybe I passed the test. Finally, when our conversation came to an end, I packed up my equipment and said goodbye to Joni, who disappeared in a stretch limo supplied by Warners. While I awaited more humble transport to take me back to the Crown Plaza Hotel, I was excited about making a programme about such a creative person.

While in LA I also interviewed Graham Nash of Crosby Stills and Nash. Graham, originally from Manchester, lived with Joni in the 1960s. I went to his house at Encino, a well known LA suburb. Most of his family were present and there was a relaxed domestic atmosphere. Graham had what looked like a a big shed at the bottom of his garden which I think was a mini-recording studio. Graham talked about Joni with candid honesty with his wife chipping in with the odd amusing comment. He had a huge respect for her abilities, but told me she wasn't an easy person to live with! A former member of the British group The Hollies, he relished moving to America and tried unsuccessfully to get other members of his family to do likewise.

He acknowledged America's weaknesses and mistakes, but for him it had worked well, getting away from the class-based rigidity of Britain. He was part of the 1960s Laurel Canyon set sneered at by the likes of Johnny Rotten and the punk movement. Graham responded by acidly pointing out that the ageing punk was now living in Beverly Hills.

While in the City of Angels, I also visited Elliot Roberts, a former manager of Joni's, now Neil Young's. His offices were in the middle of a nondescript area of Beverley Hills where every building looks the same. This was at the time of the Monica Lewinsky scandal and Elliot was a Democrat supporter. He was furious with Clinton for his behaviour: 'what can I tell my kids?' he remonstrated. I got a sense that Elliot's parting with Joni was painful. He was after all close to the Laurel Canyon crowd so it was probably like splitting with a friend not just a client. This didn't stop him appreciating her talent and giving an insight into her early years, when he helped her get up and running.

Having completed my interviews, I went to see my friend Colm Meaney who was now living in LA. He was coming to the end of his successful time in *Star Trek*. It was particularly gratifying to see a good mate, who had started playing a very small part in *Hatchet* at the Abbey, go on to do so well in TV and film. It wasn't so long ago that we were sharing a squat together in Whitechapel. It's interesting to note how many Irish actors had to go to America to establish themselves. Gabriel Byrne, Liam Neeson and Colm were all working in Dublin and London for significant periods and did good work, like a lot of other jobbing actors. However, it was difficult to get consistent employment, particularly in the English capital, unless you were embedded in the British theatre from an early stage like ex-RADA student Fiona Shaw.

As with Van Morrison, it was in the States where they found the necessary opportunities to develop their careers. Now, with advanced travel and developing media, the likes of Brendan Gleeson can stay in Ireland and be very successful. However, in those earlier, more difficult times, when Irish theatre and film were very small and you got typecast as an Irish actor in Britain, America seemed an attractive alternative. There any ethnicity would play the doctor or lawyer. Now with multi-cultural Britain, the situation is more flexible. However, in those days, Colm was brave to take the plunge. Not that success came easily. He had been working in New York for some years before moving west and getting the big *Star Trek* break. While we all change over the years, I didn't notice a huge difference in Colm's behaviour. There was still that unpretentious sense of decency and generosity, as well as his wicked sense of humour. We were still having arguments about politics and sport as we had years ago.

In fact, one of the funniest evenings I had with Colm was in Dublin in 1973 when I watched a World Cup qualifying game with him and his brother Liam. Of course, they were supporting Poland who went on to draw and qualify at England's expense. There was a very biased ITV commentary as England missed chance after chance and the Polish goalkeeper made miraculous saves. Colm and Liam made amusing comments about the prejudiced broadcaster while I defiantly cheered the three lions. Aided by a few beers, the proceedings became fairly raucous. Even though I was disappointed by the result, the evening was great fun and we've all had a good laugh about it ever since. It was very good to see such old friends again, Colm of course, but also his ex-wife Bairbre Dowling whom I knew well from my early Dublin days and, according to Dan O'Herlihy, had developed into a strong, powerful actor.

Back in Belfast, I received a disc from Peter Gabriel. I knew Peter when I was at Trinity because he was married to a fellow student's sister. Despite a busy schedule, he had still recorded his thoughts on Joni. In particular, he was illuminating about both her visual approach to music, the way she painted with sound, and her qualities as a poet. It was good to discover that like Peter, all the contributors were part of a mature, grown up pop, which made producing the programme particularly enjoyable. Sometimes entering the pop world you can find yourself meeting too many immature people with large egos, a lot of money and little talent. Unfortunately, the public massage their egos by giving them excessive adulation, wholly disproportionate to their ability. Consequently, they behave in an arrogant and dismissive manner, which can be very wearisome and unprofessional. Contrary to the tabloid 'luvvie' agenda, actors are mostly talented and have to work very hard, whereas too many pop idols are limited, often indulgent and pampered.

Another mature performer, Mary Black, presented the programme and we recorded the links at RTÉ. Mary came with a friend and proved a good choice with her warm voice giving an excellent entry point for the listener. At that time, she also regretted the lack of sufficient outlets for a more sophisticated popular music. As another contributor, jazz legend Wayne Shorter, bemoaned, 'the gatekeepers wont let us in, man', meaning music stations keep to their predictable commercial playlist. Mary had some trouble pronouncing my surname but we got there okay and she completed a good professional job. Now it was time to put the programme together and see what the listeners thought.

It transpired that the Joni Mitchell doc was well received. As with Van the Man, we had good press both before and after the transmission. Many of these articles were supported by pictures, which is the advantage of doing a programme about well known people. After experiencing the limited capacity of theatre audiences, it was very exciting to reach so many people so quickly.

54 – In Search of Mel

THE LAST DOC I PRODUCED during James Moir's tenure was about Mel Tormé, who died in 1999. This involved another trip to the USA to interview colleagues and critics. I started in LA back at the Crown Plaza in Beverly Hills Drive, where to pass the time I studiously observed baseball games without knowing exactly what was going on. I had less problem with the lift because it was so big, often full of families on a break, colourfully over-dressed people enjoying some kind of liaison or business men talking deals. So the journey was more entertaining than horrific. Most Europeans think of LA as being superficial, greedy and commercial. While that's certainly part of it, you can also meet creative and intelligent people. Like a lot of cities in America, there are sharp extremes – you could meet the biggest idiot or the most enlightening artist.

For my first interview I was going to meet the latter, a legend of American music, Mr Artie Shaw. Artie was a bandleader who in the 1930s received adulation on a Beatles-like level. A fine clarinetist, with seductively good looks, he had been married eight times to some of the most celebrated women in the entertainment indus-try, including Lana Turner, Ava Gardner, the best-selling author Kathleen Winsor and the 1940s film star Evelyn Keyes. He also had dated Judy Garland. He'd worked with Mel in the 1940s when Mel was part of a close harmony group, The Mel-Tones. Artie had also led a hugely successful band in different incarnations. In 1938, he was *Downbeat's* King of Swing, beating his main rival, Benny Goodman. Nonetheless, he still got out at the top. Fed up with re-peating the same popular songs night after night, he left the music business never to fully return. A man of left-leaning views, he was brought before the House of Un-American Activities but man-aged to survive. After spending many of his later years in Spain, he eventually returned and was now living at Newbury Park. Artie's assistant had already made formal contact:

> I spoke to Mr Shaw this morning about your request for an interview. He said that Friday 17 October at about 10.30 am is fine. He asks that you call before coming out just to make sure something else doesn't come up unexpectedly.
>
> If you need directions, let me know. If you're staying in the Hollywood area, you should allow at least 45 minutes trav-el time. Mr Shaw's address is listed below. Newbury Park

is officially part of Thousand Oaks (which is in Ventura County) and is located at the Western Edge of town.

Sincerely,

Larry Rose, Asst to Artie Shaw

This was my *Sunset Boulevard* moment, I was going to meet a 93-year-old star in greater LA. I immediately did a deal with my Iranian driver as I also needed to go to Valencia to record Mel's former manager. As we made our way to Artie's abode, the driver gave me a sight-seeing tour pointing out the Paul Getty Museum, where Sinatra used to live, and telling me how badly some stars behaved in his cab. His favourite celebrity was Pete Sampras, the seven-time Wimbledon tennis champion. 'A gentleman, absolute gentleman. Unlike some of the others that I've driven. No class. Not like Mr Sampras.'

It was a long drive and while I enjoyed the scenery and the cabbie's scandal, I got increasingly nervous as we approached chez Shaw. Artie was old and suffering from diabetes. He also had a notorious reputation for being difficult. In short, he was high maintenance. Was I walking into a nightmare?

As soon as we arrived in Ventura County, I started fiddling with my notebook, checking my questions and, most importantly, making sure that the DAT recorder was working. Once we arrived, lo and behold there was the butler, Erich von Stroheim himself, I mean Mr Larry Rose, Mr Shaw's assistant, dead on time, to the second. The door was already open and I made my way into the cosy but modest house. There in the sitting room on a wheelchair, bedecked by a tartan rug, was the man himself. Immediately I scrambled nervously around the legendary musician getting the equipment together, making banal small talk. I did a basic sound test and then I went for it. Artie was formidable but always interesting.

'What book is this for?' he growled.

'No, it's not for a book, Mr Shaw, it's a programme for the BBC.'

'Oh, right.' Then he paused and said, 'but I've just had a documentary produced by the BBC.'

'Yes, but this is for radio.'

'Oh, okay', he retorted, somewhat dismissively.

I dared to venture that I thought the doc was good.

'Yes it was okay', he admitted with reluctance.

When I asked about Mel's instrumental skills, he replied 'No, Mel wasn't a good piano player and he couldn't really play the drums, these were just things he did just to fill in.' That said, Artie was complimentary about Mel's voice and his sense of rhythm and articulation. However, apparently he was the one who first got Mel and The Mel-Tones to sing properly with an orchestra.

Although he may have been arrogant, I found his attitude refreshingly direct and honest. He was no respecter of reputations and had the confidence of an experienced bandleader. You could see how he could be a hard taskmaster, but what he said seemed to make sense. He believed in his views and never resorted to patronising clichés. Of course, while I was there I wanted to ask him about Lana Turner, Ava Gardner and Evelyn Keyes. Then there was his long time in Spain and a whole series of musical developments, let alone his literary and political side. Unfortunately, Radio 2 programmes on Artie had already been done by others and I was there to make a programme about Mel. Larry Rose, my Erich von Stroheim, had left us alone, but now he reappeared dead on cue, like the perfect butler. When I finished. I was ushered out of the sitting room while Artie remained imperious in his wheelchair. As I got to the door, I turned and said, 'Thank you Mr Shaw'.

'Okay, goodbye', he casually replied like a king sitting on his throne, dismissing a minor courtier.

Thank goodness my Iranian taxi driver had struck a deal with me. He was patiently waiting outside and was ready to go to Valencia, which was over the border from Ventura County in the northwest corner of neighbouring LA County. Valencia is a small, Hispanic-influenced town, affluent with many well planned communities, which you could reach by bike or walking. This was in contrast to central LA, where public transport was poor and seeing lots of impoverished people, mainly Hispanics, waiting in a long queue for a crowded bus was common. Amazingly, there was only one subway, which went to Long Beach. When I enquired why there wasn't a more fully-fledged system, people mentioned the soil and LA's earthquake history, but I'm not sure that the will was there when car occupancy was so high and gas relatively cheap.

In Valencia, I discovered that Dale Sheets, Mel's former manager, was an avuncular gentleman who had managed to develop an excellent elderly partnership between Mel and George Shearing. His office in Tournament Road was two-tier. You entered into a light and spacious open plan ground floor then ascended up some stairs to Dale's personal room. I got the sense that he was a stabilising influence on Mel. A genuine fan of his client, Dale looked for opportunities to restart Mel's career as fashions changed. Mel was a jazz singer but not an abstruse one. He had the same accessibility as Ella Fitzgerald. He could be marketed to an older audience who had money and memories of when both Mel and George were younger. However, rather than being a setback in their career, the partnership was a development, producing a series of superb, diverse recordings and opportunities for extensive live appearances. As I got to hear more about Mel Tormé, the thing that came across most was his professionalism and the variety of his output. Here was a singer who could manage a straight pop song, jazz with the best of them, as well as the rhythm and blues of his biggest hit 'Comin' Home Baby'.

The next day I went to meet another seasoned pro, Cy Coleman, author of *Sweet Charity*, who was also an intermittent jazz pianist. Cy had worked with Mel on an album and knew him well. I rang Cy at the Beverly Hills Plaza Hotel. A New Yorker, he was staying on the West Coast because his musical *Like Jazz* was premiering at LA's Mark Taper Forum, another concrete building and the major producing theatre in Los Angeles. He suggested we meet in the rehearsal room at the theatre. As I've never directed a musical, just plays with music, I was fascinated by the process I witnessed. It was very collaborative and there was much consultation between the choreographer, director and musical director. Rather like in opera, all these elements are so inextricably interlinked that it's difficult to proceed without everyone basically being on board. Straight theatre is also an ensemble, but there is less obvious dependency on other parts of the process.

After the rehearsal, Cy sat down and talked of his experiences with Mel. As well as rating him as an excellent jazz singer, particularly his scat which he thought was up there with best, Cy admired his use of lyrics and the way he told a story with a song. A genial Jewish New Yorker from a Russian background, Cy wrote one of my favourite musicals, *Little Me*. I'd seen it three times in the West End with Bruce Forsyth, when I was a student. Although I liked the music, I told Cy how funny it was without reference to the score. Rather the wrong emphasis when talking to the composer. Even though Neil Simon's hilarious script stole the show, I do remember singing Cy's numbers, 'Real Live Girl' and 'I've Got Your Number', admittedly rather badly.

Now it was time to say goodbye to my patient Iranian taxi driver and make my way to the airport. This was post-9/11 and I got the impression that the American authorities weren't as experienced as the British and Irish in security matters. They tended to be heavy-handed, getting passengers to virtually strip before going on board. Los Angeles wasn't as bad as New York, but you wondered if they had been properly trained for such a job.

After surviving the security assault course, I returned to the inimitable Quality Hotel on Broadway and the next day started to interview more contributors. My first visit was to meet Will Friedwald, a respected music writer and critic. Will was keen to see me at the BBC NY office but I preferred to be out on the street with my recorder. When I got to his second floor flat off 6th Avenue, I understood why he was so reluctant to meet there. The place was crowded with books and journals like a Beckettian wasteland. It was as if he just slept and read without doing anything else. It was difficult to move without falling over a book or newspaper. There were few bookcases or filing systems; it was as if an obsessive musical mind had just spilt on the floor.

I pretended not to notice, which was difficult and faintly absurd as the flat was a journalistic bombsite. Struggling to avoid the booby traps of such intellectual debris, I took out the DAT recorder from my bag and struggled through Will's paper jungle to eventually discover a small oasis of floor space. It was such a major manoeuvre that it was akin to some triumphant victory in battle where freedom is at last achieved. Will was in his early forties but his rubbish tip was like that of an old intellectual professor gone mad. Notwithstanding interviewing him in eccentric surroundings, I enjoyed his company. He has an encyclopaedic knowledge of America's popular singers and a great insight into jazz. He rated Mel highly as a major jazz singer, one who got better over the years. As I came down the stairs from Will's claustrophobic flat into the hectic activity of a New York street, full of vendors shouting, music blazing and sirens wailing, it was like taking a great breath of fresh air.

Later I visited Atlantic Records in the centre of the Avenue of the Americas. I was going to meet Ahmet Ertegun, one of the founders of the celebrated recording label. A Turkish immigrant, he founded the company with his brother, Nesuhi, who had recently died. Outside, I looked up at the massive building fearing a long haul in the lift. I waited at reception with some trepidation but was relieved to be greeted by Ahmet's PA Patti Conte, a personable, laid-back Italian-American. Gratefully, I went up in the lift with someone else, while chatting away nervously, pretending I was really in a floating room.

When we got out, it was like entering a large, exotic lounge. At the end of the corridor was a piano where musicians did their auditions. Just off the music area was Ahmet's office. The door was open and he was in the middle of an emotional phone call. Patti went and got some coffee and when Ahmet eventually got off the phone, he told me that a friend had just died. He was obviously upset. He was now eighty, an age when you are likely to attend a lot of funerals.

Ahmet didn't have to work but he obviously loved the industry. In fact, Atlantic was now owned by Warners but Ahmet remained President of the New York Atlantic subsidiary. Originally he and his brother were mainly jazz fans but they ventured into 1960s soul and managed to promote the likes of Aretha Franklin, Solomon Burke and Otis Reading to a wider audience than local labels such as Stax Records could provide. Aided by producer Jerry Wexler, who later became a co-owner, they produced a lot of distinctive, celebrated records. Mind you, this didn't necessarily suit Mel Tormé as I soon discovered.

Ahmet was cautious about Mel. For singers like Mel, the sixties were a difficult period. The Beatles factor was kicking in and the era was essentially about rock groups. For jazz singers, even accessible ones, it wasn't easy as the market was becoming saturated with only what was fashionable. 'Actually, Nesuhi, my late brother, dealt more with Mel,' said Ahmet a bit defensively. He then went on to explain that they were trying to amalgamate rhythm and blues with jazz and get Mel across to a wider audience. They certainly succeeded and 'Comin' Home Baby' is still the most frequently played Mel track. However, Mel didn't like the material he was offered. He'd already called rock 'three chord manure' so it was no surprise that when Nesuhi started jigging about in his room, illustrating various numbers, he thought that his suggested songs were 'putrid'.

'I thought you liked jazz,' Mel fulminated. He was never afraid of an opinion. In fact, I remember seeing a documentary on Duke Ellington, during which Mel boldly stated that the celebrated Ellington band were sometimes awful because none of them could read music. They were great with the Ellington tunes they knew but useless adapting to a new singer with a different repertoire. In fact, Duke and Mel had an argument about billing which ended with an unsatisfactory compromise. So being robust, I could imagine Mel's disgust at Nesuhi's musical plans.

Watching Ahmet somewhat distractedly fiddle around his desk, I could tell that he respected Mel's talent. The problem was that Mel didn't integrate easily into their commercial policy at the time. Still there was always 'Comin' Home Baby'. At least Ahmet didn't hide behind bland spin and admitted their difficulties with Mel. I enjoyed meeting him. He seemed a real gentleman. Sadly, three years later I read that he collapsed at a Rolling Stones concert and died in hospital a few weeks later.

In his latter years, Mel's closest associate was George Shearing. George was rare among British jazz musicians in going to the States (in 1947) and making it. Not only that, the Battersea-born pianist succeeded despite being blind from birth. In fact, Shearing was a perfect musical companion for Mel. Not only did they share a love of swing and bop, but they also had a great interest in classical music. Mel liked Delius and the Australian composer Percy Grainger. George admired Debussy and Satie. As I talked to George around his dining table in his New York flat on 88th Street, he told me about how he believed he had a perfect musical conversation with Mel. He'd known him for a long time but only in their latter years did they work intimately together. It was as if they rediscovered each other at the perfect time, when they could draw on the wealth of their considerable mutual experience and push each other to new heights.

In George's smart, homely flat, it was clear that his amiable wife Ellie, a former singer herself, was a considerable influence in George's personal and professional life. She got him organised as they moved between the various gigs as well as their homes in New York and Gloucestershire. This was undoubtedly a man who had triumphed over adversity. However, despite being in the States all those years, he still retained his London accent. He was still a Battersea boy at heart, which was touching, especially as that was where I had lived during my childhood. Just before I left to get into another lift, he told me, 'I miss Mel very much.'

Back in London, I'd managed to talk to various British people who'd worked with Mel, including conductor Chris Gunning, who in his twenties, was given the task of recording a London album with the American singer at the old Barnes recording studio. Chris told me that he never met Mel before the session. He just had a good telephone conversation with him but that was all. Before the recording, Chris, who had a young family at the time, had a rough night as he was putting up Phil Woods, the talented bop saxophonist, who in a moment of late night euphoria, opened one of his windows and blasted a musical riff into the West London air.

The next day, when he got to the studio, Chris received a call from Mel saying that the plane had arrived late but he was on his way. Chris continued to rehearse the band until Mel came. At the time, Mel was in the middle of an acrimonious divorce from film star Janette Scott, the beautiful daughter of British character actress Thora Hird. Consequently, Chris was a bit nervous about what to expect. After all, he was a relatively inexperienced conductor paired with a hugely respected popular singer, who was having a torrid personal time and hadn't heard any of his arrangements. Chris needn't have worried as Mel bounded in, apologised for the delay, introduced himself and proceeded to get through the session in very good time with only a few takes for each song. He was incredibly well prepared and happy with the arrangements, only making a few imaginative suggestions. In fact, what's interesting about the London Sessions album is that not only do the numbers sound fresh, and Phil Woods's solos brilliantly freewheeling, but there is genuine emotion in songs of romantic regret. Without indulgence, Mel, like a good actor, was using his most intimate experiences.

Once I'd got a couple of interviews done down the line with Ginny Mancini, Henry's genial wife, who was a leading member of The Mel-Tones group, and Johnny Mandel, one of several great arrangers who'd worked with Mel, I now needed to record the presenter. I'd booked John Dankworth and as both he and Cleo Laine were touring in the States, we recorded the links at ABC in New York. It was exciting to do this in America, even though when you have limited time, you're a little wary of working with others who may have a different way of doing things. As it transpired, I needn't have been concerned as our technician, Jeff Rider, was fine. John wasn't the greatest presenter. Sometimes he needed several takes but he had a strong command of the subject and when he made a suggestion it was helpful, not least when he noticed a mistake in Cy Coleman's piano playing on one of the selected recording tracks. Above all, he was professional and good humoured. He told us of his surprise when he was recently reintroduced to Wally Stott, the celebrated composer/arranger for such BBC programmes as *Hancock's Half Hour* and *The Goon Show*, as well as Scott Walker's Jacques Brel album. Wally had now emigrated to the States and wasn't Wally anymore but Angela Morley. 'When I was introduced after many years knowing him as Wally,' said John, 'I was a bit lost for words.'

55 – The Brilliance of Brando

AFTER JAMES MOIR'S RETIREMENT, I feared that I wouldn't get any other commissions from Radio 2. Although the Mel Tormé programme seemed to please the listeners, Lesley Douglas, Jimmy's successor, was never that keen on doing it as her musical tastes were different. However, when Marlon Brando died in 2004, an opportunity arose for a tribute and Lesley accepted my offer.

Brando was one of the most influential of performers: he modernised acting and made it relevant and exciting to a wide audience. Although in the later part of his career he lost interest and seemed to be taking a perverse delight in sending up bad films, he'd already carved out his name in movie history. Cuts in budgets meant that I couldn't travel to the States and had to use a 'stringer' to ask my questions. Although this meant I was more detached from the programme, it didn't lessen my commitment. In particular, I was determined to give air time to Brando's much neglected theatre career.

Brando came out of that exciting time on Broadway in the late 40s to early 50s when Tennessee Williams and Arthur Miller led a new wave of writing in American theatre. It's often forgotten that Brando had appeared in the theatre production of *A Streetcar Named Desire* over 700 times. In his Earls Court split level flat, I was fortunate enough to interview the distinguished actor Alec

McCowen, who as a young thespian working in summer stock, saw Elia Kazan's ground breaking Broadway production. Alec's training was more of a classical English nature, but when he saw Brando in *Streetcar* he said he had to rethink his approach to acting. He was bowled over by his performance. There was something natural, unforced, spontaneous and less coldly technical than the British method. Immediately he booked to see another performance, in which Brando did things which were sufficiently different to tantalise and intrigue. You never knew what he was going to do next, whereas too much acting of the day was flat and predictable.

Alec tried to persuade his British colleagues of the virtues of this new style of American acting, but he didn't get much of a response. For them, there was too much mumbling and behaviourism and too little light and shade. They thought that even if it worked for the shorter scenes of films, it couldn't sustain a big part in the theatre. When Alec assured them that Brando did so on stage in *Streetcar*, they remained arrogantly sceptical.

Although Brando is always labelled as a method actor, he disliked Lee Strasberg, Director of the Actor's Studio, and only attended a few classes. In fact, he was much more influenced by Stella Adler, who had detached herself from Strasberg. We interviewed Ellen Adler, Stella's daughter, who implied that Marlon had almost become part of their family, when he was a young country hick from Ohio living in the Big Apple for the first time. Stella, who was married to the distinguished director and critic Harold Clurman, split with Strasberg over interpreting Stanvislaski's system, finding Strasberg's obsession with emotional memory at the expense of the imagination counter-productive. Although she believed in research and scrutinous observation, she didn't have such an oppressively psychological approach to acting like Strasberg's.

Although I missed interviewing contributors in the States, I talked to several in London. One of these was Michael Winner, who was certainly the most arrogant man I'd yet interviewed. I approached Winner's Kensington house with trepidation. I never liked any of his films. He was a good hustler but a lousy film maker.

How he'd managed to work with such Hollywood legends as Robert Mitchum, Burt Lancaster and Orson Welles, God only knows. Probably because he was a hard-nosed, clever English salesman, who intrigued them as a foreign eccentric. As a director he was calculating, crass and insensitive.

I was greeted at the massive gates by a lady I presumed to be his genteel wife who, after ushering me inside, asked me to wait downstairs. There, in the basement, was Winner's own cinema, a dungeon of egocentricity, highlighted by a huge director's chair with his name emblazoned on the back. Opposite a giant cinema screen, I was struggling with my equipment. After a delayed pause, Winner came down. As I made small talk with him, he abruptly snapped, 'Hurry up, I haven't got all day.' I felt like telling him to go and do the proverbial and walk out of his bloody cell of self-glorification but I recovered just in time to keep my cool. Luckily, I got the recorder to work, excusing myself that these days you had to do all the technical work oneself. The stony-faced Winner was unmoved.

Winner was more interested in informing me how Marlon was a very close friend and how they got on so well and that he remained in touch with him over the years. I couldn't substantiate this but it felt like a lot of baloney. When I later talked to Stephanie Beacham, who starred with Marlon in Winner's film *The Nightcomers*, she intimated that Winner's version of working with him wasn't totally accurate, which didn't surprise me. *The Nightcomers* is a version of Henry James's *The Turn of the Screw*. Marlon is good in it as the malevolent Peter Quince, despite a variable Irish accent. However the film looks slapdash and cheap compared to Jack Clayton's *The Innocents*, which dramatises similar material with genuine vision and tension. As Winner continued to rant on about how Marlon was his best friend, a part of me was turning off. There was no exchange about what he was trying to do with the film and how Marlon was playing his part. Winner was more interested in advertisements for himself.

Someone who genuinely did have a good relationship with Marlon was Tim Seely, who was in *Mutiny on the Bounty*. Somewhat regal and no doubt a bit of a roué in his day, Tim talked to me in the sitting room of his elegant Farnham house. Many actors on *Mutiny* got fed up with Brando, who apparently instigated delays and continual script changes, which led to original director Carol Reed's departure. However, Tim seemed to retain a cordial friendship with him, probably due to a shared love of Tahiti, its women and the sun. After meeting in London for a meal not long after the movie finished, they lost touch. Then, many years later, Tim's son, while in Los Angeles, had managed by various means of miraculous subterfuge to get hold of Marlon's private telephone number. When Tim rang, the housekeeper said Marlon was asleep but she'd tell him he called. A few hours later Marlon rang Tim in Farnham and proceeded to speak to him for half an hour. I think in his later years Marlon, like Dietrich, became a bit of a phone addict, contacting people at whim all over the world.

My final interview was with Susannah York in Clapham. Susannah was more than an actress. She was a political activist involved in many causes including the release of Israeli nuclear technician Mordechai Vanunu, who was kidnapped and imprisoned after revealing his country's nuclear weapons programme. She was also involved in producing plays of new or rarely seen work in fringe venues. She told me that many of her male colleagues had given up acting as they grew old, seeing it as something rather silly to keep doing. She felt the opposite, believing it was still important and remained fully committed. However, in *Superman*, as the set collapsed and both of them were scurrying about in the rubble, Marlon turned to Susannah and said, 'this is a bloody stupid way to earn a living!'

I enjoyed putting the Brando programme together even though it was frustrating at times. American studios asked hugely exorbitant rates for short clips, totally disproportionate to my budget. Potential contributors wouldn't talk about Brando again as they'd already done so. Unfortunately, this meant that I had to resort to some old archive material. However, we did have some new and interesting insights from people like his close friend producer Jay Kantor, who reminded us that getting Marlon to do anything was difficult. Marlon was apparently lazy by inclination and getting him to go as far as committing to a movie was a major undertaking. No wonder he only made 41 films in a 54-year career.

I also met up with George Englund who directed him in *The Ugly American* and knew him from an early age. At a dark, subterranean West End hotel, he told me that because his father always put him down and his mother was an alcoholic, acting was an outlet for the acceptance he never got in his early years. It seemed that Marlon then spent quite a bit of time taking revenge on the world for his awful childhood. When he wanted to channel his experiences into his work he gave some wonderfully creative performances. Unfortunately, he didn't really stretch himself much in his later years. There were some good performances, but not on the level of his early work. I don't think he really committed himself fully to a film after *Last Tango in Paris*. I think he resented the invasion of his privacy in that role, given its intimate improvisations drawn from his own life. After that, he decided to not to engage in much emotional revelation.

Later, his personal life, already complicated by having sixteen children, spiralled out of control after the killing of his daughter Cheyenne's boy friend, Dag Drollett. His son Christian was convicted for that murder, and Cheyenne subsequently hanged herself. Maybe, he felt that he had enough personal intrusion and tragedy without exploring it in his work.

At the time of the Brando doc, Radio 2 were very much into celebrity presenting. Given this in mind, I looked for Val Kilmer to front the programme. At the time, he was in London starring in a West End production of *The Postman Always Rings Twice*. It wasn't a superficial choice. Val was inspired by Brando, and after working with him they became friends. Some of the quality newspapers were on a witchhunt against such Radio 2 presenters, Johnny Depp having already been criticised for presenting *The*

James Dean Story. However, a Radio 2 programme isn't targeted just for *Guardian* and *Irish Times* readers, and if you want to reach out to the truckers travelling around the country, you've got to get their attention quickly. If you do this with somebody who is a film star and has some knowledge of the subject, you can reach a wider listening public, which is what a national music station is all about.

When Val said yes, I went to see his theatre show and made a rather fruitless attempt to talk to him afterwards. Although you feel that some Hollywood stars come to the West End for some mythical badge of honour, Val was impressive as the central protagonist in *Postman*. Unfortunately, American actors don't move between the media and theatre in the way Irish and British actors do, but despite not appearing on stage for some time, Val did a good job.

While he was in London, it was difficult making contact. He seemed to go through a lot of PAs but eventually I tracked the latest employee down and delivered the script to an obscure Pimlico apartment. On the recording day, when Val hadn't showed up on time, I got a bit apprehensive. Then to my relief, I got a call that he was stuck in traffic. When he eventually arrived at the Sound House Studios near Shepherd's Bush, he seemed relaxed and flirted freely with our female sound engineer. I liked working with him. He took the script off the page well and responded positively to suggestions. When I asked him to record his own feelings about Marlon he was most illuminating. In an ideal world, I would have cut these into the programme. Unfortunately, I was limited by the programme's structure and omitted it. This was a pity as Val gave a very personal insight into both how as a kid he became inspired by watching Marlon on TV and how later, when working with him, he appreciated his friendship.

The Marlon Brando Story was the last doc that I produced for BBC Radio 2. It was the end of a fruitful journey for me. I never expected to be making documentaries. I came to Belfast as a drama producer and thought that my work would be just to do with plays. My development in the music documentary area was due to the new multi-tasking culture. This was a positive aspect of this policy as far as I was concerned. Even though it was very hard, slow work getting all the research done, the interviews completed and writing a suitable script, I did enjoy it. Mainly because I was genuinely interested in the subject, able to travel extensively and engage with many interesting people. It certainly brought out my greater sense of curiosity in exploring other aspects of entertainment.

At times, it dovetailed with drama, like when I produced an amusing, idiosyncratic play about the vicarious nature of Van Morrison's fans, *King of the Blues* by Neil Donnelly. I also felt that interviewing contributors helped me to listen more carefully when directing plays. Especially when amidst the madcap emotions of production pressures, you can easily go deaf and stop having a conversation. Furthermore, it was good to be at the core of popular culture. Graham Greene once said that it's wrong to be led by popular taste, but it's also fatal to ignore it. Most of my career I had been involved with well written plays that were often produced by subsidised theatres or the BBC for a mainly middle class audience. With Radio 2, prompted by great press coverage, I was breaking that mould, consistently communicating with a wider, more diverse public, many of whom had no interest in drama.

MORE RADIO DRAMAS

56 – Bi-Media Outcomes and Spangles Series

ALTHOUGH I'D PIONEERED BBC Northern Ireland production for Radio 2, it had only a marginal bearing on the Drama Department. Obsessed with continual change, the BBC was now going bi-media, which meant that radio departments would be joined with television. Our small tightly knit group was now having to merge with a bigger, more corporate department and transfer to the cold white glare of the open offices in Great Victoria Street opposite the Opera House. Here there would be no privacy or intimacy, instead Kafkesque opportunities for management to observe and judge. Still we had time for a last hurrah in our old snug in Ormeau Avenue. Around this time, I produced my only series, *Spangles*

Spangles 'n' Tights by Christopher Fitz-Simon. Episode 2. The Ambassador.
BBC Radio 4, 1998. RJ, Ali White, David Kelly, Pauline McLynn,
Christopher Fitz-Simon (writer), Sylvia Syms, Eugene O'Brien, Myrtle
Johnston (Production Assistant), Frank Kelly and Bosco Hogan.

'n' Tights, about a Dublin theatrical costumiers shop. Written by
Christopher Fitz-Simon, it was funny and camp. We had a terrific
cast which included Frank Kelly, Pauline McLynn and David Kelly,
as well as guest stars like the eccentric Sylvia Syms. We had great
fun in the studio recording the series. Maybe too much fun. Everybody seemed to find it very amusing but we were all theatrical
people. It's usually a dangerous sign when rehearsing a comedy if
actors laugh too much in rehearsal. Unfortunately, James Boyle,
the Controller of Radio 4, disliked it and my hopes of a long running series were dashed. I'd a feeling that it might have offended
his more austere Scottish sensibilty. I'd spent a lot of time working
with a good writer and getting excellent, attractive casts over the
five episodes, now all that work was going into the rubbish bin. In
one sense, Boyle was right. Despite the *Stage* describing the series
as 'an utter delight', it was possibly too high flown for radio and
needed to be projected more intimately. Maybe it was too broad
for a mid-morning transmission and should have been in another

slot. Christopher's big radio success was Ballylennon, which was much more genteel and perfect to go with elevenses. This was a broader comedy. Even so, it had great potential and we could have adjusted and developed the series if we'd been given the necessary support. For instance, BBC TV's *Only Fools and Horses* was unsuccessful in its first series but after further development it ran for years. In modern broadcasting culture you're either an instant hit or miss. Nonetheless, much to my surprise, *Spangles 'n' Tights* was recently resurrected on Radio 4 Extra, the BBC's digital radio station. So now maybe it's on the road to cult status?

57 – The Drumcree Project and BBC Politics

AFTER THIS FAILURE, I GOT involved with one of my most exciting radio projects. It was about the tensions at Drumcree where in 1996 there was rioting after the police eventually allowed an Orange march to go down the controversial Garvaghy Road. At that time, Radio 4 wanted to produce plays which immediately reflected the human stories behind the major events of the day. This was a half hour slot and the whole project needed to be turned around in two weeks and relayed live for transmission. Luckily, we had an excellent writer for the project. Gary Mitchell had been well nurtured by Pam Brighton and had already written good radio and theatre plays. Pam usually directed his work but was busy elsewhere. I talked to her about the forthcoming slot and she generously encouraged me to go ahead. Gary didn't have to do much research, as coming from a working class Protestant community he already had the fuel. What he needed to do was to get behind the headlines and find a personal story which would say something new about a tragic situation, which had not only reached a political impasse but had also led to a loss of life.

Gary chose to centre the play around two brothers, one in the RUC and the other in the Orange Order. In between was the mother trying to hold the family together. In preparation, I went on a recce with John Simpson to record marches a few miles away from Drumcree. There the mood was fairly relaxed. The bands marched and families had picnics in a big open field. Kids were playing with their parents. There were speeches but nothing of a sectarian nature. Most people were more interested in eating food than listening to the Orange dignitaries. In fact, most marches go off peacefully in the North, apart from those in a few incendiary areas, when they become nastily triumphalist and confrontational. There are certainly too many marches but for a lot of people it seems to be more of a traditional day out rather than a political statement.

We didn't record *Drumcree* in studio but on location in and around a Belfast warehouse, Tom Gray, our studio manager, using a portable DAT. This meant that the actors weren't rigidly stuck to a stationary mike but could move around and Tom would pick them up. We used different areas of the warehouse for interiors and a big, cold car park for the exteriors. There are wonderful moments in drama when content and performance perfectly coalesce. This was one of them. Our cast, Lalor Roddy, B.J. Hogg and Trudy Kelly, rose brilliantly to the challenge. Everybody had been affected by Drumcree and were concerned that it might trigger more widespread conflict. The Good Friday Agreement still seemed a long way off. You could tell by the way the company responded to the play that it really meant something to them. The production also marked the start of my relationship with Gary Mitchell, which continued in 2009 with Radio 3's *Echoes of War*, which dramatised the current marginalisation of the Protestant working class (the losers in the Good Friday agreement). After we edited *Drumcree*, we sent it down the line live to London. I remember being in studio with John Simpson as the countdown was enumerated. It was exciting and I was mighty relieved when John's finger hit the button cleanly. If we weren't directly live, it was the next best thing – nearly live!

I just wish the BBC would do more such projects. Of course, it's risky and I was lucky to have a very suitable writer, but there was a wonderful response to the play on the BBC log, most of it positive. Gary had certainly got to the heart of the drama by successfully personalising the issues in a way which illuminated the political situation. One logger (it was before comments on the BBC website) said that it was so good to hear the feelings of ordinary people about what was going on, not just officials and politicians. Another expressed concern that such issues were being dramatised while the conflict was still ongoing and that the BBC should delay transmission of such material. In contrast another listener thought that this was just what the BBC was for and applauded its bravery.

I was delighted that the play provoked such dialogue with the public. However, when I went to have an initial conversation with Robert Cooper, now head of the new bi-media drama department, he said nothing about *Drumcree*. I sat perched like a bird on one of the narrow, fixed-wall seats in his fifth floor Belfast office, as he just talked about his plans for the new department. Before I left his office, I decided to ask him what he thought. 'Lunchtime play', he replied off-handedly. If it was a minor opus why did it get such a good response from listeners and an excellent national review, Robert Hanks of *The Independent* describing it as 'a notable achievement'? It certainly wasn't a good way for Cooper to start our relationship in the new restructured department. Angered by his dismissive response, I left rather than get in to a long conversation. Cooper, tall and lean, proceeded to run his department with peremptory authority. I never felt that he had a great feeling for Ireland. It was as if his job was more of a staging post in his long career. At that time, he was in a powerful position because *Ballykissangel* was bringing in a lot of money to the department, even though the long running series had originated from World Productions, an independent company. The BBC Northern Ireland drama department produced it and it attracted a lot of viewers. Personally, I thought it was a retrograde step for TV drama, reinforcing Irish whimsy. Although it was professionally presented and employed a lot of people, it fitted the blandness of so many TV slots of those times.

Cooper knew a lot more about BBC Radio and TV than I did, but then he should have done, having worked for the corporation since the 1970s. Instead of giving me the benefit of his knowledge, he always seemed more concerned in pointing out his superiority. In fact, I had much more experience of Irish drama than he did. After all, I'd worked in nearly every major theatre north and south, and been in senior positions at two of them. Instead of tapping into that, he seemed more intent on ignoring it. His staff were always people a lot younger than him. Some were certainly talented but they were hardly in a position to challenge him. His meetings were run with a rigid, orchestrated formality. Given the interminable offers system, these were held at regular intervals. Cooper didn't live in Belfast; he was based in London at TV Centre and flew in to address his vexed staff. On taking on the reins of wider power, Cooper was critical of some of my productions at the time, such as John McClelland's *Keep Out Private*, which was actually liked by the powers that be. He also wanted my production of Christina Reid's *The Bomb Damage Sale Wedding Dress*, a modern Belfast version of *La Ronde*, to be reedited. Some of his comments were valid, but I felt that his criticisms were insufficiently balanced by a recognition of the better work I had done.

Of course, the climate was very competitive and there was huge pressure to get enough work on the slate. This made Cooper stress the tried and tested formulaic approach of the day: centring around three-act naturalistic afternoon plays with a strong opening, intriguing development and a final resolution. Certainly I learned things from him about radio, not least that it was not possible to have the more creatively meandering approach you could often apply in the theatre. In broadcasting you need to keep to the commissioning brief, whether you like it or not.

In those days, sadly, there was little leeway for the offbeat and satirical. In pitching, one needed to be precise: in getting to the core of the the story, what it's about, how it would be told and how it sounds. Cooper had to get enough TV and radio commissions accepted to prevent a serious shortfall in the department's budget. He dealt with this efficiently. It's a pity that he did so with such insensitive personal skills.

58 – The Brilliant Miniaturist

MY LATTER DAYS AT BBC Northern Ireland were difficult. It was therefore ironic that I produced some of my best work during that period. One of my favourite dramas during this time was William Trevor's adaptation of his own short story *The Property Of Colette Nervi*. Trevor is a brilliant writer with a wonderful eye for intimate detail. Like another talented Irish novelist, Brian Moore, I always felt he was somewhat marginalised by the Irish literary cognoscenti because he left the country many years ago. That sense of 'betrayal' also permeated around the Abbey where ex-Abbey actors who became successful in London, like T.P. McKenna and Jack MacGowran, were regarded irrationally by some as 'traitors'.

I enjoyed working with William, receiving very precise correspondence from his home in Devon. While we were approaching our recording dates, I thought we might be short for time, always a nightmare for a radio producer. It's always better to have a bit too much dialogue rather than too little. William thought it was sufficient but would give me some more anyway. When we came to edit the play, he was right. We didn't need the extra dialogue. He had been writing radio plays for years and had timed his drama to perfection.

His narrative starts with a very simple situation which then evolves into something much more complicated. A French couple visit a remote Irish village to see an ancient stone circle. When the woman, Colette Nervi, absent-mindedly leaves her handbag on the top of her car and it disappears, it has life-changing repercussions for Mrs Mulally the local shop keeper, her crippled daughter and a local farmer – especially after the daughter receives extravagant presents from the farmer. In a short passage of time, Trevor manages to weave a brilliant moral and dramatic maze which makes for compulsive listening. As the daughter, Marcella Riordan played well below her own age and was totally believeable. She was ably supported by Don Wycherley as the farmer and Trudy Kelly as the housekeeper, who tellingly observes, 'isn't life full of surprises even when it is not doing much more than passing?' Trudy seemed to have a knack of appearing in a lot of my better projects, the *Daily Mail* describing it as 'a gem of a production'. The play was nominated for a Prix Italia in 1999.

59 – Brian's Molly

PRODUCING DRAMA FOR RADIO 3 was always a pleasure as one was given more time and space for complex subjects. I was fortunate to direct Brian Friel's *Molly Sweeney*, a series of three brilliantly interwoven monologues centring around a woman blind from infancy, who undergoes an operation to restore her sight. The play gives you three different view points: from her husband Frank, the surgeon Mr Rice and Molly herself. Radio is in many ways drama for the blind and therefore this play fitted the medium brilliantly. No art form has a greater sense of the confessional than radio, and as each character revealed his or her most innermost thoughts, there was a real sense of the danger of intimacy.

At the centre of the drama is Molly's journey, for while her husband and the surgeon encourage her to have the operation they seem to be using her for their own ends. The reality for Molly is disparate: like the artist, she begins to see the world differently. Sight is far from restorative and contradicts the world she imagined. Her healing therefore becomes traumatic and she retreats into a 'borderline country' where 'what I see may be fantasy or indeed what I take to be imagined may very well be real.' Seeing doesn't equate with understanding, and all three characters seem alienated and exiled like so many Irish people over the years.

Sorcha Cusack was a sensitive, intelligent Molly, the blind judge's daughter. She was well complimented by Ian McElhinney as her enthusiastic husband and Alan Barry as the surgeon looking to restore his self-esteem. Book-ended by traditional Irish music, I kept the production spare and trusted the writing. Although it was very well received, I wondered whether I should have had a tougher approach to the material. If someone is dying or disabled it's easy to get sympathy. Maybe there should have been more struggle to earn that. Perhaps there should have been a greater sense that

Molly Sweeney by Brian Friel. BBC Radio 3, 1997. Myrtle Johnston (Production Assistant), Alan Barry. Sorcha Cusack, Ian McElhinney and RJ.

Molly's a person like any other with obvious foibles, who just happens to be blind, rather than an especially disabled person. The production wasn't sentimental, but there could have been more sense of the everyday to have made it more extraordinary.

Brian's agent had insisted on a casting veto in the contract. As there was no disagreement this wasn't a problem, but such a proviso worries me. Writers aren't experts about actors, and while they should be consulted, the work of bringing a play to life finally lies with those more experienced in such areas. Ireland's writers are the country's greatest artistic strength, but what we might call the Yeats factor has sometimes put them on too lofty a pedestal, immune from the necessary cooperation that is essential for working in a collaborative medium. Also, in *Molly Sweeney* we weren't allowed to change a word, which with a writer of Brian's ability I respect, but such a demand is unrealistic considering that in broadcasting there's an obvious time limit.

Good theatre writers are used to having a lot of freedom, so they're not always the best to adapt to the rigours of TV, film and radio. In fact, *Molly Sweeney* was slightly over time but we managed to rein it in by speeding up the dialogue. However, such digital innovation wasn't noticed because the amount exceeded was distributed over the two hours running time without noticeable effect.

Apparently Brian was inspired in the writing of the play by Oliver Sacks's medical cases, but I was reminded of J.M. Synge's play *The Well of the Saints*, which I saw performed in Hugh Hunt's Abbey production with Eamon Kelly and Máire Ní Dhomhnaill. In that Irish classic, a pair of blind tinkers gratefully return to being blind after a miracle cure. *Molly Sweeney* was a big success, Sorcha's performance, in particular, being universally praised. *The Independent* described it as being 'beautifully produced by Roland Jaquarello.' So that was good!

60 – Our Lady in Belfast

MY WORK FOR RADIO 3 ALSO included another fine drama, *Our Lady of Sligo* by Sebastian Barry. The play had been a success in the theatre but I was keen to have a new cast to recoin the play for radio. Sebastian's compelling drama centres around Mai Kirwan, 'the first woman to wear trousers'. In 1953, Mai is dying and being treated in a cancer ward in Dublin. The play moves between the hospital and Mai's past, particularly her volatile marriage. I had no doubt that I wanted Fiona Shaw to play the part, and I was certainly proved right. From the first reading, it was clear that this was going to be a special experience. Fiona came very prepared, even bringing various changes of clothes to accomodate being in a hospital bed. At the initial reading, she lay down a marker for a standard that everybody had to follow. Given the furtive glances from the rest of the cast when Fiona read her part, they knew the score. When a leading actor really leads, it's wonderful encouragement to all involved, not least the director.

I vividly remember one particular scene, between Fiona and Gerard McSorley, when wracked by drink Mai and Jack have a furious row. Normally I don't like doing more than two or three takes, but in this particular case I kept asking for more as I wanted to hear a certain tiredness in the voice and push the scene to the edge. When I came to the fifth take, I feared the actors would have had enough, but thankfully they responded with commitment and a fierce, savage intensity to record one of the best scenes I've ever heard in a radio production of mine. Sometimes a good actor reaches new brilliant heights. This happened in the case of Gerard McSorley who traded blows with Fiona and gave a moving and magnificent performance as Jack.

Jack had worked in the British Merchant Navy, as an engineer in the Colonial Service in Nigeria and as a Major in the British Army in Burma during World War Two. When he returned to Ireland, he was required to change his uniform. Originally from a humble background, he had modelled himself on the local upper class protestants, but after the revolution 'there were no posh protestants left in Sligo'. Later, he went on to work for the Irish Land Commission, but drink caught up with him and his negligence contributed to the loss of his and Mai's Sligo home.

An Irish Protestant like Mai, marginalised in de Valera's Catholic, nationalist, free state culture, he resorts to excessive drinking, as his marriage deteriorates. Only Mai's imminent death brings a sort of redemptive reconciliation. Gerry brilliantly caught both the charm and dissoluteness of such a character; it was a soulful interpretation of man's lost potential. Mai, his wife, was also a woman whose life had deteriorated: she'd been a student of commerce, a junior tennis champion, a dancer of grace, an elegant, intelligent partner to handsome, able Jack. However, the strain of being a nomad in the British Empire, of being alienated by her countrymen, of witnessing poverty and death in Africa and impoverishment in Ireland, fuelled her ever deteriorating state. She's raped by the local Irish doctor, loses a child which Jack blames on her drinking and behaves ever more recklessly as alcohol takes over and darkness replaces light. Fiona brilliantly brought that contradictory combination of grace and ugliness to the part. Very good actors can change emotions both quickly and truthfully, and Fiona did this to perfection. There was the memory of good times and its potential optimism, but also the anger of such waste during the 'sheer awfulness' of de Valera's Ireland. Fiona's interpretation was highly praised, being described as 'compelling' by *The Observer* and 'a bravura performance' by *The Stage*.

Sebastian was an avuncular presence at the recording. Rather than take the usual position in the control room, he preferred to remain seated in a corner of the studio. Distant but supportive, he only made comments when he felt it necessary. I'd already visited his home in Bray and he'd made the few changes needed for radio. More importantly, I'd listened to him talk about the play and absorbed his intentions. As we chatted in his study amidst the sounds of family life, it was pleasure to meet up with his charming wife Alison, an actress I remember from my time in Dublin.

Sebastian's wonderful use of language really suited radio because he paints such imaginative verbal pictures. Some think he's more of poet than a dramatist, too ethereal for the mundane crudities of conflict, but as in *Our Lady of Sligo*, the tension in his drama is often subtle, gradual and accumulative. He conveys with great insight the frustration and despair of an alienated class. Nobody writes so well about such forgotten people of Ireland. With two central performances well complimented by the powerful Aisling O'Sullivan as Mai's defiant, neglected daughter, Laura Hughes as Maria, her more practical friend who settles for being a farmer's wife, and Kevin Flood, as her loveable, adoring father, *Our Lady of Sligo* had a power and poetic resonance all of its own.

61 – The Final Reckoning

DESPITE SUCH WORK GARNERING praise, my time at BBC Northern Ireland was coming to an end. When I heard from Pat Loughrey, the region's Controller, that I was being made redundant, I wasn't happy. Although he stressed that he wanted me to work freelance, this was no compensation. I'd worked very hard during a difficult time in Radio 4 (our main commissioning outlet), with different Commissioning Editors, constant rejigging of schedules and guidelines, let alone a change of Controller and the merging of a new department. I'd come from the theatre and inevitably it would take me time to get to grips with a new medium. I'd made mistakes, but gradually I'd managed to become more familiar with the general workings, let alone the politics of the BBC.

Rationalisation, or in ordinary parlance, cuts were going to be made to make budgets viable and both Loughrey and Cooper obviously favoured their younger and cheaper staff. In fact, I only had six more years before I'd have to leave anyway, as you can't be a permanent BBC staff member beyond 60. Although I was grateful for the opportunity BBC Northern Ireland gave me, to uproot from London, leave my work in theatre and then be given such a short time in a new position was disappointing. It was as if you couldn't survive one less successful commissioning round.

I wasn't the only one who had suffered from such decisions. There's a ruthlessness behind any corporation and the wheels of the corporate juggernaut grind on remorselessly. In fact, one producer, on his last day working for the BBC, was looking to go through his e-mails when his computer totally shut down at 5.30 pm on the dot. Big Brother had spoken.

However, after calming down and reviewing the situation, there was a side of me that was glad to leave the BBC. Although I had benefitted from Cooper's experience, I didn't want to work with him anymore. In any case, his negativity towards me probably contributed to my departure. I also hated being at the centre of the offers system, which was something more akin to auction dealing than genuine artistic policy. Several BBC executives flew to the States to take business courses and I disliked what I suspected was the importation of American business techniques into a public service.

Terrified of being remote from the people, the BBC too often indulged in inane populism that lauded mediocre talents and ignored more challenging ones. Rather than using a public service to inform, educate as well as entertain, it got closer to the worst banalities of ITV. So scared of seeming elitist, they lost their nerve in revealing the innovative and challenging or exploring a subject in depth. Television was mainly to blame but during this period that culture was beginning to infect radio and there was increasingly less time to explore ideas and themes in the way you could in the theatre. Of course, having only recently started in broadcasting, I wanted to do better work in radio. It was therefore a fitting irony that by the time I left, I had become a much better radio producer. However, if BBC Northern Ireland wanted to let me go after spending so much money on my training and getting me started, I'd be better off somewhere else. I could have done even better work at Belfast if they had put greater faith in me. Instead, I put my abilities to good use mainly elsewhere – as a freelance.

FREELANCE JOURNEYS: THEATRE

62 – Belfast Upon Toon

GOING FREELANCE IS LIKE SAILING away on a journey into the unknown, hoping you'll land in some interesting places. If you fail to find anywhere, you can be cast adrift, bereft in no man's land. Luckily, over the years, I've managed to survive and work in a variety of interesting places, many times on Irish plays.

So let me start my freelance adventures by winding back to the mid-1980s, when I was Artistic Director at Live Theatre Newcastle, where I directed *The Death of Humpty Dumpty* by Graham Reid, a powerful play about the violence of the 'Troubles'. Live Theatre have more recently produced some good writing by local writers, such as Lee Hall of Billy Elliot fame, however then I felt that the company needed a contrast from one type of Geordie working class drama and Graham's play certainly provided that. Few writers write so well about the 'Troubles' from a Protestant perspective, particularly about the ravaging effects of violence. *The Death of Humpty Dumpty* centres around how such a tragedy effected a middle class family. George Sampson had witnessed two paramilitaries placing a car bomb. They see him, track him down and shoot him in his doorway. He becomes a quadriplegic. Humiliated,

The Death of Humpty Dumpty by Graham Reid, designed by Peter Ling.
Live Theatre Newcastle, 1984. Toby Byrne as George Sampson and
Nora Connolly as Sister Thompson.

having lost both his sexuality and authority, George turns viciously on this family with devastating results.

This was one of the hardest plays I've directed, not because of its style but because of its depressing content. Graham had worked as a nurse at Musgrave Park Hospital in Belfast and his experiences there informed the play. Our designer Peter Ling and I decided that it was essential to go over to Ulster to visit the various locations in the play, including the Musgrave. What I witnessed there was deeply moving. A lot of the patients were confined to bed, paralysed from the neck downwards. We were shown around the ward by an extraordinary woman, Sister Kate Grimley, who remained irrefutably cheerful and positive. She told us that in the middle of the night, there was a lot of anguish – crying, shouting, prayers and diverse sounds of desperation in a dark hell. She also mentioned that paramilitaries from opposite sides often became quite friendly with each other as a result of their disablement. Most of the victims were 'Troubles'-related, but some weren't. I remember seeing a pretty young woman with beautiful auburn hair lying paralysed, flat on her bed. When I enquired about her, the Sister told me that she was having an affair with a married man and they went out for a drive and she was the sole victim of a violent car crash.

After leaving Musgrave Park Hospital, I could only marvel at the amazing work that was done by the Sister and her staff. Her commitment was infectious. She ran the ward unsentimentally but with a humanity that was inspiring. She got the patients to be as active as possible, engaging them as if they were able-bodied, strongly believing that they could still make a life for themselves. Rarely have I been in touch with such an amazing human being. She had a commitment beyond the call of duty which was carried out with missionary zeal. Peter and I left the hospital in awe of her work.

After our visit, I felt that directing a play about the subject was trifling in comparison. In fact, there were times when I was forced to question why I was doing the play, when people were undergoing such suffering. Eventually, Peter and I concluded our work by visiting the the Giant's Ring, where in the play George goes with his lover to conduct his clandestine affair. From there we had a magnificent and invigorating view of the town.

Back in Newcastle, County Durham, Peter used the research to conjure up a flexible multi-purpose neutral grey space bounded by a cage-like steel construction, reminiscent of barriers and barricades, with an upstage gauze behind which sinister figures would sporadically appear. We assembled a good cast who worked well together and the play attracted respectable houses. Live Theatre in those days was a small-scale touring company with a lot of one-night stands, but even though it was a tough undertaking, the cast managed to maintain a high standard of performance.

Toby Byrne as George exuded an innate decency from the start, so his later laceration of the family was particularly painful. Mike Dowling, as an optimistic paraplegic, provided effective, contrasting, redemptive humour. Nora Connolly was an efficiently humane nurse and John O'Toole provided menacing black comedy as a malevolent male orderly. Dan Gordon, who had come over from Belfast, was the son who finally smothers his father to death. Maybe, the writing lurched somewhat melodramatically here, but the way Dan played the last scene, struggling with his conscience as to whether he should mercifully kill his father or not, made it very moving.

Dan, along with Amber Bourne and Julie McDonald as his sisters, and Mary Duddy as their mother, created a believable family unit at the heart of the play. To a lot of English people 'the Troubles' was just something on the news, so hopefully we managed to engage our audience with the awful human price being paid – a cost which continues to this day when you think of how many people on both sides were seriously injured, and how the consequences still affect communities: their relations and friends, the local carers, local authorities, and so on. It's a tragedy that it spirals beyond one individual long after it's off the news agenda and Graham's play expressed that brilliantly with power and sensitivity.

The production was certainly well received ('superbly produced' – *The Scotsman*; 'emotional, powerful and moving' – *Evening News*) and got a good response from audiences. On a lighter note, I also received an unusual letter from a young man who said he came to the play, liked the music and requested a playlist. Although he didn't say much about the drama or its production, I suppose it was a compliment of a kind. I'd linked the scenes with Ulster music from Van Morrison to the likes of 'Alternative Ulster' by Stiff Little Fingers and he got hooked on the score. Maybe to him it was a musical?

63 – Magical Days in Galway

ONE OF MY MOST ENJOYABLE freelance productions transpired when I was working for Druid Theatre Company in 1991. I had just left the Lyric and was feeling somewhat rudderless. Consequently, when Maelíosa Stafford asked me to direct a new play, ostensibly set in Elizabethan England, I was delighted. Maelíosa had taken over as Artistic Director while Garry Hynes was at the Abbey.

Cheapside by David Allen is about Robert Greene, a contemporary of Shakespeare's. A comparative failure himself, he resented the success of the Warwickshire upstart. Broke and impecunious, with a pregnant lover, he starts to write pamphlets for Kit Marlowe's conspiring political cronies. This brings him in contact with gossip, chicanery, the thieving Cutting Ball, half brother of his paramour, and Shakespeare himself. Exhausted by the machinations for survival, he dies exhausted, while Shakespeare's career goes from strength to strength. The play had certain parallels with Thatcher's Britain, and designer Kathy Strachan managed to find a visual language that merged it with a cutthroat Elizabethan world. This was most pronounced when Elizabeth I appeared costumed like a cross between the historical Queen and the infamous Prime Minister. Thieves were like punks and Shakespeare was an embryo yuppie. It wasn't done crudely but with innuendo and and style, so it worked. And what a difference live music makes, Brendan O'Regan's original score energising every performance.

There was a fair bit of drinking during rehearsals but nothing excessive. Without wanting to be unsocial, I didn't stay too long in Galway's colourful pubs, with their noisy chatter and searing traditional music. The bracing wind from the Irish Sea was always invigorating as I made my way back through the narrow streets and retreated to my chalet. Working with an Artistic Director who was also an actor in the play, and had cast two of the parts himself, could have been difficult. As it transpired Maelíosa's colleague Patrick Dickson, who had already played Marlowe in Australia, was a good choice and Maelíosa himself was a mesmeric, gnarled Greene. After holding auditions in a Dublin hotel, we cast Ali White, whom I knew well from the Lyric Belfast, and Phelim Drew, a talented character actor. We became a good, close-knit group.

Maelíosa was very adept at wearing two hats at the same time. I never felt the boss was in the room, just another actor. However, during rehearsals it was felt that we should be more precise with the text so it was the first time that I used the actioning technique, whereby with each thought the actor picks a transitive verb, states

246

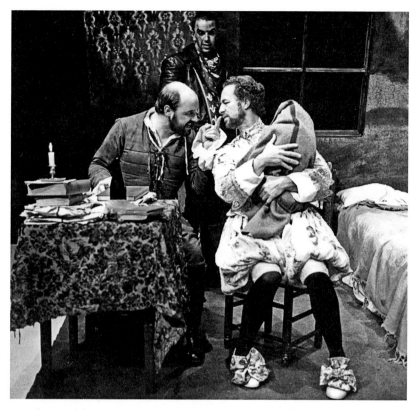

Cheapside by David Allen, designed by Kathy Strachan, Druid Theatre Galway, 1991. Maelíosa Stafford as Robert Greene, Phelim Drew as Cutting Ball and Patrick Dickson as William Shakespeare.

what he or she is doing and then demonstrates an understanding by acting it. It's a slow process but worthwhile if you're looking to get absolute clarity. With this company, it was collaborative fun. However, when you have an obsession with process, it can lead to cerebral performances that don't allow instinct to be imaginatively released, especially if there's a director who seems to prefer a good rehearsal to a successful performance. As one practitioner observed about a particular production, 'they're acting the notes not the play'. What he meant was that the cast hadn't absorbed the notes sufficiently into their own performance but had acted them in isolation as part of the director's credo. They hadn't made the connections to ensure the changes were instinctively their own. Directors haven't helped this. Over the years, I think I've given too many notes, because I've wanted to get as much out of the text as possible. However, the skill is saying the right words to give the actor the key to unlock the part. My later work in radio certainly helped me to be more succinct, but I'm still learning.

Working with such a good group and being in such a great place in the summer, I'd forgotten my Lyric blues. What was so impressive about the Druid was the company spirit. Everybody wanted to support and help the theatre. There was also a buzz around the town about any forthcoming production. Inevitably, this brought about a pressure but not one that I felt acutely. Druid wasn't a repertory company like the Lyric with constant rolling production. They produced seasonally, so there was a good focus of energies. From early on in rehearsal, I had a lot of confidence in the whole company. However, during the technical and dress rehearsal, it had apparently been usual for the crew to work into the early hours as a badge of company honour. When I stopped at 11.00 pm they looked a bit surprised. I didn't want to engage in a marathon of blood, sweat and tears. When people get tired, they make mistakes, arguments flare up and morale drops. I wanted everybody back fresh at 9.00 am.

The next day, a cheery Roger Simonsz was there to design the lighting. He created a suitably eerie world, complimenting the white floor with varied coloured backlight. Kathy's set now looked spectacular – a clever expressionistic merging of the old and new. The opening was smooth and the play much appreciated, earning an enthusiastic audience response and great reviews ('a magnificent production, one of the most clever, funny and moving pieces of theatre I've seen for a long time' – *Sunday Independent*; 'an intoxicating blend of lust, fear and greed' – *The Irish Times*). From there on, we managed to play to full houses. It was a perfect return for me working in the Republic. Unfortunately, for various reasons, the production never moved to Dublin or anywhere else in Ireland. Nonetheless, it was one of the best experiences I'd had in Irish theatre, where the work was good, the audience full and the craic excellent.

Maelíosa pulled off a terrific coup with *Cheapside*. He took a few risks and they came off. I liked both his management style as well as his acting. He's certainly one of the best Artistic Directors I've worked for. After the show, there was tremendous fun and enjoyment and we all trailed around town together attending various local hooleys. Many of the stage management came with us, which was good to see as they'd been so helpful and committed. It was upsetting to hear some years later that one of them, Bernie Walsh, died in a crash after leaving work in the early hours of the morning, leaving behind a wife and three children. His motorcycle collided with a van on the Galway-Moycullen Road. Bernie went out of his way to make my work for Druid happy and successful. He was dedicated and talented. I owed him and his colleagues a lot. However, at the time of the production, such thoughts were distant and after the post-show celebrations had died down, I extricated myself and departed, clutching the Miles Davis CD Phelim had given me as a parting gift from the company. He and Brendan were the music buffs and created the soundtrack to my visit. Knowing my love of jazz, the present was, to quote the modern vernacular, 'very cool'.

64 – Galway Postscript

THERE WAS A SOMEWHAT BIZARRE postscript to my wonderful time in Galway. Later, Roger Simonsz told me of an unusual incident. During one of the previews, he was walking back to his digs, which was the home of a psychologist who offered bed, breakfast and therapy to her patients. While doing so, he noticed a lonely figure at the nearby quay looking out to sea but thought nothing of it. Assuming that he was the last person home he closed the door and put down its heavy bolts with a clunk. Suddenly, there was frantic knocking from outside. He hastily opened the door, only to be confronted by a bewildered, bearded man pleading, 'Just don't close the door on me, just don't!' The man proceeded to run past Roger up the stairs. When his landlady emerged from the kitchen, Roger apologised to her but she assured him it was quite normal.

The man was Brian Keenan, who'd just been released after having been held hostage by Hezbollah for four and a half years.

Roger seemed to attract such drama. When in Belfast lighting at the Opera House for a Short Strand community play, he shouted 'Kill the Workers', meaning the working lights. Blissfully unaware of the IRA split between the Provos and the Workers Party (who had members from Short Strand), he nearly found himself in the midst of a mini-riot. Apparently designer James Helps calmed things down by giving an example of the eccentricities of theatrical terminology by explaining that 'hang the blacks' really means put up black curtains!

65 – Miller Again

IT WAS FITTING THAT AFTER directing *After the Fall*, I should return to the Lyric in 1993 to direct another Arthur Miller play, *All My Sons*. I was delighted that Patricia McBride, the Administrator who was running the theatre in an interim period between Artistic Directors, had given me the opportunity. After accepting, my immediate concerns were in casting. Older parts had been a problem for some years in Ireland because there wasn't a wide-ranging choice. Consequently, I didn't know anybody who could play Joe Keller, the demanding leading part, especially since some candidates like John Hewitt had already done so. In the end, I plumped for Malcolm Terris, an experienced English actor with a strong, bullish, blue collar authority, which masked inner guilt. He was partnered by Lois Baxter, who was elegant and vulnerable, determined to deny her husband's past.

All My Sons is more schematic than *After the Fall*, and has none of those jagged, unpredictable edges that made that drama so unusual. It's an earlier work – a good, solid well made play. Joe Keller allows his colleague Deever to take the rap for making faulty cylinders for planes that brought about the death of 21 pilots. As in the best Miller plays, the public and personal collide and fracture. There's a moral struggle at the heart of the play which engulfs Joe and finally forces him to commit suicide. When he hears that his eldest son Larry killed himself because of his crime, he can't live with himself or others. The play has some great heart-rending exchanges between husband and wife, father and son (Richard Croxford) and son and girlfriend (Catriona Hinds), Deever's daughter, who was previously Larry's girl. Although there's a strong sense of the perils of avoiding public responsibility, Miller seems somewhat righteous at times, too keen to prove a point. Probably in 1947, after World War Two, this was more acceptable. In the 1990s, it seemed simplistic.

I detected the influence of Clifford Odets here. Anger at people's low moral viewpoint, idealistic about a better world and some rather forced melodramatic deaths. However, even allowing for such contrivances there's still a powerful evocation of a family falling apart through cutting moral corners and trying to live a lie. More pertinently, since my production the belief that there have been cover-ups over such such issues as the Iraq War has given the play a greater contemporary potency.

We certainly managed to communicate the play well. The production was passionate but maybe lacking sufficient ambiguity. Also, there could have been a greater heightening of the more classical elements of the play, so that it could have come across with greater non-naturalistic resonance. This would have integrated it's melodramatic moments more easily. A director always needs to answer the question: what is the metaphor for a play? When you can find this, you can more easily enhance a drama, both visually and dramatically. Unfortunately, I didn't fully succeed in doing this.

However, despite such omissions, there were strong performances and an evocatively designed backyard by James Helps. James is a reassuing practitioner who has a good temperament for theatre. He doesn't waste energy on emotion, but looks at a problem with wry detachment and usually provides answers. As does the quiet and taciturn lighting designer, Gerry Jenkinson. Gerry's seen it all before in a career spanning many years, including West End shows, operas, repertory with the Glasgow Citizens as well as the celebrated *Rocky Horror Picture Show*. A green activist and biker, Gerry is a man for a crisis. I remember once all the lights at the Lyric went off just before a show. Ingeniously, Gerry solved the problem with his own inimitable relaxed adroitness and aplomb. I've always felt a bit guilty about him because scheduling in those days meant that there was too little time for lighting. We didn't have the luxury of extensive technical rehearsal. However, what he managed in the time was excellent. Never one for using battalions of lights, Gerry is great at economy of effect. His dappled backyard in *All My Sons* was a good illustration of that. Such work made me pleased to be reunited with old colleagues on such a challenging play.

66 – Comedy at the Lyric

IN 2000, AFTER I LEFT THE BBC in Belfast, I didn't immediately leave Ireland but continued to live off Upper Malone. I had a pleasant house in Greystown Avenue and decided to stay and see what emerged. Initially, my decision bore some fruit. Simon Magill, the recently appointed Associate Director at the Lyric, asked me to direct a new play, *The Butterfly of Killybegs* by Derry writer Brian Foster. It took place in the 1960s. The split level set, designed by Vanessa Hawkins, consisted of a Victorian-style bedroom with torn net curtains and the Pope's picture on the higher tier and a lower living room with 50s flying ducks decor, metal bins and rubbish. Through the windows, as a keyhole away from the prevailing domesticity, you could faintly see the outside world of ships and a dock.

Brian had written a funny drama but it was very similar in plot to Martin McDonagh's *The Beauty Queen of Leenane*. It didn't have the fashionable post-modern parodies so beloved of critics, but used stereotypes in the manner of a Restoration playwright. There was the old mother rooted to her bed dying in the remote Donegal village, locked in a bond of mutual suspicion with her plain daughter having to care for her, the attractive friend encouraging her to

The Butterfly of Killybegs by Brian Foster, designed by Vanessa Hawkins.
Lyric Theatre Belfast, 2000. Natalie Stringer as Middie O'Donnell,
Barbara Adair as Missus Doyle and Anne Bird as Mary Conlon.

get out more and the older bachelor looking for a match. A familiar story, but as an Irish comedian said, 'it's the way you tell 'em'.

Brian is an unusual playwright. The son of a prominent Derry trade unionist, he worked for twelve years at Butlins in Bognor Regis before returning to Ireland in 1985. On resettling in Derry he got encouragement from Gemma McMullan of BBC Northern Ireland and started writing in his mid-thirties. In *Butterfly of Killybegs*, he displays a great ear for dialogue and a wonderful sense of comedy. For his play to work, each character needed to be solidly rooted before being expanded theatrically. In comedy, you also need actors with a great sense of timing. A director can't give a performer such a gift but can only set up him or her to execute it properly. Thankfully, in the case of *Butterfly*, most of the chosen cast had the necessary skills.

My problem was that I had difficulty finding an actor for the mother. After a big search in Dublin, I cast Ronnie Masterson. I'd known Ronnie from my time in Dublin and admired her work with her husband Ray McAnally when they ran Old Quay Productions, and produced many good plays like *The Field* by John B. Keane and

253

The Enemy Within by Brian Friel. Ronnie understood the part well and had the much needed stature for the bedded matriarch, but she was getting old and lacked sharpness. She paraphrased lines and this meant that we sometimes lost the rhythm of the text and the necessary timing. Static characters need strong vocal projection, a new thought needing a new energy, but seemingly through smoking her voice was reedy. Consequently, Ronnie didn't attack the part and give it the size and life that it needed. She was too small-scale and passive, a supporting actor playing a leading part. Thankfully, it wasn't a disaster as she showed several personal qualities in the role – a humorous wilyness and a certain vulnerability – but it could have been so much better, especially as she didn't seem to give the role the necessary commitment and focus. She was always returning to Dublin at every opportunity and I'm not sure that helped her to sufficiently submerge into a demanding role.

The Butterfly of Killybegs by Brian Foster, designed by Vanessa Hawkins.
Lyric Theatre Belfast, 2000. Anne Bird as Mary Conlon and
John Hewitt as Patsy Doogan.

Casting is an important part of play production and my choice on this occasion could have worked out better. The trouble was that there weren't many alternatives. Getting somebody younger would have certainly given the part more energy, but I couldn't find anybody who could make such a transition successfully. In any case, I should have been tougher with Ronnie but her age and health militated against that. I tried to do it the gentle way, but it didn't really work. Unfortunately, all this made it difficult for Anne Bird, playing the frumpy unloved daughter in one of her first leading roles. Anne was terrific, both funny and macabre, and proved herself to be a young leading actor of considerable potential. Surprisingly, I don't think she has appeared in a Lyric production since.

The Butterfly of Killybegs by Brian Foster, designed by Vanessa Hawkins. Lyric Theatre Belfast, 2000. Anne Bird as Mary Conlon.

Her scenes with John Hewitt as Patsy, the middle aged bachelor, were memorably hilarious. The one where he tried to seduce her but gets into a physical tangle was particularly funny. I had worked with John previously, most notably on *The Iceman Cometh* and *Culture Vultures*. He was certainly an actor of rare talent. Maybe because he settled to work in Belfast, he got into too much of a comfort zone, but then after a series of ordinary performances he would give one as good as you'd see anywhere. I was told that there was a reluctance to cast John in TV because he was seen as having a drink problem. What a pity such judgements were so unfairly pinned on him. In the days of BBC TV's *Play for Today*, when you didn't depend on star names or pretty people and could just put a good local actor in the lead, John would have done Belfast proud. Sadly, John passed away in 2008, aged 58, so it was good to

know that in the last theatre production we did together, he produced such a wonderful comic character, an eccentric, frustrated,
lonely bachelor with a bizarre hair parting.

During *The Butterfly of Killybegs*, I'd never experienced so
much laughter in a production of mine since the Dublin days of *It's
a Two Foot Six Inches Above the Ground World*. Despite the wonderful audience response, the play didn't get a particularly good
press. The McDonagh comparison didn't help, even though Brian
swore that he'd never even seen *The Beauty Queen of Leenane*.
In any case, while I admire McDonagh's bravery in reshaping the
landscape of the Irish play, I find him a rather soulless playwright.
He certainly exhibits a fine strand of clever, malevolent comedy,
but you don't feel a great love of people in his work. Then there's
the incessant takes on other Irish plays. He's good at pastiche but
while initially this can be funny, gradually it becomes irritating,
like those French films that pay homage to celebrated directors
and spend so much time referencing other films that it mitigates
against their own creative identity. Even though we didn't win critically, Vanessa Hawkins's imposing and detailed set was deservedly nominated for an Irish Times Award and we certainly won
through with the punters. In fact, quite by chance, a neighbour of
mine in Greystown Avenue hailed me from across the road and in
no uncertain terms told me how much she enjoyed *The Butterfly
of Killybegs* more than the McDonagh play, which she'd seen at the
Opera House. Therefore I just don't understand why other Irish
theatres apart from Red Kettle in Waterford haven't really taken
up Brian Foster. The Lyric discovered a natural comic talent there.

FREELANCE JOURNEYS: RADIO

67 – Dave and Derry

IN 2001, WHILE I WAS STILL LIVING in Belfast, I directed a radio play, *From a Great Height* by Dave Duggan, who had written
the screenplay for the Oscar-nominated short film, *Dance Lexie
Dance*. It was strange attending script conferences when you were

no longer a member of staff. Although I wanted a longer break from BBC Northern Ireland, I needed the work. I didn't get a sense that there was great support for Dave's play and Robert Cooper demanded changes, which only served to remind me of my previous struggles and accelerated my efforts to look for broadcasting work outside Belfast.

From a Great Height is an imaginative drama about a young woman's love of mountaineering and the tension between her terra firma taxi driver boyfriend and her newly acquired male mountaineer. Phoebe eventually fails to find the balance between independence and commitment on or above ground. As she finally leaves Ireland on a ferry, we are left wondering if she might take up with a Frenchman she meets aboard, but somehow I doubt it. The recording went well and the comic tensions were played with verve by Susan Lynch, Lloyd Hutchinson and Conleth Hill. Gillian Reynolds, the doyen of British radio critics, gave the play a very positive review in the *Daily Telegraph* – 'Excellent cast. Imaginative production.'

One of the delights of working with Dave was to return to Derry in 2001. Dave lives not far from Northland Avenue where I had my first lodgings as a student. In my short meanderings around the city, it was terrific to see the wonderful improvements. It was a far cry from the drab environs of my student days. Derry seemed a much more positive, energised place. The peace process and the tireless work of the likes of John Hume and others had certainly brought progress, even though it had come at a tremendous cost.

68 – Britain's Brecht in Ireland

ONE OF MY REAL JOYS FREELANCING in radio was working with John Arden. I had known John and Margaretta D'Arcy, his wife and writing partner, over many years. Not only was I in the London company that performed readings of their superb epic, *The Non Stop Connolly Show*, but we also had a mutual friend in Green Fields actress Finola Keogh. John had been living in Ireland since the 1970s, but although Leila Doolan had tried to get one of his plays staged at the Abbey, no major Irish theatre company had performed his work. Given that he was a leading writer, the British Brecht as *The Guardian* called him, I find this quite extraordinary. Maybe people thought he was too formidable a presence or they believed too many unfair rumours about his and Margaretta's previous collaborations. Even allowing for this, it doesn't excuse the inertia shown towards such a significant talent being in their midst. Their loss was my gain.

I felt privileged to work with John not just because he wrote such seminal plays as *Serjeant Musgrave's Dance* but because I found him an inspiring collaborator, one who was always looking to push boundaries with content, style and language. John didn't write naturalistically but poetically. His language is heightened, supplemented by verse, doggerel and often ballad. This didn't fit in to the naturalistic formulas of the day – he was far too distinctive for that. He evolved his own style and vision. In fact, like the plays of O'Casey and Behan, John's writing contains many Jacobean features: larger-than-life characters, abrasive satirical comedy and vigorous prose. In John's case, there was also a more rigorous political vision, influenced by Brecht's epic theatre, which at its best made his writing even more challenging and exciting.

My first Irish venture with John was the Radio 4 play, *Wild Ride to Dublin* in 2003. At the centre of the drama was the unusual love affair between Spike Oldroyd, a retired right wing journalist, and Ute, a German activist who persuades Spike to examine his conscience and make a frantic journey across Ireland to free an almost innocent Republican. It was a lively, energetic piece, both amusing and pertinent. Maybe the central relationship was inspired by John's relationship with Margaretta? After all, John originally came from a Yorkshire Tory background when Margaretta met him in the mid-50s. Once he got to know her, he became a radical writer during the halcyon days of the Royal Court in the late 50s, early 60s.

At the centre of the play was Edward Petherbridge, who gave a wonderfully authoritative performance as Spike. In fact, I was very fortunate with this decision because when I cast Edward, I forgot to ask him if he could sing. So when he came to the studio, I had no idea if he could or couldn't perform John's snatches of song. Much to my relief, I discovered that he had a mellifluous voice and took on the musical challenge with gusto. In fact, Edward hadn't worked with John since his days at Olivier's National Theatre in the 1960s, so it was a good reunion. The edgy Sara Kestleman as Ute partnered him with considerable skill so the play had a very strong core. Aided by a good supporting cast, it really fizzed along as Spike raced against time to get to the besieged victim of justice.

Wild Ride was produced by Fiction Factory, an independent production company based in Greenwich and run by John Taylor, another ex-BBC producer. I enjoyed working with him and later became one of his Associate Producers. It's amazing how a new climate can reinvigorate creativity. I returned to London in the new millennium to a much more multi-cultural, energised city. A big contrast to the stiff Conservative era I'd left. I was now excited about revitalising my freelance career.

This still included producing some plays for BBC Northern Ireland, but at more of a distance. In fact, one of those was the next play I did with John Arden, *Poor Tom Thy Horn is Dry* (titled from Edgar begging in *King Lear*, disguised as an itinerant madman). It was ambitious: a picaresque drama for Radio 3 based on the life and times of Captain Thomas Ashe (1770-1835). Ashe was a Tipperary Protestant from the Irish gentry who became a soldier but encompassed so much more than that. He was clerk, tradesman, teacher, embezzler, explorer, impersonator, plagiarist, political propagandist, hack journalist and blackmailer. Just to name a few activities! A man of incredible energy and ingenuity he was ripe for dramatisation.

At the recording in west London, John was often clutching an obscure second hand book that he'd bought in Galway. He'd sometimes sit in the control room like a dedicated librarian devouring a newly acquired ancient text. The Captain Ashe story was probably one of those discoveries. The subject matter was certainly fascinating, not least being Ashe's rather sad end, where after such an eventful buccaneering life, John imagines him alone in a London park, pouring a drink out of a bottle, his life now empty, waiting to face death. Picaresque drama is by its nature episodic, so there can be a danger that such a play loses focus by rambling too much and taking too many detours. Certainly Aidan McArdle's performance as Ashe, resplendent with singing and verse, helped to hold this adventurous journey through Europe together. However, maybe, on reflection, the story could have been more focused and elicited greater tension. The fact that Ashe's life in reality, even allowing for his own hyperbolic memoirs, was so extraordinary made it very tempting to include many incidents rather than edit to the dramatic core. Nonetheless, like all John's work, it was well written and a distinctive listen. Most relevantly, it had a modern resonance about individualism and unchecked free enterprise coming to a sticky end.

Initially John, like myself, wasn't enamoured by the BBC's commissioning process. The bureaucracy of fear was so absurd at times that I heard that both Tom Stoppard and Hugh Leonard were asked to send in their CV. I was apprehensive about asking such a good established writer to write a synopsis, let alone give me a list of his credits. However, John cleverly found a way to use the system in a creative way so he could exactly pinpoint the narrative and its themes. So much so that his synopses gradually became a work of art in themselves.

When John died in 2012, I felt privileged to be asked to speak at his Dublin funeral, which emphasised his political activism. While this was important, he was above all a man of integrity and a great writer. He never took the easy careerist approach but was fuelled by a sense of artistic and political mission. I miss his commitment, talent and imagination. I just wish the Irish theatre had made more use of it.

69 – Myself Alone

My next Irish project was again recorded in west London for BBC Northern Ireland. For some years, I'd been very interested in Henrik Ibsen's *An Enemy of the People*. The idea of one person standing up against the masses for what he or she believed to be right is a principle that can be sorely tested. It's a conflict that has attracted such diverse talents as the great Indian film maker Satyajit Ray, Ian McKellen and film stars like Steve McQueen. I wasn't so interested in the original Norwegian nineteenth century setting with its tensions about the water supply, however environmentally relevant that could be. I wanted to do an Irish-based version which had immediate relevance to the current political climate.

In 2006, there had been the brave stand taken by the McCartney sisters against the IRA killers of their brother, leading to their historic meeting with President Bush. Obviously, this was an inspiration, but I didn't want a documentary drama. I preferred a modern, resonant, fictional work. I took my idea to Martin Lynch, whom I believed was the only person who could write this play. I was delighted when he agreed that the original drama would adapt perfectly to modern Belfast. It's easy for the likes of myself to talk about theoretically dramatising such subjects, but for Martin to actually do it takes courage. Especially when writers in the North have been threatened for writing similar plays.

The new modern version keeps the core of the Ibsen classic but transfers it to a modern Belfast setting. At the centre of the play is Moya McGovern looking to get justice for her murdered brother-in-law. Just like after the death of the visiting Englishman who wanted to buy land in J.B. Keane's *The Field*, the community are silent. In this case, nobody wants to cross the paramilitaries. It's left to Moya herself, aided by her strong-willed daughter Caroline, to challenge the status quo, despite the violent threats they have to endure. When Moya is finally isolated by her community and left alone, she is forced to make a very difficult decision. Susan Lynch played Moya with a moving blend of independence and vulnerability. In reality, she was too young for the role but it's the wonder of radio that actors can play many parts they'd never portray in theatre or cinema, so long as their voice is convincing. When Susan started acting, you believed her. It was a performance of mature and tragic authority, one of the best in my radio work.

An Enemy of the People was well received and won a Zebbie Award from the Irish Playwrights and Screenwriters Guild for the Best Radio Script 2007. It went on to be repeated on BBC Radio 3, an unusual occurrence. Since then, I've been trying to get a theatre version produced but without success. Maybe in the current peace climate, managements get nervous about such material. Such cowardice is short-sighted. Surely to move forward one must discuss such issues, otherwise the bubble of hatred is never burst.

70 – A First with Tom

A FEW YEARS LATER I WAS BACK in Belfast recording another Radio 3 drama, *A Whistle in the Dark* by Tom Murphy. I knew Tom from my time in Dublin. While at the Abbey I saw Tom's play *The White House* undergo eccentric changes. It's the only production I know where during the run the first half of the play reverted to being the second. Then there was the bizarre moment when Dan O'Herlihy, who was playing the John Kennedy-obsessed character, suddenly appeared on stage without warning with a facsimile Kennedy wig, much to the surprise of the other actors. Despite these upheavals another version of this material later became one of Tom's best plays, *Conversations on a Homecoming*. At that time, Tom was back in Ireland after a period living in England, where the first production of *A Whistle in the Dark* had been produced at the Theatre Royal Stratford East, home of Joan Littlewood's Theatre Workshop, which also presented the early Behan plays and *Oh What a Lovely War*. In those days, Tom was a frequenter of the Queens Elm Pub off the Fulham Road, which housed artists, bohemians, sportsmen and other waifs and strays. In fact, Tom told me that it was there that he met none other than Johnny Haynes, the Fulham and England football captain. Johnny was a great player and the Beckham of his day, given he was regularly advertising Brylcreem, then a fashionable hair lotion. He used to come down from the ground to carouse with some of the team. Another regular at this watering hole was Michael Craig, a British film star. Good looking and talented, he appeared in many features of the day. Craig read *A Whistle in the Dark* and was one of its prime movers.

The Royal Court had flirted with Tom's work over the years but could never commit. Later, when I was there in the early 1970s, there was a Sunday Night Production without decor of his powerful play *Famine*. It was hideously under-rehearsed and deserved much better. The Royal Court should have also produced *A Whistle in the Dark* as Tom's play was way ahead of its time, but they foolishly missed the opportunity. Eventually, this wrong was corrected many years later, when Druid brought their successful revival to the same London venue.

A Whistle in the Dark is raw, powerful, violent and truthful, an honest dramatisation of an immigrant Irish family in the early 1960s. As a child growing up in London at the time, I remember seeing adverts in Earls Court shops prominently stating 'no blacks or Irish'. Although you probably wouldn't want the likes of the Carney family roistering in a flat above you all night, it doesn't excuse the racist notices. The 1960s was a seminal era, but it was only later in the decade when radical change started to emerge. I'd always admired Tom's work, particularly *A Whistle in the Dark*, which is a tight, taut piece. Some of the later plays, like *The Morning After Optimism*, which I saw while I was at the Abbey, I found imaginative and audacious, but sometimes over-written and too long. Nonetheless, *Optimism* was a beguiling and arresting production featuring a wonderful performance by Colin Blakely prancing about in a forest as a malevolent spiv, well supported by Eithne Dunne, a leading Irish actress of substance.

During the run of *Optimism*, I witnessed Tom and Colin singing raucous duets together at the Dublin Festival Club. I think Colin was living in the Republic at that time to escape the British tax authorities, who were rumoured to have made appearances at the

Royal Court Theatre, where he was appearing with Paul Scofield in *Uncle Vanya*. Apparently, he had to leave Britain by midnight on the day of the last performance. I believe it was a hell of a rush from Sloane Square to Heathrow to escape the tax hounds. Her Majesty's tax inspectors' loss was the Abbey's gain, and he brought a real buzz to the company. Here was a major Irish actor setting high standards and inspiring the company. While I was directing at the Eblana, I also frequented Tom in Groomes, where he often sang beautifully. Amidst the drunken caterwauling, his voice was like an angel coming out of the ether. Therefore I wasn't surprised that in his fine play, *The Gigli Concert*, one of the characters wants to sing like the celebrated Italian tenor.

A Whistle in the Dark is Tom's most performed play but it had never been previously produced for radio. I was determined to make it work for a new audience. Although Irish emigration to the UK is now largely middle class, the play still has a great resonance with working class emigration around the world. There was limited time for me to talk with Tom, but I enjoyed meeting him again after many years. We made some pertinent adjustments for radio, while keeping the core of the original. Although these changes worked well I was intrigued that Tom mentioned that there was a film script of the play, written for Peter Rogers, producer of *Carry On* fame. Later, I was nagged by the thought that maybe I should have requested to read it with a view to seeing how much the play had been opened out and if any of that script could be used for radio. On such hesitancy do you live or die. In the end, I decided that I needed to go ahead to meet the forthcoming deadline. In any case, I had a very good script and most things worked through the characters and Tom's excellent use of language.

A good cast was led by John Kavanagh, who gave a terrific performance as Dada, a menacing visiting Irish patriarch. Dada's tribal world suffocates the aspirations of his son Michael (Aidan McArdle), who wants to start a new life with his English wife (Emma Amos). The play takes place in Coventry which suffered severe bombing during World War Two. By the early 1960s, with the pacifist Benjamin Britten's especially commissioned *War Requiem* opening the newly built Coventry Cathedral, the English midlands was beginning to come out of austere post-war rationing and herald a revival in manufacturing industry. This was in marked contrast to Ireland's economic blight. Whilst such regeneration was taking place, the likes of the Carneys were on the rampage. Michael, the resident immigrant, is a man invaded and finally destroyed by his past and his family, unable to stem the tide of tribal assertion. The mild mannered Michael, aggressively taunted and derided by his visiting brothers, finally breaks out in frustration and commits a savage act of violence. Fear of change, fear of being different, fear of the educated in a harsh, competitive world, all pertinent today, contribute to the tragedy.

Some areas of my production did show the stage origins too much, and for the opening music maybe I should have used something from the *War Requiem* as an ironic counterpoint. Nonetheless, the essential claustrophobic intensity of the drama was there and so were the performances. What the play did more than anything else was to remind me what a brilliant playwright Tom is. Radio brings you closer to the intimacy of the word and in *Whistle* every character seems to have a brilliantly crafted, distinct voice. This accentuates the individual sense of alienation and despair that lies behind the camaraderie, joking and macho posturing. Also, the bigger speeches are beautifully expressed, like musical arias encapsulating a whole life. When they come, they're dramatically earned not imposed purple passages. Maybe, the female character, Michael's wife Betty, could be more developed but on radio giving her a distinct English midlands accent rooted her within that community and accentuated her status. You get a strong sense of her own decency and of a woman having an increasing sense of foreboding about the outcome of the family's visit. Her husband, Michael is the outsider in turmoil, wanting to lead a better life but still loving his family despite despising their tribalism. This familial conflict evolves with all the tragic predictability of a Greek drama. The play ends in a maelstrom of violence which is still very alarming. Although the Abbey during the Blythe years rejected the play and the English critics unjustly dismissed it, it impressed Harold Pinter. His play *The Homecoming* is certainly influenced by *A Whistle in the Dark*. In *The Homecoming*, the situation is reversed: an academic returns with his wife from America to his old working class home in North London. At the end, the violence is more contained as the academic departs alone, his wife preferring to stay with his family.

In 1965 Edward Bond's *Saved* caused a rumpus at the Royal Court for its central scene dramatising the stoning of a baby, but got support from the likes of Laurence Olivier. At that time, the climate was ripe for breaking taboos. Unfortunately, a few years earlier Tom's play was left isolated in the world of Lord Chamberlain censorship, middle class respectability and some anti-Irish racism. It took too long for it to become the modern classic it is now. The play was certainly recognised by the Irish Playwrights and Scriptwriters Guild, who awarded it a Zebbie Award for the Best Radio Script 2011, despite it being over 50 years since it was originally written. The play had made a big impact on a new, younger audience. You couldn't pay Tom's writing a bigger compliment than that.

71 – Carlo and I

I FIRST WORKED WITH CARLO GÉBLER on his dramatisation of Sam Hanna Bell's classic Ulster novel *December Bride* in 2001, a frenetic experience for me as it was the first time I'd returned to a Belfast studio as a freelance and much had changed. Although Carlo's script was well written, it had too many time consuming short scenes and it took too long to edit. However, when put together, it worked well and the story set in 1909 of a pregnant servant girl (a powerful Monica Dolan) caught between the competing affections of two brothers (Lalor Roddy and Gerard Crossan) and unwilling to name the child's father, travelled well over two episodes. However the production had its *Last Tango* and *Wild Bunch* moments. There's something absurdly surreal about an actor thrusting to mike to get convincing ejaculation sounds, or a cabbage being beaten to pulp to evoke a violent going over. But that's the fun of radio: titillating the imagination through sound.

My next collaboration with Carlo was in 2011 on his Radio 3 play *Charles and Mary* about the relationship between siblings Charles and Mary Lamb, the authors of the celebrated *Tales from Shakespeare*. While writing, Charles was working full-time in the City of London and Mary was looking after her ageing and infirm parents. The strain took a terrible toll on Mary, who suffered from fits, and led to her killing her mother. Charles managed to stop Mary going to bedlam and eventually got her released from an asylum on condition that he looked after her. It was during this period that they wrote their famous book together. It was a great success and became an established classic. Unfortunately, Mary's mental stability later worsened and she spent the rest of her life in institutions and finally a nursing home, not fully aware of the increasingly alcoholic Charles's death.

Carlo wrote a skilful and compassionate account of this relationship. It never pandered to the sensational aspects of the murder but looked to dramatise the moving bond between brother and sister and how circumstances changed the nature of their relationship. It sensitively dramatised the love and devotion shared between them and how it survived family tragedy and built a seminal creative bond. There was a genuine sense of the effects of old age, mental illness and the strain of Georgian life on two young people who had to grow up quickly. The way their increasing difficulties brought them closer together as both siblings and writers was very moving.

At the centre of the production, I was very fortunate to have two players of high quality in the leading roles. Paul Rhys is a Welsh actor with a genuine poetic sensibility. There's a feeling of soulful sensitivity in his interpretation, while Lia Williams made a disturbed murderer a complex creative person with whom one could sympathise. With support from an excellent cast including Dudley Sutton, who was in the first production of *A Whistle in the*

Dark, and the redoubtable Marcella Riordan, one of Ireland's best radio actresses, we had a real sense of actors 'taking it off the page', not reading but speaking for the first time, vital in radio drama.

Carlo is a good writer and one of Ireland's most professional practitioners. As well as his undoubted literary ability, his background as a TV director makes him have a good understanding of what's needed in broadcasting. He writes to time, gets drafts in by the agreed date and absorbs the brief. These attributes may sound boring but they're necessary to be free to do the work well. In today's pressurised broadcasting culture, the writer needs to be very disciplined. The more relaxed world of long rehearsals and Richard Burton and the taffia sinking a few pints at The George before recording *Under Milk Wood* are over, whether we like it or not. Therefore a writer has to work creatively within restraints. Those who adapt to such restrictions flexibly are more likely to succeed; those who are more rigid tend to flounder. For instance, if I discover while recording that I'm running over time, I could ask the writer for a cut later in the schedule, whatever the quality of the writing. Unfortunately, something has to go.

I remember learning a lesson about cutting when I was working with Lindsay Anderson on *The Contractor* at the Royal Court. Bill Owen, well known latterly for BBC TV's *Last of the Summer Wine*, was told that a very well written speech had to be cut. His response was to bemoan the omission: 'But this was the reason I took the part. This tells me everything about the man. It's a wonderful piece of writing.'

'Yes, exactly,' argued Lindsay, 'that's why we're cutting it. It tells us too much.'

David Storey's play had been written with oblique and sparse dialogue. Then suddenly, in the middle of a scene, Bill's character had a lengthy Ibsenite purple passage, explaining himself too literally. The speech was out of keeping with the play's style and stood out like a sore thumb, therefore it had to go, despite being well written. Initially, Bill went into a bit of a sulk, especially when the rest of the cast were very non-committal, but eventually he realised that the cut was necessary and he integrated the content of the speech into the way he developed the part.

Carlo has a good understanding of such decisions and how to use them to positive advantage. He has a rare ability to move seamlessly between the literary and broadcasting worlds.

72 – RTÉ Pursuits

IN 2000, WHILE STILL LIVING in Belfast, I worked on two challenging plays for RTÉ: *The Man with No Ears* by Dave Duggan, about an Irish company setting up a project in Africa, and *Innocent Refuge* by Sean Moffatt, about a Romanian refuge trying to survive in Ireland. They dramatised respectively modern Ireland's business colonisation and its immigrant challenge.

While working at RTÉ, I stayed at a Ballsbridge hotel which was still being built. In fact, if you turned the wrong way to the breakfast room you could have disappeared down a big black hole, if it wasn't for a hastily arranged tarpaulin safeguarding the area. Not exactly what I envisaged regarding health and safety regulations but this was the Celtic Tiger and Dublin was going building mad. It seemed to be a case of making hay while the sun shines. I found it difficult at RTÉ. Unlike the BBC, there were no PAs available and no preparation time with a studio manager. I had to find the effects and music myself in a system which was unfamiliar. What's more, I was working at weekends when there were few staff available, so I felt very isolated. Thankfully, I met up with Daniel Riordan, whom I knew previously as a good actor and was now an RTÉ Drama Producer. It was due to Dan's courteous diligence that I was steered in the right direction.

Despite these frustrations, overall I enjoyed working at RTÉ. The studios were excellent, real state-of-the-art and much better than those in Belfast. Philip Cooke, the sound supervisor, was both amenable and efficient. At night he played in a rock band in a Dublin pub – another Irish renaissance man. Still not as bad as the LA dentist who, while wrenching a producer's tooth out, asked if his script could be read as he was really a screenwriter! The casts at

RTÉ were the equal of those at the BBC and they responded well to working on the material. When I finished the two plays I left, got paid and didn't hear much more about them. They seemed to go well but I suppose during that transitional period, I was just holding the line. Thankfully, RTÉ got through that uncomfortable phase when consultants were prowling the building noting your activities with an ironic friendly smile. There was a lot of apprehension around and to some I appeared a threat, which I wasn't. Now, the department seems to be thriving, exploring different forms and giving many new writers the chance of a voice. Long may that continue.

MY IRISH JOURNEY

73 – Final Thoughts

IT'S FIFTY YEARS SINCE I FIRST stepped foot in Ireland as a student. Since then Ireland, north and south, have come a long way. Despite the 2008 recession, the Good Friday agreement and the Republic's entry into the European Union have brought huge changes to both the peace and prosperity within the island. Although culturally there is closer contact between north and south than there was in the past, I still think that there is some way to go. For those outside Ireland, it's strange that people talk about wanting a united country when they haven't yet united the football team. Funnily enough, such an event, if it came to pass, could well trigger greater cultural rapprochement. However, breaking through many self-interested barriers wouldn't be easy.

I remember when I saw the Ulster Theatre Company in the 1960s I thought that they had some of the best Irish actors available, but none of them ever figured in the Abbey company, nor have the plays of several seminal Ulster playwrights like Sam Thompson, Robin Glendinning and Martin Lynch, or in the latter's case, not since 1984. At least the Abbey is starting to produce a new generation of northern playwrights like Owen McAfferty and David Ireland. This is a positive development as plurality is the real challenge for the future. Not only by educating people at a very early age to understand and respect all the cultural, political and religious traditions within the island, but also to integrate a new wave of immigrants into a more multi-cultural society, both north and south.

British society went through the Notting Hill riots of the 1950s, the racism of the early 1960s, Enoch Powell's 'Rivers of Blood' speech in 1968 and the 1993 Stephen Lawrence murder before black people were more fully integrated into the country. Although Europe is now much more liberal and Ireland, in particular, has made amazing progress on issues such as gay marriage, the fragility of the Eurozone, the alienation of globalisation and the increasing waves of desperate immigrants from Africa and the Middle East have already shown the potential for unpleasant right wing parties to emerge. Therefore it's important that Ireland remains steadfast and looks boldly to integrate such communities into the country, and to develop an audacious theatrical culture that reflects such diversity.

My own personal Irish journey has been invigorating and life-enhancing. Ireland not only gave me chances to develop my work but it also gave me the opportunity to experience another culture and review one's own. From such evaluation, views change and one's personality evolves. I believe Ireland has helped me to mature more fully. Some people have said that my engagement with the country hasn't helped my career, as many prospective English employers haven't seen the many productions I've done there. That may or may not be true, but whatever the judgement, I believe I've experienced something more profound than moving up the greasy pole of theatrical politics – an immersion in a uniquely exciting dramatic culture over a long period of time. A culture that certainly in the Republic is impressively at the heart of the nation.

That hasn't made me change my passport and try to be Irish when I'm clearly not, like some other English practitioners. I don't believe that such superficial gestures are really respected. Birth is a fact you can't choose, attitude is something you develop. While still retaining my own identity, I've come to have a deep affection for Ireland, its people and its culture. I don't see the opportunities Ireland has given me as a fork in the road to some higher calling elsewhere, but at the core of my personal and professional life.

My relationship with Irish institutions hasn't been always easy. Like most experienced directors, I've had my share of both success and failure. However, despite my ups and downs, wherever I am based, I still feel very committed to Ireland and Irish theatre, both north and south. Not only did the country's humour and conviviality help me to loosen up, but I think its culture inspired me to expand my horizons, not least in understanding a wider compassion and the value of passion and commitment. Through working in Irish drama and broadcasting I've manage to learn and develop my craft and engage with audiences across these islands. This doesn't mean that I haven't been critical of some of the country's more hallowed myths and political shenanigans. Yet, despite such insular navel gazing, I retain the same excitement and commitment to Irish drama, when as a student, I first came on that boat to Belfast all those years ago. I have to thank the Irish people for that.

Index

Index